Self-Determined Learning Theory

Construction, Verification, and Evaluation

The LEA Series on Special Education and Disability
John Wills Lloyd, Series Editor

Self-Determined Learning Theory

Construction, Verification, and Evaluation

Edited by

Dennis E. Mithaug
Teachers College, Columbia University

Deirdre K. Mithaug
St. John's University

Martin Agran
University of Northern Iowa

James E. Martin
University of Oklahoma

Michael L. Wehmeyer
University of Kansas

 LAWRENCE ERLBAUM ASSOCIATES, PUBLISHERS
2003   Mahwah, New Jersey   London

Lawrence Erlbaum Associates, Inc., Publishers
10 Industrial Avenue
Mahwah, New Jersey 07430

Cover design by Kathryn Houghtaling Lacey

Library of Congress Cataloging-in-Publication Data

Self-determined learning theory : construction, verification, and evaluation /
Dennis E. Mithaug . . . [et al.].
    p.   cm.
Includes bibliographical references and index.
ISBN 0-8058-3698-5
    1. Learning, Psychology of.   2. Adjustment (Psychology).   3. Autonomy
(Psychology).   I. Mithaug, Dennis E.

LB1060 .S39   2003
370.15′23 — dc21   2002024115
                                                                         CIP

Books published by Lawrence Erlbaum Associates are printed on acid-
free paper, and their bindings are chosen for strength and durability.

Printed in the United States of America
10 9 8 7 6 5 4 3 2 1

Contents

Preface

We wrote this preface to prepare you for the task that lies ahead, which is to introduce to you a different way of explaining learning. We appreciate that there may be obstacles to accepting our explanation, mainly because there are many beliefs about learning you could hold that are different from the one in this book. Knowing this, we ask you to set aside those beliefs for the next 14 chapters. Then, after reviewing our case for self-determined learning theory, you can decide for yourself whether those beliefs need adjusting in light of what you have learned. We look forward to your review and, of course, any adjustments you may make toward adopting our explanation for learning.

In the upcoming chapters you will learn that self-determined learning theory is based on the claim that learning *is* adjustment. We explain this by showing a causal connection between opportunities to learn, engagement in those opportunities, adjustments to them, and learning. These factors function as follows. Opportunities for gain provoke engagement, engagement affects adjustments, and adjustments determine what is learned. This is self-determined learning theory in a nutshell. It explains why, how, and what people learn. People learn when they are provoked by an event that interrupts their goal pursuits—the *why* of learning. They engage the event by altering their expectations, choices and actions to control the event—the *how* of learning. And they adjust by altering their beliefs and patterns of responding to the event—the *what* of learning.

Self-determined learning theory explains this process of learning through adjustment by claiming that when provocative opportunities are as favorable as possible for engagement (optimal opportunities) and when the resulting adjustments to those opportunities are as effective as possible under the circumstances (optimal adjustments), then learning is likely to maximize. Hence, the theory claims that optimal opportunities and optimal adjustments maximize learning.

In the book we offer compelling reasons for using this theory to explain learning. One is that if learning is adjustment, then improving the ability to adjust will improve the ability to learn. Throughout the book we show this to be the case for students at risk for learning in that they tend to be poor adjusters. However, when they improve their capacity to adjust, they improve their ability to learn. This, in turn, improves their prospects of adjusting and learning in situations at school, home, and the community.

Another reason for using this learning-as-adjustment explanation is that it solves the learning transfer conundrum yet to be adequately explained by existing theory. Claiming that adjustment is learning leads to the conclusion that failure to generalize to new situations is due to poor adjustment. Therefore, by learning to adjust, students learn to transfer what they know to new situations. In the book we show how improving students' ability to adjust increases their generalization of appropriate learning to different situations.

The third reason for considering this account is that it places learning where it occurs naturally, as a reaction to a provoking necessity, interest, or curiosity. Learning occurs when students are provoked into figuring out *what to expect* from a new circumstance, *how to choose* what to do, and then *how to act* on choice to produce a predictable result from the circumstance. These discovery elements of learning through adjustment require thinking, acting, and evaluating in order to deal with the provocation. In the book we identify the instructional elements of provocative choice opportunities that sustain engagement sufficiently for students to produce the adjustments needed to maximize their learning.

This leads to the last of our compelling reasons for explaining learning as adjustment. It accounts for why learners learn more when they experience freedom of choice than when they are denied choice. This is because the prerequisite to enjoying freedom is being able to deal with adjustment challenges in ways that advance one's interests. Learners who are free to adjust as they wish to get what they need and want learn more about various pursuits than do learners who are not free to adjust as they wish. Self-determination advocates argue similarly, claiming that learning in adult life is driven by being free to engage in one's pursuits. In fact, adult learning theorist Candy (1991) went further, claiming that self-determined learning or "learning for oneself is the prototype of all learning" (p. 30). And he cited the following 1866 passage by Craik from *The Pursuit of Knowledge Under Difficulties* to prove his case.

Originally, all human knowledge was nothing more than the knowledge of a comparatively small number of such simple facts as those from which Galileo deduced the use of the pendulum for the measurement of time, and Newton the explanation of the system of the heavens. All the rest of our knowledge, and these first rudiments of it also, a succession of individuals have gradually discovered, each his own portion, by their own efforts, and without having any teacher to instruct them. In other words, everything that is actually known has been found out and learned by some person or other, without the aid of an instructor. There is no species of learning, therefore, which self-education may not overtake; for there is none which is not actually overtaken. All discoverers (and the whole of human knowledge that has not been divinely revealed) in the creation of discovery have been self-taught, at least in regard to that which they have discovered. [1866, p. 13]. (Candy, 1991, p. 30)

In the book we show how self-determined learning theory explains these claims about learning-as-adjustment. The theory explains why building students' adjustment capacities maximizes learning, and why it also improves students' ability to generalize learning to new situations. The theory explains why instruction through provocative challenges engages students to make adjustments needed to learn what they need and want to know. And, most important, the theory explains why learning to adjust to meet one's own needs and interests is necessary for self-determination in life. Again, Dewey (1909/1975) was right when he argued that the goal of education is to prepare young people for life in the free society.

We divided the book into theory construction, theory verification (two parts), and theory evaluation—and then organized the 14 chapters using the four steps of *Learning to Theorize: A Four-Step Strategy* (Mithaug, 2000). The first step of that approach defines a problem of not understanding something as a discrepancy between what we know and what we don't know about a circumstance. The second step searches for information and explanations to change the condition of not knowing into a condition of knowing. The third step evaluates the credibility and worth of the explanation constructed in step 2. The fourth step adjusts existing beliefs so they are consistent with the new theory (Mithaug, 2000, p. x).

We completed the first step of the four-step strategy—defining the problem—in chapter 1, "Understanding the Engagement Problem," by defining our problem of understanding as a discrepancy between what we know about engagement and what we don't about its effect on learning. We completed step 2—find reasons and an explanation for the discrepancy—in chapters 2 and 3. In chapter 2, "How Engagement Affects Adjustment," we identify the factors that connect engagement with adjustment. In chapter 3, "How Adjustment Affects Learning," we solve the discrepancy problem with a theory that explains how the factors identified in chapter 2 explain what we didn't know about how engagement affects learning.

We completed step 3—evaluating the credibility and worth of a theory—in the remaining chapters of the book. In chapters 4 through 13 we describe studies that test the new theory's predictions and prescriptions. And in chapter 14, "The Credibility and Worth of Self-Determined Learning Theory," we evaluate the theory's credibility by assessing its coherence, validity, and verifiability and then we evaluate the theory's worth by assessing its significance, scope, and utility.

We left step 4—adjusting beliefs—for you to complete. It is beyond the scope of the book because only you can decide whether the theory we have proposed is credible and valuable enough to adopt and, if it is, whether adopting it will require that you adjust other beliefs you hold about learning.

REFERENCES

Dewey, J. (1975). *Moral principles in education.* London: Feffer & Sons. (Original work published 1909)

Candy, P. C. (1991). *Self-direction for lifelong learning: A comprehensive guide to theory and practice.* San Francisco: Jossey-Bass.

Mithaug, D. E. (2000). *Learning to theorize: A four-step strategy.* Thousand Oaks, CA: Sage.

I

THEORY CONSTRUCTION

1

Understanding the Engagement Problem

Dennis E. Mithaug
Deirdre K. Mithaug
Martin Agran
James E. Martin
Michael L. Wehmeyer

In this book we introduce a theory of learning that explains why learning maximizes during self-engagement. We review past research on factors associated with engagement and original research on the credibility and worth of a theory that predicts learning will maximize when engagement produces optimal adjustments to new challenges. The theory explains that this happens when learners believe their opportunities for gaining something from a circumstance are valuable and manageable *and* when they know how to regulate their expectations, choices, and actions to produce results they expect from the circumstance. Then they engage the situation to optimize their adjustments and maximize their learning. The theory also predicts that as students acquire the knowledge and skills they need to deal with new situations, they experience sufficient control over the results of their efforts to believe subsequent opportunities for gain from the situation will give them more of what they need and want to know. This is how they become self-determined learners.

Unfortunately, self-engagement and learning like this are rare in school, as the following examples illustrate. Example A presents a general education classroom version of the problem as described by Zimmerman, Bonner, and Kovach (1996). Example B presents the special education version of the problem as described by Sands and Wehmeyer (1996).

EXAMPLES OF LEARNERS

Example A: Disengaged General Education Learners

Calvin, a bright sixth grader who has never experienced much success in school, has dreamed of achieving better and even thinks he may try to be the first person in his family to graduate from high school. Considering his family's low level of education, it is not surprising that Calvin has not developed many essential study skills and has many unfortunate habits, such as procrastinating, skimming reading assignments, cramming for tests at the last minute, and writing in a haphazard manner. He has a low sense of self-efficacy about improving his grades in school and generally appears poorly motivated in class.

Maria is an eighth-grade student who enjoys a wide social network. She diligently completes her work but only in a superficial way. Although she tries hard in school, schoolwork is less important to her than her friends, and as a result she gets only average grades. She is very popular among her classmates, and she usually "studies" daily with friends — sharing answers to math or science problems and reading her assignments cursorily between extended discussions about the day's events. Maria prepares minimally for tests, usually cramming the night before the exam, and her writing skills are a year below grade level. She has only a moderate amount of self-efficacy about doing well academically and tries not to think much about the future. (Zimmerman et al., 1996, pp. 6–7)

Example B: A Disengaged Special Education Learner

Carey is a sociable sixth grader who lacks determination in all that she does. She is a poor student, dislikes school, avoids homework, and spends much of her time watching television and hanging out with friends. She dreams about what she might be when she grows up but lacks confidence that she will ever become what she wants to be. Moreover, she has no idea what steps are necessary to pursue her dreams. When asked what grades she expects to earn each semester, she gives inconsistent answers. Sometimes she says she will get all A's, and other times she says she expects to fail all her courses. This is typical of how she looks at the future. Her goals are either so high she cannot achieve them or so low she is certain of achieving them. Either way, she has no intention of changing what she does or how she thinks. This is because when she sets expectations that are too high, no amount of planning and working will make any difference, and when she sets expectations that are too low, any amount of planning and working will be effective. Consequently, there is never any connection between what Carey expects and what she does. Frequently, this causes her to feel depressed and helpless because she depends so much on external events or people for direction and stimulation. She doesn't know what to improve about herself or how to improve herself, and she doesn't know how to enhance her opportunities.

She is a poor self-regulator, too. Carey lacks self-determination. (Mithaug, 1996, p. 148)

Students like Maria, Calvin, and Carey don't appear to have discovered the intrinsic rewards of controlling their own learning. As a result, they never have that "flow" experience Mihali Csikszentmihalyi described for people whose engagement in self-imposed challenges enhances their sense of control over their circumstances.

> The optimal state of inner experience is one in which there is order in consciousness. This happens when psychic energy — or attention — is invested in realistic goals, and when skills match the opportunities for action. The pursuit of a goal brings order in awareness because a person must concentrate attention on the task at hand and momentarily forget everything else. These periods of struggling to overcome challenges are what people find to be the most enjoyable times of their lives. . . . A person who has achieved control over psychic energy and has invested it in consciously chosen goals cannot help but grow into a more complex being. By stretching skills, by reaching toward higher challenges, such a person becomes an increasingly extraordinary individual. (Csikszentmihalyi, 1990, p. 6)

Self-determined learning theory identifies the conditions that provoke students like Calvin, Maria, and Carey to engage the learning challenges described by Csikszentmihalyi (1990). It explains the *why* and *how* of self-engagement. Students engage themselves when they have optimal opportunities to choose what they will do and how they will do it — the *why* factor. And they stay engaged to the extent they adjust their expectations, choices, and actions effectively enough to produce the gain they expect from those opportunities — the *how* factor. In other words, students get and stay engaged to the extent they adjust optimally to opportunities that provoke them into adapting to new and challenging circumstances. This applies to all students, with or without disabilities and across cultures and time. The theory predicts that students who are motivated to adapt to challenging opportunities will be like Doris in example C. They will enjoy learning enough to become life-long achievers.

Example C: An Engaged Learner

> *Doris* is a bright . . . sixth-grade student who has learned to regulate her behavior to get what she wants over the long haul. She is an experienced achiever. She is determined to do well in school because she knows that good grades will help her get what she wants after she graduates. Doris also knows what she can do and how to compensate for what gives her difficulty. She sets goals that are consistent with her needs and interests, strives to achieve them, and then experiences great satisfaction when she makes

progress. Most important, Doris expects to achieve goals that are *just beyond* what she achieved in the past, which often requires more work and better methods of producing gain than what she has done previously. No one tells her what goals she should set or how she should meet them, although she often seeks advice when she gets confused and does not know where to begin. Doris has the habit of performing at or near her capacity in most of what she does. After meeting one goal she sets a slightly more ambitious goal the next time. This increases her capacity and improves her opportunity to act in self-determined ways. (Mithaug, 1996, p. 147)

We know much about students like Doris who pursue new opportunities to achieve all they can. These students believe they are causal agents in dealing with their circumstances. They enjoy the challenge of learning, and they persist even when their pursuits present difficulties. Students like Doris thrive on having choices about what and how to adapt in order to learn because then they can regulate their actions to take advantage of their strengths and to compensate for their weaknesses. They are free to adjust their expectations to new situations and to set goals that are consistent with what they can do. And when students are motivated to produce results that are important to them, they strive to develop plans that will help them learn as much as they can, which leads them to believe their decisions and actions are the cause of their success or failure. Consequently, when they fall short of expectations, they know what to do to improve, and when they get results they want they feel in control because they know what they did to succeed. Finally, when students' feelings of control persist their experience of engagement is similar to that described by Csikszentmihalyi (1990) as "flow."

This chapter identifies the antecedents to engagement that are likely to discourage students from becoming self-determined learners like Doris. One of these is the learning opportunity that can either motivate or discourage students who face challenges to adjust in order to learn. The evidence suggests that a student's perceptions of a circumstance can discourage engagement by interpreting it to be unimportant or impossible to control. Because every circumstance is filtered through these personalized views of what constitutes an opportunity or an obstacle for gain, students' beliefs will affect their engagement and learning.

Indeed, teachers act on this view implicitly when they make learning opportunities match student needs and abilities so that some learning occurs. Using principles of individualized instruction, they tailor the demands and rewards of each challenge to match student perceptions of what they can do to produce gain toward a valued outcome, and this encourages them to learn. Used skillfully, this matching of challenges to *existing* perceptions of opportunity guarantees that every student learns something. For some educators, *this* is effective teaching.

What emerges across various commentaries is the image of effective teachers taking an active, direct role in the instruction of their students. These educators give many detailed and redundant instructions and explanations when introducing a new concept.... They give ample opportunity for guided practice with frequent reviews of student progress.... They check for understanding, using such techniques as questioning, consistent review of homework, and review of previous day's lessons before moving on to new areas. Such teachers move among students when they are involved in practice seatwork. Feedback is provided frequently and with meaningful detail. Effective teachers use feedback strategies for positive reinforcement of student success. Feedback also provides the basis for reteaching where necessary. Effective teachers take an active role in creating a positive, expectant, and orderly classroom environment in which learning takes place. To accomplish these climate objectives effective teachers actively structure the learning process and the management of time, guiding in such things as signals for academic work and maintaining student attention by group alerting and accountability techniques and through variation in educational tasks. (Berliner, 1984, cited in Bickel & Bickel, 1986, pp. 492–493)

Although effective by some indicators, we suggest that this approach can also have the undesirable effect of teaching students to expect all learning opportunities to be perfectly matched to their needs, interests, and abilities. This in turn causes them to leave the learning-friendly environment lacking the capacity to adjust to unfamiliar circumstances on their own. Hence they exhibit the same learned helplessness that placed them in those optimized situations in the first place. Ellis (1986) described the problem as follows.

Instructors may facilitate retention of dependency on others by the nature of strategies being taught, as well as corrective feedback, reinforcement and structures used in the classroom.... Feedback which is heavily teacher-oriented (i.e., "Let me check your answers ... I think you did a good job here ... now I want you to ...") may over the long run, subtly encourage the student to be more dependent on others for metacognitive processes such as monitoring and reinforcement. In turn, feedback which is student-oriented (i.e., "How well do you think you did? What are the best parts of your work? What should we focus on next to make it better?") facilitates students' use of metacognitive processes related to strategy use.

In addition, classroom structures which provide little daily and weekly opportunity for students' input or selection of instructional goals, activities and rule setting can subtly reinforce an external locus of control, e.g., classroom environments which are highly structured, assignments are predetermined by the teacher without considering the students' goals, little opportunity for students to participate in the decision making process regarding their education, little opportunity for the student to verbally state what is being learned and why. In short, efforts by some teachers to run highly or-

ganized and tightly structured classrooms may inadvertently reduce student opportunities to learn and use metacognitive skills of self-structuring
and monitoring. While satisfying the need to help students by frequently
acting as a controlling agent and too frequently or unnecessarily offering
help, teachers can be training their students to be more dependent on the instructor for problem solving, guidance, and feedback. (Ellis, 1986, p. 67)

EXPLAINING DISENGAGEMENT

This is the problem we want to understand. We want to figure out what
causes disengagement so we can explain how engagement produces
learning. Fortunately, on the question of disengagement, there are several
explanations. One is that students who believe they are helpless in controlling the content and course of their learning are likely to avoid it when
they can. Diener and Dweck (1978) offered support for this theory of
learned helplessness in a study reporting that students who held beliefs
that they were helpless in the face of challenge were less likely to improve
their achievement than were children who believed they were in control
of their circumstances. Although mastery children spent time finding new
ways of improving poor outcomes, learned helpless children spent time
explaining why they failed. Other theories have offered similar explanations. Rotter's (1966) locus of control theory claims that people who exhibit an external locus of control are less likely to take action to improve
their circumstances than are people who exhibit an internal locus of control. Weiner's (1976) theory of causal attribution claims people who attribute their success and failure to factors outside of their control are less
likely to persist in the quest to succeed than are people who attribute success and failure to factors they control. And Bandura's (1982) self-efficacy
theory postulates a connection between beliefs and engagement, claiming
that people with low self-efficacy perceptions are less likely to persist and
succeed in their pursuits than are people with high perceptions of self-
efficacy. Finally, Corno and Mandinach (1983) claimed that negative perceptions interact with the process of adjusting to classroom challenges to
affect cognitive engagement.

> Students come to classroom task situations with numerous past experiences
> and knowledge, with skills and dispositions of various kinds. Among these
> knowledge networks may or may not be a schema for attacking a variety of
> cognitive tasks like those encountered in classrooms and other achievement
> situations. Students higher in general mental ability are more likely to have
> developed a self-regulated learning schema, as measures of general ability,
> call forth self-regulation processes. . . . These "aptitudes" set in motion *stu-
> dent interpretations of the instructional environment*, which act in consonance

with characteristic features of classroom instruction to determine the amount and kind of cognitive engagement a student will demonstrate on a given task. (Corno & Mandinach, 1983, p. 102, italics added)

When students interpret (perceive) the demands of the instructional challenge inadequately, their adjustments yield poor results and lower self-efficacy perceptions.

Ineffective or inefficient interpretations of task information, such as a failure to reduce and organize, may yield lower initial performance expectations if students are aware of their limitations. Initial expectations (both for outcomes and success) and the form of cognitive engagement that results once the task is begun, in turn, affect continued self-efficacy. (Corno & Mandinach, 1983, p. 102)

On the other hand, when students succeed in controlling difficult learning situations through their self-regulatory behavior, they believe they are responsible for controlling the situation.

When the student determines he or she has performed a difficult task successfully, favorable attributions should result. If either self-regulation, resource management, or task focus were actually engaged, a strategy attribution (i.e., "I used the right approach") would be expected. Strategy attributions are internal and controllable, by Weiner's categories. (Corno & Mandinach, 1983, p. 102)

The model in Fig. 1.1 describes the causal sequence implied by these theories. When students hold negative beliefs about learning opportunities, they tend to underperform to produce undesirable results and generate experiences of helplessness. This in turn tends to reinforce beliefs about being unable to control new challenges. As you can see from the arrows connecting these factors, a self-perpetuating pattern emerges that sustains negative beliefs, underperformance, and undesirable results. The idea behind learned helplessness is that instead of learning beliefs and behavior patterns that yield positive results and experiences, underachieving students learn beliefs and behaviors that yield negative results and experiences. Hence they learn to be helpless in the face of new challenges.

EXPLAINING SELF-ENGAGEMENT

The causal model depicted in Fig. 1.1 also suggests ways of breaking cycles of learned helplessness. It suggests, for example, that interventions to change student beliefs, performance, or results will replace experiences of

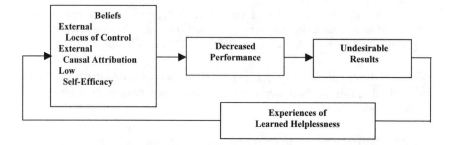

FIG. 1.1.   Beliefs, actions, results, and experiences during learned helplessness.

learned helplessness with experiences of learned control. Indeed, this was
the basis of Wang's (1983) recommendation for teaching underachievers
in general and special education.

> It appears that instructional intervention programs can shift students' per-
> ception of locus of control toward the internal orientation. Moreover, re-
> search shows a relationship between changes in student perceptions of locus
> of control and improvements in school performance. In light of these re-
> search and development efforts, it seems that the next appropriate step is to
> design and study the processes and effects of learning environments that at-
> tempt to maximize student learning through the development of students'
> sense of personal control. (Wang, 1983, p. 216)

She argued that teaching students to be effective self-regulators would increase their sense of internal locus of control, which in turn would increase engagement and learning:

> (a) When students are taught the prerequisite skills for managing their
> learning behaviors and learning situations, they can successfully take on
> self-management responsibility; (b) as students gain increasing capability to
> exert control over their school learning, their task performance improves; (c)
> it is possible to design intervention programs to foster the development of
> students' sense of personal control; (d) students' belief in their personal con-
> trol may be an important factor in allowing them to resist the adverse effects
> of teacher expectations; and (e) learning environments that are effective in
> fostering perceptions of self-responsibility need organizational and curricu-
> lar structures that allow students to acquire both academic and self-
> management skills. (Wang, 1983, pp. 242–243)

Proponents of self-determination made similar claims for students with
disabilities. They argued that when students with disabilities learn to take
control of their learning by improving their beliefs, self-regulation, and

TABLE 1.1
Three-Component Classifications of 18 Self-Determination Elements

Beliefs	Self-Regulation	Adjustment
1. Knowing needs and strengths	1. Self-advocacy skills	1. Self-monitoring skills
2. Knowing interests	2. Self-instructional skills	2. Self-evaluation skills
3. Having an internal locus of control	3. Problem-solving skills	3. Self-reinforcement skills
4. Making internal causal attributions	4. Choice-making skills	4. Goal-attainment skills
5. Having positive perceptions of self-efficacy	5. Decision-making skills	5. Adjustment skills
6. Having optimal opportunities for choice	6. Goal-setting skills	
	7. Performance skills	
1. Powers et al. (1998)	—	—
2. Sitlington & Neubert (1998)	—	—
3. —	Dolls & Sands (1998)	—
4. Carpenter (1998)	Carpenter (1998)	—
5. Curtis (1998)	Curtis (1998)	—
6. Fullerton (1998)	Fullerton (1998)	—
7. Gothelf & Brown (1998)	Gothelf & Brown (1998)	—
8. Halpern (1998)	Halpern (1998)	—
9. Van Reusen (1998)	Van Reusen (1998)	—
10. Wehmeyer (1998)	Wehmeyer (1998)	—
11. —	Agran (1998)	Agran (1998)
12. —	Hughes & Presley (1998)	Hughes & Presley (1998)
13. Martin & Marshal (1998)	Martin & Marshal (1998)	Martin & Marshal (1998)
14. Mithaug, Wehmeyer, Agran, Martin, & Palmer (1998)	Mithaug et al. (1998)	Mithaug et al. (1998)

adjustments, they increase their engagement and achievements during school and beyond. Wehmeyer and Sands (1998) identified many of the methods believed to produce these changes. Table 1.1 lists them according to their purported improvement in beliefs, self-regulation, and adjustment. The first row identifies interventions that target each causal category. The first column lists six types of information that improve beliefs about new challenges. The second column lists seven types of self-regulation skills that affect adjustments. And the third column lists five strategies that improve adjustment outcomes. The second row identifies published articles making these claims. As you can see, two articles identify strategies to improve beliefs. Ten articles describe strategies to improve self-regulation, beliefs and self-regulation, or self-regulation and adjustment. But only two articles describe approaches to improving beliefs, self-regulation, and adjustment.

WHAT WE KNOW AND DON'T KNOW

This is what we know about disengagement and how to deal with it. Persistent disengagement is due to self-defeating cycles of beliefs, actions, and results that can be reversed with interventions that alter those modes of believing, self-regulating, and adjusting. Moreover, those interventions are effective to the extent they give students control over their engagement and learning. When this happens, cycles of control replace cycles of learned helplessness.

The causal model in Fig. 1.2 explains how this might work. The upper half of the model represents engaged learning and the lower half represents disengaged learning. The upper half shows how positive beliefs, effective self-regulation, and successful results lead to learned control, and the lower half shows how negative beliefs, ineffective self-regulation, and unsuccessful results lead to learned helplessness. The explanation for learning suggested by this model is that beliefs about circumstances (left box) provoke self-regulation (middle box), which yields an adjustment (right box) that the learner interprets (attributions for success and failure) as being a gain or a loss for the valued pursuits.

When students are fully engaged in attempts to overcome difficult challenges, they adapt to those circumstances in order to learn as much as they can from them. Doris did this when she set successively higher goals for herself, but did Carey? Does the adaptive process depicted in Fig. 1.2 offer clues to an answer? We think it does. We suspect that the adaptive factors explaining why students engage new learning challenges in order to succeed also explains why they avoid new challenges. The model in

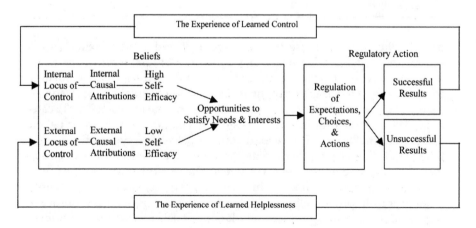

FIG. 1.2. Causal factors leading to experiences of learned control and learned helplessness.

Fig. 1.2 suggests, for example, that one factor is how students *perceive* their circumstances. Another is how they *act* on their perceptions to improve their situation, and a third is how they *feel* about the changes they make. It is very likely that these factors interact, as indicated in the model, to affect prospects of engaging new circumstances in the future. The question to be answered is, how do these factors interact to produce adjustments that maximize learning?

There is also much we do not know about disengagement and its instructional solutions. We don't know, for example, why some beliefs and perceptions tend to be provocative and to increase engagement whereas other beliefs and perceptions do not. Nor do we know why some episodes of engagement lead to adjustments that maximize learning and other episodes do not. The problem is that this ignorance about what instigates and sustains engagement limits our ability to explain why some instructional interventions work and others do not. Right now the best we can say is that some adjustments are self-defeating and that sometimes instruction works to reverse those patterns and produce learning. Why this occurs or under what conditions we cannot say.

We will search for answers to these questions by defining learning as *an adaptation to a new circumstance*. This will direct us to find reasons that explain why and how students engage challenges that require them to adjust in order to learn. It will lead to an examination of how students' beliefs and perceptions affect their actions to engage a new circumstance (cognitive factors), how those actions alter a circumstance to produce various outcomes (behavioral factors), and how feelings about the resulting adaptation affect subsequent beliefs about new circumstances (affective factors).

WHAT THE BOOK EXPLAINS

In this chapter we reviewed what we know about engagement and learning. In the next chapter, "How Engagement Affects Adjustment," we review research on the factors identified in the causal model of Fig. 1.2. This will help us understand how engagement produces those adjustments that are responsible for new learning. In chapter 3, "How Adjustment Affects Learning," we summarize the reasoning in chapters 1 and 2 to explain why learning maximizes when opportunities and adjustments optimize.

This is the theory of self-determined learning. It explains why and how opportunities to learn affect learning. The *why* factor is the optimality of the learning opportunity, which indicates how favorable the challenging situation appears to the learner. The *how* factor is the optimality of the adjustment, which indicates how effective the learner regulates expectations, choices, and actions to produce expected gain from the situation. According to the theory, when opportunity and adjustment conditions are as favorable as possible for the learner, self-engagement persists, a sense of control over the challenging circumstance develops, and learning maximizes. During these two optimality conditions, engagement persists because it produces results learners expect and want. They feel in control of gain production because they know exactly what to do to produce those results. They maximize learning because their beliefs, perceptions, and actions are sufficiently adapted to the situation to produce predictable gain from it.

According to this explanation for learning, the *adaptation* learners create to deal with a new situation *is what they learn*. They learn a new pattern of engagement. They experience a new feeling of control over the situation. They acquire a new set of beliefs and perceptions about the new circumstance. And as a result of this change in their adaptive states, the circumstance that was once new and challenging to them because it was *unknown and uncontrolled* becomes old to them because it is *known and controlled*. Table 1.2 presents this explanation for learning through adjustment.

In parts II and III of the book, we present studies to verify this explanation for engagement and learning. In part II we test the predicted effects of optimal opportunities and adjustments by comparing students with known differences in their self-engagement, sense of control, and learning. In part III we test prescriptions for instruction by determining whether an improvement in one or both optimality factors produces a corresponding increase in engagement, sense of control, and learning.

The studies in part II compare the opportunities and adjustments of students with reputed differences in engagement, sense of control, and achievement. We reasoned that because students with and without disabilities are reported to be different on these indicators, they are likely to

TABLE 1.2
Self-Determined Learning Theory: How Optimal Opportunity
Maximizes Engagement, Sense of Control, and Learning

---

1. The closer to optimal the opportunities for experiencing gain, the more likely is the regulation of expectations, choices, and actions to produce gain.
2. The more often the regulation of expectations, choices, and actions to produce gain, the more likely is it that adjustments optimize as expectations, choices, actions, and results become adaptive, rational, efficient and successful.
3. The closer to optimal the adjustments to an opportunity, the more persistent is the engagement to produce gain, the greater is the feeling of control over gain production, and the closer to maximum is the learning from that adaptation.
4. Therefore, the closer to optimal the opportunities for experiencing gain, the more persistent is the engagement, the greater is the sense of control, and the closer to maximum is the learning.

exhibit corresponding differences in the optimality of their opportunities and adjustments. Chapters 4 through 8 test the predictions that:

1. Students with disabilities have less favorable beliefs about their regulatory capacity to self-determine than do students with disabilities.
2. Differences in beliefs about regulatory capacity to self-determine are present among adults with and without disabilities.
3. Differences in beliefs about regulatory capacity to self-determine are present among students with and without disabilities in other countries.
4. Differences in beliefs about regulatory capacity to self-determine are due in part to differences in disability conditions.
5. Students in special education are less effective self-regulators during both optimal and suboptimal learning opportunities than are students in general education.

Part III tests the claim that if suboptimal opportunities and adjustments are responsible for lowered persistence, sense of control, and learning, then instruction to improve those conditions will produce a corresponding increase in persistence, sense of control, and learning. Chapters 9 through 13 test this by determining whether learners become more engaged and achievement oriented when their opportunities and adjustments become more favorable. Specifically, these studies examine whether:

1. Instructional strategies that improve learning opportunities and that make self-regulated adjustments more adaptable, rational, efficient, and successful will increase engagement and learning of young children with severe learning and behavior problems.

2. Teaching problem-solving strategies to secondary students with disabilities will improve their learning opportunities and self-regulatory behavior and, as a result, will increase their sense of control and achievement.

3. Teaching problem-solving strategies to secondary students with disabilities will improve their learning opportunities and self-regulated adjustments and, as a result, will increase perceptions of their ability and opportunity to self-determine.

4. Teaching problem-solving strategies to adults with severe disabilities will improve their learning opportunities and self-regulated adjustments and, as a result, will improve their job placements.

5. Improving the optimality of learning opportunities and self-regulated adjustments of prospective special education teachers will increase their practicum pupils' self-directed learning.

The last section of the book evaluates the theory. Chapter 14 assesses the theory's credibility by examining its coherence, validity, and verifiability, and it evaluates the theory's worth by considering its significance, scope, and utility.

WHAT'S NEXT?

The next chapter builds on the suggestion in this chapter that the beliefs, self-regulation, and adjustments identified in Fig. 1.2 may explain what provokes engagement, how engagement produces adjustment, and how adjustment affects learning. In that chapter, we use a modified version of the causal model in Fig. 1.2 to review research on the claim that discovering something new about a circumstance depends on being provoked by it sufficiently to solve problems of knowing how to produce desirable gain from it.

REFERENCES

Agran, M. (1998). Student directed learning strategies. In M. L. Wehmeyer & D. J. Sands (Eds.), *Making it happen: Student involvement in education planning, decision making, and instruction* (pp. 355–377). Baltimore, MD: Paul H. Brookes.

Bandura, A. (1982). Self-efficacy mechanism in human agency. *American Psychologist, 37*(92), 122–147.

Bickel, W. E., & Bickel, D. D. (1986). Effective schools, classrooms, and instruction: Implications for special education. *Exceptional Children, 53*(6), 489–500.

Carpenter, W. D. (1998). Become your own expert! A self-advocacy curriculum for secondary school-age students with learning disabilities. In M. L. Wehmeyer & D. J. Sands (Eds.), *Making it happen: Student involvement in education planning, decision making, and instruction* (pp. 263–277). Baltimore, MD: Paul H. Brookes.

Corno, L., & Mandinach, E. B. (1983). The role of cognitive engagement in classroom learning and motivation. *Educational Psychologist, 18*(2), 109–124.

Csikszentmihalyi, M. (1990). *Flow: The psychology of optimal experience.* New York: Harper & Row.

Curtis, E. (1998). It's my life: Preference-based planning for self-directed goals. In M. L. Wehmeyer & D. J. Sands (Eds.), *Making it happen: Student involvement in education planning, decision making, and instruction* (pp. 241–261). Baltimore, MD: Paul H. Brookes.

Diener, C. I., & Dweck, C. S. (1978). An analysis of learned helplessness: Continuous changes in performance, strategy, and achievement cognitions following failure. *Journal of Personality and Social Psychology, 36*(5), 451–462.

Doll, B., & Sands, D. J. (1998). Student involvement in goal setting and educational decision making: Foundations for effective instruction. In M. L. Wehmeyer & D. J. Sands (Eds.), *Making it happen: Student involvement in education planning, decision making, and instruction* (pp. 45–74). Baltimore, MD: Paul H. Brookes.

Ellis, E. S. (1986). The role of motivation and pedagogy on the generalization of cognitive strategy training. *Journal of Learning Disabilities, 19*(2), 66–70.

Fullerton, A. (1998). Putting feet on my dreams: Involving students with autism in life planning. In M. L. Wehmeyer & D. J. Sands (Eds.), *Making it happen: Student involvement in education planning, decision making, and instruction* (pp. 279–296). Baltimore, MD: Paul H. Brookes Publishing Co.

Gothelf, C. R., & Brown, F. (1998). Participation in the education process: Students with severe disabilities. In M. L. Wehmeyer & D. J. Sands (Eds.), *Making it happen: Student involvement in education planning, decision making, and instruction* (pp. 99–121). Baltimore, MD: Paul H. Brookes Publishing Co.

Halpern, A. (1998). Next S.T.E.P.: Student transition and educational planning. In M. L. Wehmeyer & D. J. Sands (Eds.), *Making it happen: Student involvement in education planning, decision making, and instruction* (pp. 167–185). Baltimore, MD: Paul H. Brookes Publishing Co.

Hughes, C., & Presley, J. A. (1998). Self-management and self-instruction: The benefits of student involvement in individualized education program implementation. In M. L. Wehmeyer & D. J. Sands (Eds.), *Making it happen: Student involvement in education planning, decision making, and instruction* (pp. 329–354). Baltimore, MD: Paul H. Brookes.

Martin, J. E., & Marshal, L. H. (1998). ChoiceMaker: Choosing planning, and taking action. In M. L. Wehmeyer & D. J. Sands (Eds.), *Making it happen: Student involvement in education planning, decision making, and instruction* (pp. 211–240). Baltimore, MD: Paul H. Brookes.

Mithaug, D. E. (1996). The optimal prospects principle: A theoretical basis for rethinking instructional practices for self-determination. In D. J. Sands & M. L. Wehmeyer (Eds.), *Self-determination across the life span: Independence and choice for people with disabilities* (pp. 147–167). Baltimore, MD: Paul H. Brookes.

Mithaug, D. E., Wehmeyer, M. L., Agran, M., Martin, J. E., & Palmer, S. (1998). The self-determined learning model of instruction: Engaging students to solve their learning problems. In M. L. Wehmeyer & D. J. Sands (Eds.), *Making it happen: Student involvement in education planning, decision making, and instruction* (pp. 299–328). Baltimore, MD: Paul H. Brookes.

Powers, L. E., Turner, A., Westwood, D. H., Loesch, C., Brown, A., & Rowland, C. (1998). TAKE CHARGE for the future: A student-directed approach to transition planning. In M. L. Wehmeyer & D. J. Sands (Eds.), *Making it happen: Student involvement in education planning, decision making, and instruction* (pp. 187–210). Baltimore, MD: Paul H. Brookes.

Rotter, J. B. (1966). Generalized expectancies for internal versus external control of reinforcement [Special issue]. *Pscyhological Monographs, 80*(1).

Sands, D. J., & Wehmeyer, M. L. (1996). *Self-determination across the life span: Independence and choice for people with disabilities.* Baltimore: Paul H. Brookes Publishing Co.

Sitlington, P. L., & Neubert, D. A. (1998). Transition assessment: Methods and processes to determine student needs, preferences, and interests. In M. L. Wehmeyer & D. J. Sands (Eds.), *Making it happen: Student involvement in education planning, decision making, and instruction* (pp. 75–98). Baltimore, MD: Paul H. Brookes.

Van Reusen, A. K. (1998). Self-advocacy strategy instruction: Enhancing student motivation, self-determination, and responsibility in the learning process. In M. L. Wehmeyer & D. J. Sands (Eds.), *Making it happen: Student involvement in education planning, decision making, and instruction* (pp. 131–152). Baltimore, MD: Paul H. Brookes.

Wang, M. C. (1983). Development and consequences of students' sense of personal control. In J. M. Levine & M. C. Wang (Eds.), *Teacher and student perceptions: Implications for learning* (pp. 213–247). Hillsdale, NJ: Lawrence Erlbaum Associates.

Wehmeyer, M. L. (1998). Student involvement in education planning, decision making, and instruction: An idea whose time has arrived. In M. L. Wehmeyer & D. J. Sands (Eds.), *Making it happen: Student involvement in education planning, decision making, and instruction* (pp. 3–23). Baltimore, MD: Paul H. Brookes.

Wehmeyer, M. L., & Sands, D. J. (Eds.). (1998). *Making it happen: Student involvement in education planning, decision making, and instruction.* Baltimore, MD: Paul H. Brookes.

Weiner, B. (1976). Attribution theory, achievement motivation, and the educational process. *Review of Educational Research, 42,* 201–215.

Zimmerman, B. J., Bonner, S., & Kovach, R. (1996). *Developing self-regulated learners: Beyond achievement to self-efficacy* (pp. 6–7). Washington, DC: American Psychological Association.

2

How Engagement Affects Adjustment

Dennis E. Mithaug
Deirdre K. Mithaug
Martin Agran
James E. Martin
Michael L. Wehmeyer

In this chapter we examine the relationship between opportunities, engagement, and adjustment. Our claim is that when learners believe a circumstance offers a valuable and manageable opportunity for gain, they engage it by regulating their expectations, choices, and actions to produce a result that yields a satisfactory change in circumstances — usually a gain toward some end. This in turn produces an experience of control over the circumstance that positively affects subsequent beliefs about the opportunities for gain in that situation. This is how opportunities affect engagement and how engagement affects adjustment.

We show how these effects are expressed in beliefs that interpret circumstances as being opportunities or obstacles for gain, in engagement that regulates expectations, choices, and actions to produce new adjustments, and in an adjustment optimality that affects feelings of control over the circumstance. This process of adjustment to a circumstance explains why learning depends on self-regulated engagement. Figure 2.1, which we developed from Fig. 1.2 in the preceding chapter, illustrates the adjustment process. Beginning on the left side of the diagram, *beliefs* about *circumstances* produce an opportunity effect that defines events as being favorable enough to engage. The *self-regulated engagement* provoked by these opportunities adjusts expectations, choices, and actions to produce desirable change in the circumstance. The resulting *adjustment* affects experiences of control, which in turn affects subsequent *beliefs about opportunities* for gain. According to this adjustment model of learning, engagement moves learners from one adaptive state to another as their self-regulated adjustments in expectations, choices, and actions produce

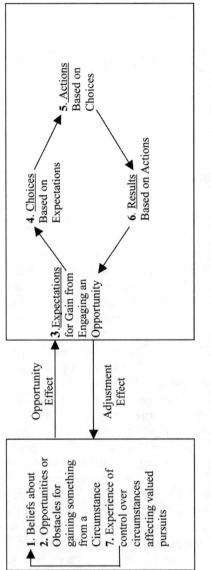

FIG. 2.1. Effects of beliefs about circumstances, self-regulation, and experiences of control on opportunities and adjustments during engagement and learning.

changes in circumstances that feed back to alter beliefs about opportunities for gain from the situation. These new adaptive states are what learners learn from new situations.

The key factors in this process are *beliefs* about *circumstances* (factors 1 and 2), the *opportunity effect* produced by these factors, the regulation of *expectations, choices, actions,* and *results* (factors 3–6), the *adjustment* effect produced by that self-regulation, and the experience of *control* associated with that adjustment (factor 7). We consider these influences next.

BELIEFS ABOUT CIRCUMSTANCES

First let's consider the effect of beliefs about circumstances on engagement, factors 1 and 2 in Fig. 2.1. Our claim is that beliefs affect learning by influencing engagement. By defining environmental events as opportunities, obstacles, or as irrelevant to valued pursuits, beliefs determine whether we act or avoid acting on a circumstance. Beliefs are constructed as we acquire information about the cause of a circumstance, its consequences for pursuits, and the actions likely to advance or protect an interest. For example, when we have information that suggests the cause of an unfavorable circumstance, that the event will adversely affect our pursuits, and that we can act to prevent it, we act.

In this sense, beliefs about opportunities interpret information about how events affect pursuits. So when learners believe they know the cause of a circumstance but that it will not affect their pursuits, they do not act because the situation is irrelevant to their pursuits. On the other hand, when they do not know what to believe about the cause of a circumstance but believe it will adversely affect their pursuits, they act to find the source of the problem and what they can do to prevent its undesirable consequences.

Therefore, when learners believe they know the cause of a circumstance and when that knowledge implies action to advance or protect an interest, they act to produce gain toward the advancement or protection of that interest. On the other hand, when they believe they do not know the cause of a new circumstance but believe its consequences will affect their interests, they act to find out more. This is how beliefs about a situation produce different effects on engagement. In the first case, *knowing what to believe* leads learners to act in ways they "know" will advance or protect an interest. Their responding is predictable here in that it is explained by the interest. This is not so in the second case, where the learner *does not know what to believe*. Here the learner is provoked *to discover* what might advance or protect an interest (Mithaug, 2000).

This claim that beliefs affect engagement has been around for some time. It was first investigated early last century in Max Weber's (1864–

1920) ambitious effort to show that the Protestant ethic was responsible for the entrepreneurial engagement that prompted the industrial revolution. In his famous work *The Protestant Ethic and the Spirit of Capitalism* (1930/1958), Weber claimed that people who believed in the ethic were more likely to be engaged in discovery to find out about events affecting their pursuits than were people who did not believe in it. Sociologist Robert Merton (1957) investigated the claim in the 1950s using historical data to show a correlation between beliefs about personal control and scientific inquiry. He found that people who believed they were in control of their circumstances were likely to engage in scientific problem solving to figure out how things work (Mithaug, 1993, p. 90). Christopher Lasch (1979) used a similar argument to connect American individualism with belief in personal responsibility.

> The Protestant work ethic stood as one of the most important underpinnings of American culture. According to the myth of capitalist enterprise, thrift and industry held the key to material success and spiritual fulfillment. America's reputation as a land of opportunity rested on its claim that the destruction of hereditary obstacles to advancement had created conditions in which social mobility depended on individual initiative alone. The self-made man, archetypical embodiment of the American dream, owed his advancement to habits of industry, sobriety, moderation, self-discipline, and avoidance of debt. He lived for the future, shunning self-indulgence in favor of patient, painstaking accumulation; and as long as the collective prospect looked on the whole so bright, he found in the deferral of gratification not only his principal gratification but an abundant source of profits. (Lasch, 1979, p. 106)

In the 1950s, psychologists sought to trace the intergenerational transmission of beliefs by studying independence training of people who succeeded in science. They found that parents of accomplished scientists held beliefs about causal agency and that their child-rearing practices correlated with those beliefs about personal control (McClelland & Liberman, 1949). Decades later a similar line of inquiry connected efficacious beliefs with success in life. Gallup and Gallup (1986) found that successful people believed in personal responsibility, self-reliance, control, and the ability to get things done. Garfield (1986) reported that peak performers in business, science, sports, and the arts tended to believe that persistent adjustment to challenge would lead to success in their pursuits. And Griessman (1987) found that belief in the ability to engage valued pursuits persistently through both good and bad times was associated with success in life.

This work illustrates the positive function of beliefs; that is, they can encourage engagement. Their negative function was described in the last chapter in terms of external locus of control (Rotter, 1966), low self-efficacy (Bandura, 1982), and external causal attributions (Weiner, 1976). For these beliefs, the function was to discourage engagement. Indeed several researchers have suggested that students who hold these negative beliefs tend to avoid challenge and exhibit learned helplessness (Bailer, 1961; Bendell, Tollefson, & Fine, 1980; Butkowski & Willows, 1980; Chapman & Boersma, 1979; Dudley-Marling, Snider, & Tarver, 1982; Floor & Rosen, 1975; Gozali & Bialer, 1968; Hallahan, Gajar, Cohen, & Tarver, 1978; Lewis & Lawrence-Patterson; 1989; Licht, 1983; Licht, Kistner, Ozkaragoz, Shapiro, & Glausen, 1985; Pearl, 1985; Pearl, Bryan, & Donahue, 1980; Wehmeyer, 1993; Wehmeyer & Kelchner, 1996; Weisz, 1979).

OPPORTUNITY EFFECTS

Of course, beliefs do not function independently of circumstances to affect action. To illustrate, consider two very different opportunity effects provoked by beliefs. One occurs when a circumstance is consistent with the belief that acting one way produces more gain from a circumstance than acting another way. Here the opportunity effect produced by the belief produces an expectation for gain and choices to respond that yield that expected gain for the learner. Hence the adjustment correlates with reinforcement maximization and can be explained by Herrnstein's Matching Law, which predicts that *when actors know what to expect* from a situation, their engagement matches their prospects for reinforcement (Herrnstein, 1970). According to the law, engagement and opportunity for gain (reinforcement) correlate positively over time.

But matching does not occur *when beliefs are inconsistent with circumstances* because then actors do not know what to expect from the situation. Consequently, they do not know how to respond to its opportunities for gain. Still they must act if they are to reach their goals. So instead of acting to produce the gain they hope for, they adjust their expectations, choices, and actions *to get information on what to do* to produce gain. This is what John Dewey's traveler did when he came to a fork in the road and did not know which path to take. He experienced an inconsistency between his belief that he was on the correct path to his destination and the fact that there was not one path but two. He was provoked into discovering what to expect, how to choose and what to do. The following account illustrates this opportunity effect on his engagement (Mithaug, 2000).

A man traveling in an unfamiliar region comes to a branching of the road. Having no sure knowledge to fall back upon, he is brought to a standstill of hesitation and suspense. Which road is right? And how shall his perplexity be resolved? There are but two alternatives: he must either blindly and arbitrarily take his course, trusting to luck for the outcome, or he must discover grounds for the conclusion that a given road is right. Any attempt to decide the matter by thinking will involve inquiring into other facts, whether brought to mind by memory, or by further observation, or by both. The perplexed wayfarer must carefully scrutinize what is before him and he must cudgel his memory. He looks for evidence that will support belief in favor of either of the roads — for evidence that will weigh down one suggestion. He may climb a tree; he may go first in this direction, then in that, looking, in either case, for signs, clues, indications. He wants something in the nature of signboard or a map, and his reflection is aimed at the discovery of facts that will serve this purpose. (Dewey, 1933, p. 14)

Circumstances like these motivate us to act because they contradict what we believe will get us where we want to go. They provoke us into resolving uncertainties. When Dewey's traveler encountered a situation that contradicted his belief, he felt compelled to find out more. He looked in one direction and then another in search of a sign indicating which path led where. And when he found what he needed to know, he chose the path leading to his destination.

All actors change their patterns of self-regulation when their beliefs are inconsistent with their circumstances. Nonhuman actors do too. When they do not know the consequences of pursuing one option rather than another, they engage in problem solving to discover the best choice. They behave like Herrnstein's laboratory animals who "do not know" that lever pressing or disk pecking produces food (Horne & Lowe, 1993; King & Logue, 1990). They search their environments to learn more.

SELF-REGULATED ENGAGEMENT

According to this analysis there are two self-regulation effects, one provoked by beliefs that are consistent with circumstances and the other provoked by beliefs that are inconsistent with circumstances. The first type of provocation occurs when actors know what to expect from a situation. The resulting engagement is a previously learned pattern of self-regulation, one that produces gain as expected from existing beliefs about the situation. Hence it does not yield new learning. In these situations, the Matching Law's prediction of a correlation between engagement and gain (reinforcements) holds because actors know exactly what gain to expect by engaging the circumstance. Consequently, they spend their time and behavior acting on those events that produce the gain that they want.

The second type of provocation occurs when actors do not know what to expect from a situation, when their beliefs are inconsistent with their circumstances. The engagement resulting from this provocation is a different pattern of responding and therefore *does yield new learning.* Consider what Dewey's traveler was provoked to learn when he came to an unexpected fork in the road and realized he did not know which way to go. The unexpected circumstance interrupted his travel plans and provoked him to find more information about the forked road. To get that information, he climbed trees, took short trips down each path, looked for signs indicating where to go, and so forth. When he finally *learned what he needed to know* about the situation, he used that information to regulate his behavior to progress (make gain) toward his destination.

Indeed, the self-regulation strategy actors use to discover what they need to know about an unusual circumstance is well documented. Dewey (1910/1991) claimed the strategy included five phases: "(i) a felt difficulty; (ii) identifying location and definition; (iii) suggesting possible solutions; (iv) developing reasons on the bearings of the suggestion; and (v) observing and experimenting to accept or reject the conclusion of belief or disbelief" (p. 72). Newell and Simon (1972) identified the same strategy a half-century later by observing test subjects find solutions to difficult problems. They reduced it to four steps:

1. Identify the discrepancy between the goal state of a solved problem and the actual state.
2. Search for an operation to reduce that discrepancy.
3. Apply the operator likely to reduce the discrepancy.
4. Repeat the steps until the actual state equals the goal state.

Then Newell and Simon (1972) also showed how the strategy could be used in a computer program to solve complex problems in chess, memory, learning, physics, engineering, education, rule induction, concept formation, perception, and understanding (pp. 661–784). Its use in solving the everyday problem of getting a child to nursery school was also demonstrated, as follows.

> I want to take my son to nursery school. What's the difference between what I have and what I want? One of distance. What changes distance? My automobile. My automobile won't work. What is needed to make it work? A new battery. What has new batteries? An auto repair shop. I want the repair shop to put in a new battery but the shop doesn't know I need one. What is the difficulty? One of communication. What allows communication? Telephone ... and so on. (p. 416)

This example reveals how the strategy resolves a sequence of inconsistencies between circumstances and beliefs. For example, when Newell (or Simon) got into the car, he believed it would get the child to school on time. But when the car contradicted that belief by not starting, Newell did not know what to believe. The following sequence traces the provocative effects of several inconsistencies. The first was controlled by the belief that the car would get the child to school. It provoked the routine of getting ready to use the car. The next four episodes were controlled by not knowing what to believe, which provoked problem solving to find out why the car did not start, what to do about it, and how to use that information to get the car to start. The last episode was controlled by the belief that the car would start and get the boy to school.

> *My Goal*: Get my son to nursery school.
> 1. *Problem*: How to reduce distance from home to nursery school.
>   *Solution*: Use car to take son to nursery school.
>   2. *Problem*: Car won't start, battery is dead.
>   *Solution*: Get new battery to start car.
>   3. *Problem*: Don't have new battery at home.
>   *Solution*: Get new battery at repair shop.
>   4. *Problem*: Repair shop doesn't know I need a new battery.
>   *Solution*: Telephone repair shop to bring out new battery and install it.
>   5. *Action*: Telephone repair shop.
>   *Consequence*: Auto repairman came and installed new battery.
>   *Evaluation*: Car will start now.
>   6. *Action*: Drive son to nursery school
>   *Consequence*: Son is at nursery school.
>   *Evaluation*: I have met my goal. (Mithaug, 1993, p. 54)

Table 2.1 compares different discovery strategies that have been used to explain similar events. The first is Dewey's practical reasoning, the second is Newell and Simon's means–ends problem solving, the third is the scientific method, and the fourth is Mithaug's constructive theorizing. All of these strategies employ similar steps. The first step — awareness of the problem — is recognition of an inconsistency between a belief and a circumstance. It provokes the other three. For Dewey the first step is a felt difficulty, for Newell and Simon it is a discrepancy between a goal state and an actual state, for the scientific method it is a discrepancy between a theory and the facts, and for constructive theorizing it is a discrepancy between knowing and not knowing reasons for an unusual circumstance. The remaining steps include searching for possible solutions (step 2), comparing them with the new circumstance (step 3), and returning to step 1 to assess the status of not knowing and repeating the sequence as necessary until the problem of not knowing is eliminated (step 4).

TABLE 2.1
Strategies for Self-Regulated Problem Solving to Learn Something New

Dewey's Practical Reasoning	Newell & Simon's Means-Ends Problem Solving	The Scientific Method	Mithaug's Constructive Theorizing
1. Define and locate a felt difficulty	1. Compare a current situation with goal situation to detect one or more differences between them	1. Define problem as an inconsistency between facts of a circumstance and a theory	1. Define problem as a discrepancy between knowing and not knowing about a fact, value, or action associated with a circumstance
2. Suggest a possible solution and find reasons for it	2. Find an operator associated with these differences that will reduce the differences	2. Collect data on discrepancy in order to formulate a hypothesis to explain the discrepancy	2. Find reasons to explain these discrepancies between knowing and not knowing
3. Conduct further observations and experiments to test the solution	3. Apply the operator	3. Conduct tests of the hypothesis	3. Evaluate the credibility and worth of these reasons and explanation
4. Return to step 1 to accept or reject the solution	4. Return to step 1 and repeat steps if difference still exists	4. Based on test results, return to step 1 to adjust the theory	4. Return to step 1 to adjust existing beliefs

For most learners, problems of not knowing something are resolved quickly and easily following some version of this strategy. It may take some people longer to find out what they need to know simply because they are not systematic in their problem solving. And sometimes people act *before* knowing enough about the situation to deal with it effectively. So when they fail to get what they want and wonder why, they take the problem more seriously, this time regulating their expectations, choices, and actions with a problem-solving strategy.

Unfortunately, many students fail to learn how to learn because they are unaware of inconsistencies between their beliefs and circumstances or because they don't know how to resolve inconsistencies once they are aware of them. Hence, they never learn to adjust when situations change. Whitman (1990) claimed that persons with mental retardation are poor adjusters for these reasons.

On one hand, persons with retardation seemingly are unable to realize that similar situations often require similar responses and on the other hand, that dissimilar situations may require different responses. Because of this type of problem it seems that mental retardation might be better described as a self-regulatory disorder. Such a re-conceptualization is compatible with general descriptions of persons with retardation as being dependent and having an external locus of control. . . . Because of their inability to effectively self-regulate their behavior and the negative consequences associated with failure, they look to others for assistance. (p. 348)

Others have made similar claims about students with learning, emotional, and behavior problems. Table 2.2 lists these studies, which also link deficiencies in self-regulated problem solving to poor adjustments at school.

In chapter 1 we linked ineffective self-regulation to the poor adjustment and underachievement of Calvin, Maria, and Carey. Calvin dreamed of being the first person in his family to graduate from high school but regulated his behavior poorly when presented with new challenge. He procrastinated, skimmed reading assignments, crammed for tests at the last minute, and wrote in a haphazard manner. Maria also self-regulated poorly. She tried hard in school but attended more to her friends than her schoolwork. When she studied, she did it with her friends by sharing answers to math or science problems and by reading her assignments cursorily between extended discussions about the day's events. She prepared minimally for tests and crammed the night before the exam

TABLE 2.2
Studies Linking Disability, Self-Regulation Deficiencies,
and Maladaptive Adjustments

Students with Emotional and Behavioral Problems	Students with Learning Disabilities	Students with Mental Retardation
Arnold & Clement (1981)	Aponik & Dembo (1983)	Floor & Rosen (1975)
Bolstad & Johnson (1972)	Brown & Palincsar (1982)	Litrownick & Steinfeld (1982)
Erickson, Wyne, & Routh (1973)	Ellis (1986)	Litrownik, Cleary, Lecklitner, & Franzini (1978)
Finch, Deardorff, & Montgomery (1974)	Graham, Harris, & Reid (1992)	Litrownik, Freitas, & Franzini (1978)
Finch, Kendall, Deardorff, Anderson, & Sitarz (1975)	Harris & Graham (1985)	Weisz (1979)
Finch & Spirito (1980)	Hallahan, Kauffman, & Lloyd (1999)	Whitman (1990)
Finch, Wilkinson, Nelson, & Montgomery (1975)	Licht (1983)	
Guevremont, Osnes, & Stokes (1986)	Licht, Kistner, Ozkaragoz, Shapiro, & Clausen (1985)	
Montgomery & Finch (1975)	Lloyd (1980)	
Neilans & Israel (1981)	Shelton, Anastopoulos, & Linden (1985)	
Nelson, Finch, & Hooke (1975)	Wiens (1983)	
Varni & Henker (1979)	Wong (1980)	

(Zimmerman, Bonner, & Kovach, 1996, pp. 6–7). Carey fit a similar profile but for different reasons. She disliked school, avoided homework, and spent her time watching television and hanging out with friends. She dreamed about what she might be when she grew up but lacked confidence that she would ever become what she wanted. Also, she never connected her actions with the realization of her dreams. When asked what grades she expected, she gave inconsistent answers. Sometimes she expected all A's, and other times she expected all F's. This was typical of how she set goals. They were either so high nothing she did could achieve them or so low that anything she did would achieve them. Either way, she never had to change what she believed, what she expected, or how she acted. By setting expectations too high, no amount of new regulation would make a difference. By setting expectations too low, any self-regulation would be effective. Hence, there was never a connection between what Carey believed, what she expected, and how she acted (Mithaug, 1996, p. 148).

ADJUSTMENT TO CIRCUMSTANCES

Clearly, self-engagement provoked by beliefs that are inconsistent with circumstances is more interesting than engagement provoked by beliefs that are consistent with circumstance because the former produces the most learning. The latter, in contrast, reflects learned patterns of adjustment that have a track record of producing expected gain toward desired ends. Little new learning is required to produce these adjustments. Self-regulated engagement provoked by inconsistencies between beliefs and circumstance, in contrast, leads to new adjustments, gain, and hence new learning about circumstances. On this score there is much variability in adjustment and learning. The adjustment's optimality reflects this in that the closer to optimal the adjustment, the more favorable it is for producing desired gain. Self-regulation engagement is responsible for these adjustments because as it becomes effective, adjustments become favorable.

Research conducted by Zimmerman and Martinez-Pons (1986, 1988, 1990) supports this proposition with studies of high- and low-achieving students. That work found that high-achieving students were more likely to engage in effective patterns of self-regulation than were low-achieving students. The former were more likely to engage in goal setting and strategic planning (setting expectations and making choices), in strategy implementation and monitoring (taking actions), in strategy outcome monitoring (results monitoring), and in evaluation and monitoring (adjusting subsequent expectations, choices, and actions). These differences in self-regulatory behavior were also correlated positively with membership in high- and low-achieving groups. In fact, these behaviors predicted group

membership at 93% accuracy. Biemiller and Meichenbaum (1992) reported similar findings in a 10-year literature review of self-regulation
studies.

> Research conducted in the last 10 years suggests that one source of the dif-
> ferences between the highest- and the lowest-achieving children is the de-
> gree to which they become self-regulators of their own learning. High-
> achieving students engage in a number of helpful strategic skills, including
> goal setting, planning, self-interrogating, self-monitoring (checking an-
> swers), asking for help, using aids, and using memory strategies.... In ad-
> dition, more competent students bring a greater knowledge to school tasks.
> Self-regulated learners behave in ways that often characterize adult ex-
> perts.... Their "budding expertise" is evident in the complexity of their
> skills; the amount and structure of their knowledge; the strategic nature of
> their behavior; and the motivated effort they make, especially in response to
> failure. (p. 75)

Biemiller and Meichenbaum concluded that high achievers succeed because they ask questions that *guide the regulation of their expectations, choices,
actions, and results*. They ask: What can I *expect* (setting expectations)? What
should I do (*making choices*)? What am I *doing* (monitoring behavior)? What
results did I get (comparing results with expectations)?

Self-regulation theory explains how self-regulation behaviors affect the
optimality of adjustments (Mithaug, 1993). It claims that when factors 3–6
in Fig. 2.1 optimize, adjustments become as favorable as possible. This occurs when actors regulate their expectations, choices, actions, and results
to the best of their ability. Hence, their expectations reflect the most they
can accomplish given their ability and experience (optimal expectations).
Their choice of how to produce gain is the most likely way of producing
the gain they expect given their alternatives (optimal choosing). Their actions are as effective as possible given their ability (optimal responding).
And their results match their expectations as closely as possible given
their situation (optimal results). In sum, they have regulated the four factors in Fig. 2.1 as effectively as possible given their capacity and their circumstances. Hence, their adjustments are optimal and the gain toward the
goals is maximal. This is how optimal adjustments maximize gain
(Mithaug, 1993).

THE EXPERIENCE OF CONTROL

Central to this view of learning though adjustment is the experience of control associated with each new adjustment. This is factor 7 in the causal
model in Fig. 2.1. When self-regulation produces an adjustment that makes

a difficult circumstance favorable enough for a pursuit, the feeling of control associated with that new state supports the belief that the circumstance can be improved again in favor the pursuit, as Mithaug (1993) illustrated.

> Optimal experience is a byproduct of transforming suboptimal conditions into optimal opportunities. Writer May Sarton discovered it in writing poetry: "I'm absolutely alone then and I'm in a state of great intensity of feeling and intellect. I'm perfectly balanced and nothing else exists. Time doesn't exist." Composer Burt Bacharach found it in writing music: "The music is hard, but I like going back to the room and writing. I'm happy because I push myself into a discipline. I get into a groove where I'm playing the piano and melodies start to flow and I'm happy." And futurist writer John Naisbitt found it while fulfilling his potential. "People who work for a sense of personal worth keep working at it. They want to push and stretch. They want to experience their potential. They want to get right out there to the edge, and that's what they keep pushing for." (Mithaug, 1993, pp. 149–150)[1]

Experiences of control can also be produced by cycles of engagement and adjustment that improve circumstances one engagement episode at a time. As feelings of control increase and the probability of engagement increases, actors become adept at regulating their behavior effectively. They discover what to expect from new challenges (optimal expectations), how to choose actions that are effective (optimal choosing), how to act effectively (optimal responses), and how to predict exactly what they can produce (optimal results). Csikszentmihalyi (1990) described these feelings as *optimal experiences.*

> Contrary to what we usually believe . . . the best moments in our lives . . . are not the passive, receptive, relaxing times—although such experiences can also be enjoyable, if we have worked hard to attain them. The best moments usually occur when a person's body or mind is stretched to its limits in a voluntary effort to accomplish something difficult and worthwhile. Optimal experience is thus something that we make happen. For a child, it could be placing with trembling fingers the last block on a tower she has built, higher than any she has built so far; for a swimmer, it could be trying to beat his own record; for a violinist, mastering an intricate musical passage. For each person there are thousands of opportunities, challenges to expand ourselves. (Csikszentmihalyi, 1990, p. 3)

Of course contrary experiences can occur too, even when actors do their best to overcome obstacles preventing them from getting what they want.

---

[1]Sarton, Bacharach, and Naisbitt quotes are from Wholey (1986, pp. 109, 175, and 66, respectively).

TABLE 2.3
How the Experience of Control Affects Beliefs About Self-Regulatory
Capacity During Conditions of Optimal and Suboptimal Opportunity

Postadjustment Experiences of Control	Preadjustment Belief That a Circumstance Presents an Optimal Opportunity for Gain	Preadjustment Belief That a Circumstance Presents a Suboptimal Opportunity for Gain
Experience of high control after repeated production of expected gain	Postadjustment belief that *competent* self-regulation is responsible	Postadjustment belief that *intelligent* self-regulation is responsible
Experience of low control after repeated failure to produce expected gain	Postadjustment belief that *incompetent* self-regulation is responsible	Postadjustment belief that *unlucky* self-regulation is responsible

And when these experiences persist, they can feel so helpless that they believe nothing they do will make a difference. This, in turn, can promote avoidance rather than engagement. Weiner's attribution theory (1976) makes this prediction by claiming that when actors fail repeatedly, they tend to believe that they have insufficient ability or they have bad luck. Either way, they have no reason to engage new challenges.

Table 2.3 shows that these predictions are in line with those suggested by the causal model in Fig. 2.1. Column 1 identifies the experiences of control resulting from repeated success (row 1) and from repeated failure (row 2), and columns 2 and 3 identify the circumstances that provoke engagement and adjustments to those challenges. Column 2 represents opportunities judged to be favorable (optimal) for pursuits, and column 3 represents opportunities judged to be unfavorable (suboptimal) for pursuits. Note that the cell predictions are similar to those of Weiner's attribution theory (1976).

First consider the effects of repeated success on beliefs about the cause and consequences of new challenges (row 1). When actors produce the gain they expect during optimal opportunities (cell 1), they believe their success is due to competent adjustments to that circumstance. On the other hand, when they produce the gain they expect during difficult circumstances (cell 2), they believe their success is due to intelligent adjustment. Now consider the effects of repeated failure on beliefs about the cause and consequences of new challenges (row 2). When actors fail to produce the gain they expect during favorable opportunities, they believe their failure is due to incompetent adjustments (cell 3). On the other hand, when they fail to get what they expect during unfavorable circumstances (cell 4) they believe their failure is due to their bad luck.

WHAT WE KNOW ABOUT LEARNING THROUGH ADJUSTMENT

In this chapter we developed an explanation for learning through adjustment that claims *beliefs* about *circumstances* produce *opportunities* that provoke *self-regulated* engagement, which in turn produces adjustments that influence *experiences of control*. According to this account, learning results when adjustments produce new adaptive states. Hence, learning is a change in beliefs and patterns of adjustment associated with that change.

We described how these factors work together to produce learning. We argued that when beliefs about circumstances are inconsistent with events, actors are provoked into problem solving as they alter their engagement. This produces new adjustments to circumstances, and new feelings of control over the situation. The resulting adaptive state is what is learned. It consists of *beliefs* about the causes and consequences of an unusual or challenging circumstance, the self-regulated *behavior* provoked by beliefs about those events, and *feelings* of control associated with the adjustments produced by that self-regulation. Hence, learning includes the believing, acting, and feeling associated with adaptive change. In the next chapter, we make these claims explicit by describing a theory of learning based on this model of adjustment. It explains why optimal opportunities and optimal adjustments maximize learning.

REFERENCES

Aponik, D. A., & Dembo, M. H. (1983). LD and normal adolescents' causal attributions of success and failure at different levels of task difficulty. *Learning Disability Quarterly, 6,* 31–39.

Arnold, J. H., & Clement, P. W. (1981). Temporal generalization of self-regulation effects in under-controlled children. *Child Behavior Therapy, 3*(4), 43–67.

Bailer, I. (1961). Conceptualization of success and failure in mentally retarded and normal children. *Journal of Personality, 42,* 1099–1107.

Bandura, A. (1982). Self-efficacy mechanism in human agency. *American Psychologist, 37*(92), 122–147.

Bendell, D., Tollefson, N., & Fine, M. (1980). Interaction of locus-of-control orientation and the performance of learning disabled adolescents. *Journal of Learning Disabilities, 13,* 32–35.

Biemiller, A., & Meichenbaum, D. (1992). The nature and nurture of the self-directed learner. *Educational Leadership,* 75–80.

Bolstad, O. D., & Johnson, S. M. (1972). Self-regulation in the modification of disruptive classroom behavior. *Journal of Applied Behavior Analysis, 5,* 443–454.

Brown, A. L., & Palincsar, A. S. (1982, April). Inducing strategic learning from texts by means of informed, self-control training. *Topics in Learning and Learning Disabilities,* pp. 1–17.

Butkowski, I. S., & Williows, D. M. (1980). Cognitive-motivational characteristics of children varying in reading ability: Evidence for learned helplessness in poor readers. *Journal of Educational Psychology, 72*(3), 408–422.

Chapman, J. W., & Boersma, F. J. (1979). Learning disabilities, locus of control, and mother attitudes. *Journal of Educational Psychology, 71*, 250–258.

Csikszentmihalyi, M. (1990). *Flow: The psychology of optimal experience.* New York: Harper & Row.

Dewey, J. (1933). *How we think: A restatement of the relation of reflective thinking to the educative process.* Boston: D. C. Heath.

Dewey, J. (1991). *How we think.* Buffalo, NY: Prometheus Books. (Original work published 1910)

Dudley-Marling, C. C., Snider, V., & Tarver, S. G. (1982). Locus of control and learning disabilities: A review and discussion. *Perceptual Motor Skills, 54*, 503–514.

Ellis, E. S. (1986). The role of motivation and pedagogy on the generalization of cognitive strategy training. *Journal of Learning Disabilities, 19*(2), 66–70.

Erickson, E. A., Wyne, M. D., & Routh, D. K. (1973). A response-cost procedure for reduction of impulsive behavior of academically handicapped children. *Journal of Abnormal Child Psychology, 1*, 350–357.

Finch, A. J., Jr., Deardorff, P. A., & Montgomery, L. E. (1974). Reflection-impulsivity: Reliability of the Matching Familiar Figures Test with emotionally disturbed children. *Psychological Reports, 35*, 1133–1134.

Finch, A. J., Jr., Kendall, P. C., Deardorff, P. A., Anderson, J., & Sitarz, A. M. (1975). Reflection-impulsivity, persistence behavior, and locus of control in emotionally disturbed children. *Journal of Consulting and Clinical Psychology, 43*(5), 748.

Finch, A. J., Jr., & Spirito, A. (1980). Use of cognitive training to change cognitive processes. *Exceptional Education Quarterly, 1*(1), 31–39.

Finch, A. J., Jr., Wilkinson, M. D., Nelson, W. M. III, & Montgomery, L. E. (1975). Modification of an impulsive cognitive tempo in emotionally distrubed boys. *Journal of Abnormal Child Psychology, 3*(1), 49–52.

Floor, L., & Rosen, M. (1975). Investigating the phenomenon of helplessness in mentally retarded adults. *American Journal of Mental Deficiency, 79*(5), 565–572.

Gallup, G., & Gallup, A. M. (1986). *The great American success story: Factors that affect achievement.* Homewood, IL: Dow Jones-Irwin.

Garfield, C. (1986). *Peak performers: The new heroes of American business.* New York: Avon.

Gozali, J., & Bialer, I. (1968). Children's locus of control scale: Independence from response set bias among retardates. *American Journal of Mental Deficiency, 72*, 622–625.

Graham, S., Harris, K. R., & Reid, R. (1992). Developing self-regulated learners. *Focus on Exceptional Children, 24*(6), 1–16.

Griessman, B. E. (1987). *The achievement factors: Candid interviews with some of the most successful people of our time.* New York: Dodd, Mead.

Guevremont, D. C., Osnes, P. G., & Stokes, T. F. (1986). Preparation for effective self-regulation: The development of generalized verbal control. *Journal of Applied Behavior Analysis, 19*, 99–104.

Hallahan, D. P., Gajar, A. H., Cohen, S. B., & Tarver, S. G. (1978). Selective attention and locus of control in learning disabled and normal children. *Journal of Learning Disabilities, 11*, 231–236.

Hallahan, D. P., Kauffman, J. M., & Lloyd, J. W. (1999). *Introduction to learning disabilities* (2nd ed.). Boston: Allyn & Bacon.

Harris, K. R., & Graham, S. (1985). Improving learning disabled students' composition skills: Self-control strategy training. *Learning Disability Quarterly, 8*, 27–36.

Herrnstein, R. J. (1970). On the law of effect. *Journal of the Experimental Analysis of Behavior, 13*, 243–266.

Horne, R. D., & Lowe, C. F. (1993). Determinants of human performance on concurrent schedules. *Journal of the Experimental Analysis of Behavior, 59*, 29–60.

King, G. R., & Logue, A. W. (1990). Humans' sensitivity to variation in reinforcer amount: Effects of the method of reinforcer delivery. *Journal of the Experimental Analysis of Behavior, 53*, 33–45.

Lasch, C. (1979). *The culture of narcissism: American life in an age of diminishing expectations.* New York: Warner Books.

Lewis, S. K., & Lawrence-Patterson, E. (1989). Locus of control of children with learning disabilities and perceived locus of control by significant others. *Journal of Learning Disabilities, 22*, 255–257.

Licht, B. G. (1983). Cognitive-motivational factors that contribute to the achievement of learning-disabled children. *Journal of Learning Disabilities, 16*(8), 483–490.

Licht, B. G., Kistner, J. A., Ozkaragoz, T., Shapiro, S., & Glausen, L. (1985). Causal attributions of learning disabled children: Individual differences and their implications of persistence. *Journal of Educational Psychology, 77*(2), 208–216.

Litrownik, A. J., Cleary, C. P., Lecklitner, G. L., & Franzini, L. R. (1978). Self-regulation in retarded persons: Acquisition of standards for performance. *American Journal of Mental Deficiency, 83*(1), 86–89.

Litrownik, A. J., Freitas, J. L., & Franzini, L. R. (1978). Self-regulation in mentally retarded children: Assessment and training of self-monitoring skills. *American Journal of Mental Deficiency, 82*(5), 499–506.

Litrownik, A. J., & Steinfeld, B. I. (1982). Developing self-regulation in retarded children. In P. Karoly & J. J. Steffen (Eds.), *Improving children's competence: Advances in child behavioral analysis and therapy* (pp. 239–296). Lexington, MA: Lexington Books.

Lloyd, J. (1980). Academic instruction and cognitive behavior modification: The need for attack strategy training. *Exceptional Education Quarterly, 1*(1), 53–63.

McClelland, D. C., & Liberman, A. M. (1949). The effect of need for achievement on recongition of need-related words. *Journal of Personality, 18*, 236–251.

Merton, R. K. (1957). *Social theory and social structure.* Glencoe, IL: Free Press.

Mithaug, D. E. (1993). *Self-regulation theory: How optimal adjustment maximizes gain.* Westport, CT: Praeger.

Mithaug, D. E. (1996). The optimal prospects principle: A theoretical basis for rethinking instructional practices for self-determination. In D. J. Sands & M. L. Wehmeyer (Eds.), *Self-determination across the life span: Independence and choice for people with disabilities* (pp. 147–165). Baltimore, MD: Paul Brookes.

Mithaug, D. E. (2000). *Learning to theorize: A four-step strategy.* Thousand Oaks, CA: Sage.

Montgomery, L. E., & Finch, A. J., Jr. (1975). Reflection-impulsivity and locus of conflict in emotionally distrubed children. *Journal of Genetic Psychology, 126*, 89–91.

Neilans, T. H., & Israel, A. C. (1981). Towards maintenance and generalization of behavior change: Teaching children self-regulation and self-instructional skills. *Cognitive Therapy and Research, 5*(2), 189–195.

Nelson, W. M. III, Finch, A. J., Jr., & Hooke, J. F. (1975). Effects of reinforcement and response-cost on cognitive style in emotionally disturbed boys. *Journal of Abnormal Psychology, 84*, 426–428.

Newell, A., & Simon, H. A. (1972). *Human problem solving.* Englewood Cliffs, NJ: Prentice Hall.

Pearl, R. (1985). Cognitive-behavioral interventions for increasing motivation. *Journal of Abnormal Child Psychology, 13*(3), 443–454.

Pearl, R. A., Bryan, T., & Donahue, M. (1980). Learning disabled children's attributions for success and failure. *Learning Disability Quarterly, 3*, 3–9.

Rotter, J. B. (1966). Generalized expectancies for internal versus external control of reinforcement [Special issue]. *Pscyhological Monographs, 80*(1).

Shelton, T. L., Anastopoulos, A. D., & Linden, J. D. (1985). An attribution training program with learning disabled children. *Journal of Learning Disabilities, 18*(5), 261–265.

Varni, J. W., & Henker, B. (1979). A self-regulation approach to the treatment of three hyperactive boys. *Child Behavior Therapy, 1*(2), 171–192.

Weber, M. (1958). *The Protestant ethic and the spirit of capitalism* (T. Parsons, Trans., with Foreword by R. H. Tawney). New York: Charles Scribner's Sons. (Original work published 1930)

Wehmeyer, M. L. (1993). Gender differences in locus of control scores for students with learning disabilities. *Perceptual and Motor Skills, 77*, 359–366.

Wehmeyer, M. L., & Kelchner, K. (1996). Perceptions of classroom environment, locus of control and academic attributions of adolescents with and without cognitive disabilities. *Career Development for Exceptional Individuals, 19*(1), 15–30.

Weiner, B. (1976). Attribution theory, achievement motivation, and the educational process. *Review of Educational Research, 42*, 201–215.

Weisz, J. R. (1979). Perceived control and learned helplessness among mentally retarded and nonretarded children: A developmental analysis. *Developmental Psychology, 15*(3), 311–319.

Whitman, T. L. (1990). Self-regulation and mental retardation. *American Journal on Mental Retardation, 94*(4), 347–362.

Wholey, D. (1986). *Are you happy?* Boston: Houghton Mifflin.

Wiens, J. W. (1983). Metacognition and the adolescent passive learner. *Journal of Learning Disabilities, 16*(3), 144–149.

Wong, B. Y. L. (1980). Activating the inactive learner: Use of questions/prompts to enhance comprehension and retention of implied information in learning disabled children. *Learning Disability Quarterly, 3*, 28–37.

Zimmerman, B. J., Bonner, S., & Kovach, R. (1996). *Developing self-regulated learners: Beyond achievement to self-efficacy.* Washington, DC: American Psychological Association.

Zimmerman, B. J., & Martinez-Pons, M. (1986). Development of a structured interview for assessing student use of self-regulated learning strategies. *American Educational Research Journal, 23*, 614–628.

Zimmerman, B. J., & Martinez-Pons, M. (1988).Construct validation of a strategy model of student self-regulated learning. *Journal of Educational Psychology, 80*, 284–290.

Zimmerman, B. J., & Martinez-Pons, M. (1990). Student differences in self-regulated learning: Relating grade, sex, and giftedness to self-efficacy and strategy use. *Journal of Educational Psychology, 82*, 51–59.

3

How Adjustment Affects Learning

Dennis E. Mithaug
Deirdre K. Mithaug
Martin Agran
James E. Martin
Michael L. Wehmeyer

Our view is that adjustments affect learning by changing the experiences, beliefs, and behaviors that define new adaptations to situations. Self-determined learning theory is based on this understanding that when a circumstance that is perceived to be an opportunity for gain provokes frequent and persistent engagement to produce new adjustments, the resulting adaptive changes are the maximum possible for that situation. Hence, learning is the maximum possible too. The theory in Table 3.1 uses the causal factors described in chapter 2 to make this claim explicit. Proposition 1 claims that when opportunities to learn about an unknown situation are as favorable as possible under the circumstances, engagement increases as actors regulate their expectations, choices, and actions to produce desirable changes in the situation. Proposition 2 claims that as engagement increases, adjustments optimize as expectations become adaptive, choices become rational, actions become efficient, and results become successful. Proposition 3 claims that with this optimization of adjustments, engagement persists, and control over learning maximizes. Proposition 4, which is a deduction from propositions 1–3, claims that because opportunities affect adjustments and adjustments affect engagement, control, and learning, opportunities also affect engagement, control, and learning. In other words, as opportunities optimize, engagement, control, and learning maximize.

The core of the explanation is the first two propositions that link the characteristics of the circumstance—the learner's beliefs about the opportunity—with characteristics of the learner—the learner's capacity to regulate those events. When these factors match sufficiently to engage the learner, adjustments optimize, and engagement, control, and learning maximize.

TABLE 3.1
Self-Determined Learning Theory: How Opportunities
Affect Engagement, Control, and Learning

Proposition 1: The closer to optimal the opportunities for producing gain toward a desired end, the more likely is the regulation of expectations, choices, and actions to produce that gain.
Proposition 2: The more often the regulation of expectations, choices, and actions to produce gain, the more likely is it that adjustments optimize as expectations, choices, actions, and results become adaptive, rational, efficient and successful.
Proposition 3: The closer to optimal the adjustments to an opportunity, the more persistent is the engagement to produce gain, the greater is the control over gain production, and the closer to maximum is the learning from that adaptation.
Proposition 4: Therefore, the closer to optimal the opportunities for experiencing gain,
   the more persistent is the engagement, the greater is the sense of control, and the
   closer to maximum is the learning.

This theory answers the question "What causes engagement and maximizes learning?" by claiming that *opportunities* and *adjustments* are responsible. When they are optimal (maximally favorable from to the
learner's point of view), then engagement, control, and learning maximize. This is the upper limit of what learners learn from new circumstances. The lower limit occurs when conditions are suboptimal: when circumstances are perceived to be important but unmanageable, manageable
but unimportant, or unimportant and unmanageable. Under these conditions, engagement, control, and learning decrease proportionately.

This chapter reviews research on our central claim that the optimality
of a student's opportunities and adjustments affects his or her learning.
Figure 3.1 structures the review by specifying the types of cognitive and
behavioral interventions that tend to improve opportunities or adjustments and, as a result, produce new learning. It suggests that these interventions work because they alter student beliefs about circumstances or
because they increase student capacity to adjust. In either case, they in-
duce change in adaptive states and cause students to learn something new
about those circumstances. Moreover, to the extent that these interventions produce adaptations that are significantly different from previous
ones, student learning is substantial. And to the extent that they produce
the greatest change possible between adaptive states, student learning
maximizes. This is predicted by the theory, which states that as adjustments optimize, learning maximizes.

OPPORTUNITY INTERVENTIONS

According to self-determined learning theory, a circumstance is perceived
to be optimal when an actor believes a change in it will benefit a valued
pursuit (the opportunity is valuable) *and* when the actor believes he or she

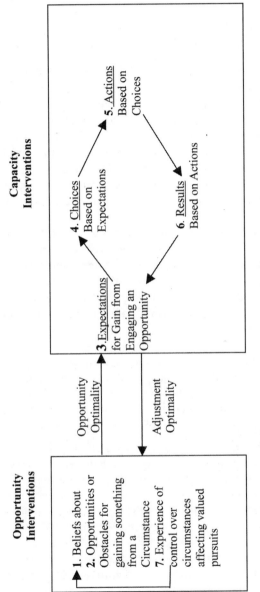

Capacity Interventions

5. <u>Actions</u> Based on Choices

4. <u>Choices</u> Based on Expectations

6. <u>Results</u> Based on Actions

3. <u>Expectations</u> for Gain from Engaging an Opportunity

Opportunity Optimality

Adjustment Optimality

Opportunity Interventions

1. Beliefs about
2. Opportunities or Obstacles for gaining something from a Circumstance
7. Experience of control over circumstances affecting valued pursuits

FIG. 3.1. Opportunity and capacity interventions affecting beliefs, self-regulation, adjustment, and learning.

can make that change (the opportunity is manageable). When these conditions are present, the actor is likely to act on the circumstance. This is the meaning of proposition 1, which states that the closer to optimal the opportunities for producing gain toward a desired end, the more likely is the regulation of expectations, choices, and actions to produce that gain.

Much research has been conducted on interventions showing the effects of optimal opportunities. Cognitive interventions that improve beliefs about one's capability in dealing with difficult challenges make circumstances appear manageable enough to be engaged. Behavioral interventions that make challenging circumstances valuable by providing reinforcements for completed work and that make them manageable by reducing the task demands also optimize opportunities and increase engagement. And choice-based opportunity interventions that allow actors to choose work that matches their interests and abilities optimize opportunities, too, and produce a similar increase in engagement. We consider each in turn.

Cognitive approaches that optimize opportunities are based on the view that learner beliefs about challenges affect their performance and achievement. For example, learners who believe their failures are due to insufficient ability rather than insufficient effort tend to avoid learning challenges and underachieve (Chapin & Dyck, 1976; Dweck, 1975; Fowler & Peterson, 1981; Thomas & Pashley, 1982). Licht (1983) summarized this argument as follows.

> Children who believe that their difficulties are due to factors that are stable and beyond their control, particularly insufficient ability, tend to display a maladaptive pattern of achievement-related behaviors. When confronted with difficulty, these children are likely to show a deterioration in their effort and their problem-solving strategies, resulting in a level of performance that is below their capabilities. These children also are likely to avoid the tasks on which they have previously experienced difficulty. In contrast, children who attribute their difficulties to controllable factors, particularly insufficient effort, tend to maintain their effort and problem-solving strategies, even in the face of failure. At times, failure may even prompt these children to use more sophisticated strategies than they had shown earlier. (p. 484)

The cognitive interventions that alter these self-defeating attitudes employ some form of belief enhancement. Schunk (1984) did this to increase arithmetic performance of regular education students, and Schunk and Cox (1986) used self-efficacy enhancements with self-regulation instruction to improve academic performance of students with learning disabilities. Another approach is to teach students to set proximal rather than distal objectives. This tends to increase their self-efficacy and performance

(Bandura & Schunk, 1981). Bandura, Barbaranelli, Caprara, and Pastso-relli (1996) summarized these studies as follows: "Children who believe they can exercise some control over their own learning and mastery of coursework achieve success in their academic pursuits" (p. 1217). Indeed researchers have shown that perceptions of self-efficacy correlate positively with the attainment of short-term goals (Lent, Bron, & Larkin, 1984). Apparently, students who set intermediate objectives to meet distant goals tend to have higher levels of self-efficacy, and this tends to increase their academic performance (Schunk & Swartz, 1993).

Behavioral opportunity interventions increase engagement by making instructional challenges both doable and valuable for the learner. This is most evident in direct instruction, which has a long history of success with difficult-to-teach learners (Greer, 1994, 1996; Greer & McDonough, 1999; Haring & Scheifelbusch, 1976; Lindsley, 1964; Lovitt, 1967; Tawney & Gast, 1984). It is based on two claims. The first is that responses are learned when they come under the control of an instructional cue. The second is that this relationship is strengthened when a reinforcing consequence is contingent on correct responses to that cue. Hence, the more often an instructional cue is followed by a response that in turn is reinforced, the more likely it is that learning will occur. Greer and McDonough (1999) explained the effects of direct instruction in terms of a learn unit that locks teachers and students in patterns of mutual adjustment, which predicts what students learn and how rapidly they learn it.

The learn unit consists of the interlocking operants of instruction that incorporate particular student and teacher interactions that predict whether student behaviors will be controlled by particular stimuli and setting events (Greer, 1994). The learn unit is present when student learning occurs in teaching interactions and is absent when student learning does not occur in teaching interactions. It is a countable unit of teacher and student interaction that leads to important changes in student behavior. That is, the behavior of the student comes under the control of the target discriminative stimulus (S^D) within the motivational conditions in which the behavior will produce a particular consequence to form a discriminated operant. For this to happen, the teacher must respond in certain ways to the presence of the student and to the resulting behavior or its absence. In effect, the teacher "learns" from the responses of the student; that is, the teacher learns what to do next just as a researcher follows the organism's behavior in a laboratory (Sidman, 1960). Thus, the learn unit captures the behaviors of both the teacher and the student that are needed to produce a particular outcome. (Greer & McDonough, 1999, p. 6)

Thus, all learning is a function of this association between a cue, a response, and reinforcement. When it is present, learning occurs. When it is not, learning does not occur. And when it is present at high levels, learning maximizes.

> Research shows that learn units (i.e., those that are done for planned instruction or even incidental ones) are found in effective instruction in various forms or functions and are not found in ineffective instruction. Learn units, or their lack, are observable in preschool classrooms, graduate classes, tutoring settings, group lectures, lecture discussions, courses that use the personalized system of instruction, automated instruction, one-minute timings, one-to-one instruction laboratory courses, writing exercises, and problem solving projects in various behavioral topographies (e.g., spoke, written, or otherwise). What makes instruction effective is a high rate of learn units. (Greer & McDonough, 1999, p. 9)

The key to direct instruction, therefore, is the systematic arrangement of cues and consequences throughout the adjustment-learning process. Teachers must match instructional cues to student response repertoires for optimal reactions (provide manageable learning opportunities), and they must deliver consequences for those responses that are reinforcing (provide valuable opportunities). Then they must present these optimized opportunities in scripted curricula that move student adjustments toward teacher-set goals. The result is, as explained by self-determined learning theory, optimal opportunities provoking optimal adjustments to maximize learning.

Of course, the approach has little effect on underachievement that occurs when teachers are not present to direct those adjustments and learning. In these situations, students who do not know how to optimize circumstances disengage and cease learning. The third intervention type, the choice opportunity, is useful here in that it encourages students to regulate their own problem solving in order to adjust. This tends to increase their capacity in that it allows them to learn to set expectations for gain, make choices to produce it, and then take action to follow through. Indeed, research has shown that the choice opportunity alone is sufficient to motivate many of these regulatory behaviors.

Consider, for example, the early studies using choice opportunities to increase engagement and learning in difficult-to-teach students. In one pair of studies, teachers gave students with severe mental retardation opportunities to choose between preferred and nonpreferred tasks. This provoked them into setting expectations for gain (reinforcement derived from different work), making choices, then following through by distributing work according to their choices (Mithaug & Hanawalt, 1978; Mithaug & Mar, 1980). Parsons, Reid, Reynolds, and Bumgardner (1990) used a similar approach to provoke and maintain engagement in adults with severe disabilities. Participants observed in these situations were more engaged during choice than during non-choice conditions. Dunlap et al. (1994) reported similar results for students with behavior problems. On-task behavior and assignment completion rates were higher during choice than during non-choice conditions.

Fisher, Thompson, Piazza, Crosland, and Gotjen (1997) attempted to explain these effects by employing a concurrent-operants procedure to control for the reinforcing influence of the option selected during the opportunity (value of the opportunity). They found that even with this control in effect, the choice opportunity rather than the reinforcing event chosen was associated with increased engagement. In one experiment, they yoked participant selections across conditions to equalize differential reinforcement effects of selected events and found that the opportunity to choose was responsible for enhanced performance. In a second experiment they found that the choice opportunity was most effective when participants chose between low- and high-preference items.

In an equally intriguing study, Hanley, Piazza, Fisher, Contrucci, and Maglieri (1997) found that even when choice opportunities do not improve performance, they still reflect participant preference. In this study, the researchers compared two interventions to decrease destructive behavior, a functional communication procedure that included a choice-control feature and a noncontingent reinforcement procedure that did not. They found that although both treatments reduced destructive behavior, the functional communication treatment was preferred to the noncontingent reinforcement treatment. The researchers concluded that

> although control over reinforcement may not alter treatment efficacy, it may influence client preferences (i.e., clients may prefer to control when and if reinforcement is delivered). That is, both participants showed a clear preference for a procedure in which control over reinforcement was available (FCT) over one in which control over reinforcement was not available (NCR). (p. 470)

This finding is reminiscent of a study by Arlin and Whitley (1978) that reported a positive correlation between choice opportunities experienced by students and beliefs about academic control. When these researchers assessed year-end changes in perceptions of control among 566 fifth-, sixth-, and seventh-grade students, they found that student beliefs about opportunities for self-managed instruction correlated positively with perceptions of academic control. Apparently, the choice opportunity produces feelings of control over a circumstance, which improves perceptions of its manageability and hence its optimality.

In summary, our view of these opportunity interventions is that they provoke engagement and learning because they alter learner views about their challenges. Cognitive interventions improve beliefs about being able to deal effectively with new challenges. Direct instruction arranges learning challenges so they are valuable and manageable, which has the effect of optimizing every learning opportunity. And choice interventions present challenges as options for learners to consider in deciding how to respond to a challenge. According to self-determined learning theory, learners perceive opportunities presented by these interventions to be more valuable and doable than they would be otherwise. In other words, learners engage during these interventions because they present optimal opportunities for getting what they need or want.

CAPACITY INTERVENTIONS

Of course intervening on the opportunity side of the adjustment model is not the only way to increase learning because, according to Fig. 3.1, capacity interventions can also improve students' ability to learn. This makes sense in that many students fail to learn because they do not know how to adjust to new challenge. Indeed the expectation, choice, action, and result factors on the capacity side of the figure reveal the ways that a student can fail to adjust optimally to new circumstances.

The *expectation variable* reflects how optimally students regulate their expectations for gain, given what is possible for them in that situation. The *choice* variable indicates how optimally they regulate their choices to meet their expectations. The *action* variable indicates how optimally students regulate their actions when acting on their choices. The *result* variable indicates how optimally they regulate gain production to match their expectations. According propositions 2 and 3 of the theory, students adjust optimally to the extent their expectations are *adaptive*, their choices are *rational*, their actions are *efficient*, and their results are *successful*. When each of these factors is regulated as effectively as possible under the circumstances, then the resulting adjustment is optimal and the gain produced from those circumstances is maximum (Mithaug, 1993). Under these conditions, the student learns as much as he or she can, given his or her opportunities and capacity to adjust to them.

An examination of these four factors also reveals why learners underachieve. Sometimes they neglect to find out what to expect from a new circumstance before adjusting to it. Occasionally, they fail to choose based on that knowledge of what is possible in that situation. Sometimes they fail to act effectively on their choices. And sometimes they fail to monitor results well enough to adjust appropriately the next time they attempt to get what they think is possible from the situation. The problem is that underachievement can result from any one of these failures because the four interact to amplify the effects of success or failure. Hence, the gain produced by the suboptimal adjustment can be substantially less than what is possible from more effective self-regulation.

In this section, we review the intervention strategies that have helped solve these types of underachievement problems. We have organized them according to their effects on the self-regulation variables identified in Fig. 3.1. The review of interventions on expectations focuses on methods that help students discover what to expect from new situations. The review on choice interventions identifies the methods that help students choose rationally based on their understanding of the situation. The review of action interventions describes the problem-solving strategies that help students act effectively on their choices, and the review of result interventions identifies strategies that help students evaluate outcomes in order to improve subsequent adjustments in expectations, choices, and actions. According to self-determined learning theory, these interventions improve engagement, control, and learning because they increase students' *capacity* to adjust to new challenges.

Interventions That Optimize Expectations

Knowing what to expect from a new situation is the first challenge to knowing how to adjust to it. Recall what happened to John Dewey's traveler when he came to a fork in the road. *He didn't know what to expect.* For example, did the right path lead to New York City, or did the left path lead there? Recall also how he adjusted his expectations. He engaged in problem solving, the thinking strategy specifically designed for discovering what is new about strange situations. This strategy yielded information indicating, for example, that the right path led to New York City and the left path led to Chicago, which he used to adjust his expectations and choices in a new plan of action.

Unfortunately, many students adapt poorly simply because they do not *find out what to expect* from new situations before acting on them. In the previous chapter we cited Whitman's (1990) claim that people with mental retardation fail to adapt for this reason, and then cited other sources that made the same claim for students with learning disabilities and students with behavior problems. The recommended solution was to teach students to use problem-solving strategies. Belmont, Ferretti, and Mitchell (1982) and Whitman, Burgio, and Johnston (1984) demonstrated the effectiveness of this approach for persons with mental retardation. Carlson and Tully (1985) used it to help students with learning disabilities. Francescani (1982), Lochman and Curry (1986), and Lochman and Lampron (1986) reported similar benefits for students with emotional and behavior problems.

Apparently, when students learn to solve problems on their own, their learning and production increase (Achenbach & Zigler, 1968; Budoff &

Corman, 1976; D'Zurilla & Goldfried, 1971; Horner, 1987), their mental functioning increases (Haley, 1976; Stark, Reynolds, & Kaslow, 1987) as do their social adjustments (Camp & Bash, 1982; McFall & Dodge, 1983; McGinnis, Sauerbry, & Nichols, 1985; Spivack, Platt, & Shure, 1976; Spivack & Shure, 1974; Yu, Harris, Solovitz, & Franklin, 1986).

The reason for this wide-ranging success, according to self-determined learning theory, is that problem-solving instruction is a generic capacity-building intervention. It is generally effective in discovering what people need to know about their unusual circumstances. Indeed, Mithaug (1993) revealed this to be the generic feature in such therapeutic strategies as behavior modification (D'Zurilla & Goldfried, 1971), cognitive-behavioral training (Whitman et al., 1984), social behavior therapy (Haaga & Davison, 1986), group therapy (Rose, 1986), critical thinking (Valett, 1986), and school-to-work adaptability training (Agran, Blanchard, & Wehmeyer, 2000; Mithaug, Martin, & Agran, 1987).

Interventions That Optimize Choices

Still, using an information-gathering strategy alone is probably insufficient for the optimal adjustment. This is because having accurate knowledge about usual circumstances does not always lead to good choices about how to act in those situations. This was certainly the case for Dewey's traveler, who knew that hitching a ride would get him to town faster than walking, but was uncertain about whether he should hitch a ride to the Bronx or to Brooklyn. Table 3.2 presents this dilemma about which was better *for him*, a Bronx ride that promised to be less expensive but more risky, or a Brooklyn ride that promised to be more expensive but safer. To solve the problem of knowing how to choose, he had to weigh the costs and benefits of the two options against his needs (the value of the option) and abilities (the manageability of the option).

Problems like these are common in everyday decision making. Air travelers know what to expect when they book a flight from New York to Chicago, but may be less certain about the exact time or the best carrier given their particular circumstances. Students know when they enroll in degree programs that they will take many courses, but they may be less certain about the number of courses to take given their need to work part-time to raise a family. In all such cases, *knowing the facts of a situation* is necessary but insufficient for *knowing how to choose a course of action that matches one's needs and capabilities*. Making a rational choice in these situations demands a search for the option that best matches what we know about the circumstance with what we know about ourselves.

The recommended approach to dealing with these difficulties is usually a decision strategy much like the generic problem solving that discov-

TABLE 3.2
Making an Optimal Choice

When Dewey's traveler learned what to expect from the fork in the road, that the left path led to Chicago and the right to New York, he could choose and act in a way that was consistent with his needs and interests, which was to get to Manhattan. But, of course, turning right did not completely solve his problems. *Instead it started a series of problem solving episodes he had to regulate toward that end.* His additional concern was to get there *on time,* which required that he decide to hitch a ride or to walk. Fortunately, there was sufficient traffic that getting a ride would not be a problem. In fact, as soon as he waived for one, two cars stopped with offers to get him there. One promised to drop him off in Brooklyn where he could get a cab to Manhattan and the other to drop him off in the Bronx where he could take the subway to the city.

This problem was different from dealing with the fork in the road because here there was no question about what to expect. He knew exactly where he would end up in both cases. The question was which of the two options was better to meet his particular needs, which were to be at Columbia in time for his first class at 1 p.m. Should he go to Brooklyn and cab it to Manhattan and Columbia or go to the Bronx and take the train? The question was, which was the better choice? Which one fit his particular needs and interests better? Because Dewey's traveler was a student, money and time were important. Cabbing the remainder of the trip to Manhattan might be too expensive, whereas taking the train would not. On the other hand, the cab driver would get him on time because most cab drivers work Brooklyn and upper Manhattan routinely. On the other hand, taking the train from the Bronx to Manhattan requires changing trains at Yankee Stadium and getting off at the 125th Street station, where he would have to walk several blocks through unfamiliar neighborhood. Which was the better choice? Should he take a cab costing $40 that would probably be safer and more efficient, or should he take the train for $1.50 and risk getting lost, getting mugged, and missing his first class? Which choice was optimal, given his circumstances?

ers new information. Janis and Mann (1977) illustrated one of these with their seven-step approach to good decisions:

1. Consider a wide range of alternative courses of action.
2. Survey the full range of objectives to be fulfilled and values implicated by the choice.
3. Carefully weigh the positive and negative consequences of each alternative.
4. Intensely search for new information and evaluate alternatives.
5. Correctly assimilate new information.
6. Reexamine positive and negative consequences of alternatives.
7. Detail provisions for implementing chosen alternatives.

Hogarth (1980) also had a seven-step strategy for good decision making:

1. Structure the problem.
2. Assess consequences.

3. Assess uncertainties.

4. Evaluate alternatives.

5. Analyze sensitively.

6. Gather information.

7. Choose.

Indeed, many strategies like these have been used to teach students to make better decisions (Adelman, Lusk, Albarez, & Acostsa, 1985; Adelman, MacDonald, Nelson, Smith, & Taylor, 1990; Kaser-Boyd, Adelman, & Taylor, 1985; Taylor, Adelman, & Kaser-Boyd, 1983, 1985). Some focused on the decision making of young children (Davidson, 1991; Davidson & Hudson, 1988; Gregson-Paxton & John, 1995; Reyna & Ellis, 1994; Weithorn & Campbell, 1982). Some used the strategy for adolescents (Baron & Brown, 1991; Beyth-Marom, Fishchhoff, Quadrel, & Furby, 1991; Friedman & Mann, 1993; Furby & Beyth-Marom, 1992; Galotti & Kozberg, 1996; Gordon, 1990; Lewis, 1981; Mann, Harmoni, & Power, 1989). Others focused on the decision making of students with learning disabilities (Phillips, 1990) and students with mental retardation (Hickson & Khemka, 1999; Hickson, Golden, Khemka, Urv, & Yamusah, 1998; Ross & Ross, 1978; Tymchuk, Andron, & Rahbar, 1988; Tymchuk, Yokota, & Rahbar, 1990; Wehmeyer & Kelchner, 1996; Wehmeyer & Lawrence, 1995).

Our view is that these strategies function similarly during adjustment in that they prescribe actions that are consistent with the facts of the situation and with the learner's needs and abilities. This is what Dewey's strategy did for him. It identified options that promised to get him where he wanted to go (the availability of rides to New York City) and that matched his capacity to act (the Brooklyn ride was safe). Then all he had to do was to act on his choice.

Interventions That Optimize Actions

Now we face the third obstacle to constructing an optimal adjustment, responding effectively to the situation. This obstacle is nearly always present because (1) improving a circumstance usually requires action and (2) we don't always act as effectively as we can. Dewey's traveler understood this because his ride options required different actions to get to class. The Brooklyn ride required that he find a cab driver in Brooklyn who could get him to campus on time and the Bronx ride option required that he remember to transfer to the D Train at Yankee Stadium and walk to Columbia from the 125th Street exit. Dewey's traveler understood that if he didn't follow through on whichever choice he made, he would jeopardize his chance of adjusting optimally by getting to class on time.

Many students underachieve on this score alone. They do not follow through on their plans. They may plan to study before a test, but never do it adequately enough to pass. This was Zimmerman, Bonner, and Kovach's (1996) explanation for the underachievement of Calvin and Maria. Even though Calvin knew he had to study rather than play to achieve, his "unfortunate habits, such as procrastinating, skimming reading assignments, cramming for tests at the last minute, and writing in a haphazard manner" prevented him from getting the results he wanted. The same was true for Maria, who read her "assignments cursorily between extended discussions about the day's events," and prepared "minimally for tests, usually cramming the night before the exam."

Some researchers claim this problem is due to students being cognitively disengaged during schoolwork (Brown, 1988; Corno, 1986, 1989; Ellis, 1986; Zimmerman, 1985). They underperform because they do not pay attention to what they are studying. They don't set expectations for what they believe they can accomplish (no goal setting), nor do they consider their options before making choices about the best way to meet goals (no choice making). As a result, there is no connection between thinking about learning and taking action to learn. To solve this problem, researchers have instructed students to use self-regulation strategies to guide the activities of learning (Baird & White, 1982; Borkowski, Carr, Rellinger, & Pressley, 1990; Borkowski, Estrada, Milstead, & Hale, 1989; Bos & Van Reusen, 1991; Corno, 1986, 1989; Corno & Mandinach, 1983; Ghatala, 1986; Graham & Freeman, 1986; Loper, Hallahan, & Ianna, 1982; Pressley, Borkowski, & Schneider, 1987; Pressley, Ross, Levin, & Ghatala, 1984; Reeve & Brown, 1985; Wong, 1980; Wong & Jones, 1982; Zimmerman, 1990; Zimmerman & Martinez-Pons, 1986). And this seems to work because when students set goals and make choices about what they plan to do, they are more likely to monitor their behavior as they work on their plans. Hence, they exhibit that "cognitive engagement" that researchers claim is associated with learning and achievement (Deshler, Schumaker, & Lenz, 1984; Ellis, Deshler, Lenz, Schumaker, & Clark, 1991; Paris, Lipson, & Wixson, 1983; Weinstein & Meyer, 1986).

Interventions That Optimize Results

Cognitive engagement is also important in dealing with the fourth and final obstacle to the optimal adjustment: figuring out how to *adjust repeatedly* to meet challenging goals. Here paying attention is clearly needed because difficult situations can be so confusing that the learner doesn't know which of his or her expectations, choices, or actions are appropriate and which are not. Unless the learner pays close attention to *discrepancies* between results and expectations, he or she will never figure out what to change in subsequent adjustments to improve the prospects for success.

The most successful strategy to solve this problem is some version of the scientific method, which regulates all adjustments toward reducing discrepancies between expectations (from a theory or hypothesis) and results. Indeed, when scientists develop hypotheses (expectations) they specify what they believe is true about the unusual circumstance. They deduce test procedures (choices) based on their hypothesis. And they conduct tests (take effective action) to evaluate their beliefs (expectations). Then they complete the most important step of all. They *compare* their results with their hypothesis (expectations) to confirm or reject their beliefs about the cause of the event. Moreover, they conduct these tests *repeatedly* until they find an expectation (belief) that is consistent with results. In other words, they adjust their beliefs and actions many times to find what works best. Then they claim that they understand the situation sufficiently to know what to do about it (Mithaug, 2000).

Cognitive-behavioral researchers have used versions of the strategy to help students learn to adjust on their own. Some of these strategies have improved correspondence between students' choices and actions (Burgio, Whitman, & Reid, 1983; Dickerson & Creedon, 1981; Felixbrod & O'Leary, 1974; Glynn, 1970; Lovitt & Curtiss, 1969; Miller & Kelley, 1994; Olympia, Sheridan, Jenson, & Andrews, 1994), between their choices and results (Wang & Stiles, 1976), and between their actions and results (Glynn, Thomas, & Shee, 1973; Schloss & Wood, 1990; Sowers, Verdi, Bourbeau, & Sheehan, 1985). A few studies have employed strategies that focused on all four adjustment variables at once. Not surprisingly, they produced learning gains that maintained and generalized across settings and time (Fantuzzo & Clement, 1981; Stevenson & Fantuzzo, 1984, 1986).

In our view, these strategies work because they lead to the optimization of expectations, choices, actions, and results. The strategies work like the scientific method in that they get beliefs about an opportunity to match with the facts of the situation. Just as an experiment gets a theory or hypothesis in line with the facts of an unusual situation, the close monitoring of one's expectations, choices, actions, and results produces adjustments that correspond with circumstances. Systematic self-monitoring of the adjustment process yields optimal adjustments.

The scientific method works exactly the same way. It requires scientists to evaluate their beliefs (theories) by making predictions about what will happen (optimal expectations), choosing the right experiments to test those predictions (optimal choosing), conducting the experiments correctly (optimal acting), and then evaluating results by matching them to the predictions. If they match, then their expectations, choices, and actions have produced an optimal result in that it matched the prediction (Mithaug, 2000).

Using a discovery strategy like this is perhaps they best way of adjusting optimally and learning maximally from an unusual circumstance. But it is very demanding in that it requires continuous monitoring and regulating of the adjustment indicators. We must monitor what we expect to make certain it is consistent with the facts of the situation (setting adaptive expectations). We must monitor our choices to make certain the option we choose is consistent with the facts and with what we expect to gain (making rational choices). We must monitor our actions to make certain they are consistent with our choices (effective actions). And we must monitor results to verify whether they are consistent with expectations and if not repeat the process by adjusting our expectations, choices, and actions until we find a combination that works. Of course, when we finally produce a result that matches expectations (successful result), we know why it occurred and what to do next time if we want the result again. Then we have optimized our adjustments and maximized our learning from the situation.

MAXIMIZED LEARNING

In this chapter we used propositions from self-determined learning theory to argue that learning is a function of a learner's opportunities and adjustments. We claimed that when new circumstances are perceived by learners to be valuable and doable opportunities for gain, they engage them (proposition 1). Moreover, when their engagement increases, their adjustments in expectations, choices, and actions to produce gain during these opportunities tend to optimize (proposition 2). As adjustments to new opportunities optimize, learners' engagement, sense of control, and learning tends to maximize (proposition 3). Therefore, we concluded that as opportunities for gain optimize, learning from those opportunities maximizes (proposition 4). In other words, to the extent that students are provoked by a new challenge to engage new circumstances frequently and continuously over time, their adjustments to those events tend to optimize and their learning about those events tends to maximize.

This is the upper limit for learning. It is that point where additional adjustment will not significantly alter what the actor knows, or how he or she acts or feels about a situation. It is where learning maximizes. In the following passage, Brim (1992) reflected on this process as it unfolds in the act of striving to optimize adjustments and maximize gain. The passage suggests that overachievement is similar to underachievement in that it too is a function of adjusting expectations, choices, and actions in order to produce a desirable, expected result.

> When we win, the response is to increase the degree of difficulty. We set a shorter timetable for the next endeavor, *raising expectations* of how much we can achieve, even broadening out and adding new goals. We will try to get

there earlier or faster, and to get more or better. . . .

Winning raises our hopes; losing lowers them. As Tocqueville wrote about democracy in the United States when it was a new nation, social movements are not caused by failure and frustration but spring from rising strength. And so it is today. Recently at Howard University, the leading primarily black university in the United States, students escalated a demonstration after achieving their goal of forcing the resignation of the Republican Party chairman, Lee Atwater, from the college's board of trustees. The protesters went on to disrupt classes and demand assurances of financial aid and improved campus housing. It is when inequality declines that aspirations rise and rebellions occur. T. George Harris, former editor of *Psychology Today*, spoke of this to me as "the snake of hope"; prison riots, he notes, start when the food is getting better, not worse.

There are broad implications here for what happens to people when they are successful at work. Once you get good at a particular job, it no longer takes most of your ability to do it well. So you set your sights higher and push on to more demanding work. . . .

But here's the hitch. People can become psychologically trapped by their own success as they race to keep up with the rising expectations bred by each new achievement. With each success, they raise their level of difficulty, climbing up the ladder of subgoals, moving faster, *raising aspirations, and at some point reaching the limit of their capacity.* (Brim, 1992, pp. 31–32, italics added)

REFERENCES

Achenbach, T., & Zigler, E. (1968). Cue-learning and problem-learning strategies in normal and retarded children. *Child Development, 39,* 827–848.

Adelman, H. S., Lusk, R., Albarez, V., & Acosta, N. K. (1985). Competence of minors to understand, evaluate and communicate about their psychoeducational problems. *Professional Psychology: Research and Practice, 16,* 426–434.

Adelman, H. S., MacDonald, V. M., Nelson, Pl., Smith, D. C., & Taylor, L. (1990). Motivational readiness of children with learning and behavior problems in psychoeducational decision making. *Journal of Learning Disabilities, 23,* 171–176.

Agran, M., Blanchard, C., & Wehmeyer, M. L. (2000). Promoting transition goals and self-determination through student-directed learning: The Self-Determined Learning Model of Instruction. *Education and Training in Mental Retardation and Developmental Disabilities, 35,* 351–364.

Arlin, M., & Whitley, T. W. (1978). Perceptions of self-managed learning opportunities and academic locus of control: A causal interpretation. *Journal of Educational Psychology, 70*(6), 988–992.

Baird, J. R., & White, R. T. (1982). Promoting self-control of learning. *Instructional Science, 11,* 227–247.

Bandura, A., Barbaranelli, C., Caprara, G. V., & Pastorelli, C. (1996). Multifaceted impact of self-efficacy beliefs on academic functioning. *Child Development, 67,* 1206–1222.

Bandura, A., & Schunk, D. H. (1981). Cultivating competence, self-efficacy, and intrinsic interest through proximal self-motivation. *Journal of Personality and Social Pscyhology, 41*(3), 586–598.

Baron, J., & Brown, R. V. (1991). *Teaching decision-making to adolescents*. Hillsdale, NJ: Lawrence Erlbaum Associates.

Belmont, J. M., Ferretti, R. P., & Mitchell, D. W. (1982). Memorizing: A test of untrained mildly mentally retarded children's problem solving. *American Journal of Mental Deficiency, 87*, 197–210.

Beyth-Marom, R., Fishchhoff, B., Quadrel, M. J., & Furby, L. (1991). Teaching decision-making to adolescents: A critical review. In J. Baron & R. V. Brown (Eds.), *Teaching decision-making to adolescents* (pp. 19–59). Hillsdale, NJ: Lawrence Erlbaum Associates.

Borkoswki, J., Estrada, M., Milstead, M., & Hale, C. (1989). General problem-solving skills: Relations between metacognition and strategic processing. *Learning Disability Quarterly, 12*, 57–70.

Borkowski, J., Carr, M., Rellinger, E., & Pressley, M. (1990). Self-regulated cognition: Interdependence of metacognition, attributions, and self-esteem. In B. F. Jones & L. Idol (Eds.), *Dimensions of thinking and cognitive instruction* (pp. 53–92). Hillsdale, NJ: Lawrence Erlbaum Associates.

Bos, C. S., & Van Reusen, A. K. (1991). Academic interventions with learning disabled students: A cognitive/metacognitive approach. In J. E. Obrzut & G. W. Hynd (Eds.), *Neuropsychological foundations of learning disabilities* (pp. 659–683). San Diego: Academic Press.

Brim, G. (1992). *Ambition: How we manage success and failure throughout our lives*. New York: Basic Books.

Brown, A. (1988). Motivation to learn and understand: On taking charge of one's own learning. *Cognition and Instruction, 5*, 311–321.

Budoff, M., & Corman, L. (1976). Effectiveness of a learning potential procedure in improving problem-solving skills of retarded and nonretarded children. *American Journal of Mental Deficiency, 81*, 260–264.

Burgio, L. D., Whitman, T. L., & Reid, D. H. (1983). A participative management approach for improving direct-care staff performance in an institutional setting. *Journal of Applied Behavior Analysis, 16*(1), 37–53.

Camp, B., & Bash, M. (1982). *Think aloud*. Champaign, IL: Research Press.

Carlson, J., & Tully, P. (1985, Summer). Learning-by-doing centers: A program to foster problem-solving skills of learning disabled students. *Teaching Exceptional Children*, pp. 305–309.

Chapin, M., & Dyck, D. G. (1976). Persistence in children's reading behavior as a function of N length and attribution retraining. *Journal of Abnormal Psychology, 85*, 511–515.

Corno, L. (1986). The metacognitive control components of self-regulated learning. *Contemporary Educational Psychology, 11*, 333–346.

Corno, L. (1989). Self-regulated learning: A volitional analysis. In B. J. Zimmerman & D. H. Schunk (Eds.), *Self-regulated learning and academic achievement: Theory, research, and practice* (pp. 111–141). New York: Springer.

Corno, L., & Mandinach, E. B. (1983). The role of cognitive engagement in classroom learning and motivation. *Educational Psychologist, 18*(2), 109–124.

Davidson, D. (1991). Children's decision-making examined with an information-board procedure. *Cognitive Development, 6*, 77–90.

Davidson, D., & Hudson, J. (1988). The effects of decision reversibility and decision importance on children's decision-making. *Journal of Experimental Child Psychology, 46*, 35–40.

Deshler, D. D., Schumaker, J. B., & Lenz, B. K. (1984). Academic and cognitive interventions for LD adolescents: Part I. *Journal of Learning Disabilities, 17*, 108–117.

Dickerson, E. A., & Creedon, C. F. (1981). Self-selection of standards by children: The relative effectiveness of pupil-selected and teacher-selected standards of performance. *Journal of Applied Behavior Analysis, 14*, 425–433.

Dunlap, G., DePerczel, M., Clarke, S., Wilson, D., Wright, S., White, R., & Gomez, A. (1994). Choice making to promote adaptive behavior for students with emotional and behavioral challenges. *Journal of Applied Behavior Analysis, 27*(3), 505–518.

Dweck, C. S. (1975). The role of expectations and attributions in the alleviation of learned helplessness. *Journal of Personality and Social Psychology, 31,* 674–685.

D'Zurilla, T., & Goldfried, M. (1971). Problem-solving and behavior modification. *Journal of Abnormal Psychology, 8,* 107–126.

Ellis, E. S. (1986). The role of motivation and pedagogy on the generalization of cognitive strategy training. *Journal of Learning Disabilities, 19*(2), 66–70.

Ellis, E. S., Deshler, D. D., Lenz, B. K., Schumaker, J. B., & Clark, F. L. (1991). An instructional model for teaching learning strategies. *Focus on Exceptional Children, 23*(6), 1–23.

Fantuzzo, J. W., & Clement, P. W. (1981). Generalization of the effects of teacher and self-administered token reinforcers to nontreated students. *Journal of Applied Behavior Analysis, 14,* 435–447.

Felixbrod, J. J., & O'Leary, K. D. (1974). Self-determination of academic standards by children: Toward freedom from external control. *Journal of Educational Psychology, 66,* 845–850.

Fisher, W. W., Thompson, R. H., Piazza, C. C., Crosland, K. A., & Gotjen, D. (1997). On the relative reinforcing effects of choice and differential consequences. *Journal of Applied Behavior Analysis, 30,* 423–438.

Fowler, J. W., & Peterson, P. L. (1981). Increasing reading persistence and altering attributional style of learned helpless children. *Journal of Educational Psychology, 73,* 251–260.

Francesscani, C. (1982, May). MARC: An affective curriculum for emotionally disturbed adolescents. *Teaching Exceptional Children,* pp. 217–222.

Friedman, I. A., & Mann, L. (1993). Coping patterns in adolescent decision-making: An Israeli–Australian comparison. *Journal of Adolescence, 16,* 187–199.

Furby, L., & Beyth-Marom, R. (1992). Risk taking in adolescence: A decision-making perspective. *Developmental Review, 12,* 1–44.

Galotti, J. M., & Kozberg, S. (1996). Adolescents' experience of a life-framing decision. *Journal of Youth and Adolescence, 25*(1), 3–15.

Ghatala, E. S. (1986). Strategy-monitoring training enables young learners to select effective strategies. *Educational Psychologist, 21,* 43–54.

Glynn, E. L. (1970). Classroom applications of self-determined reinforcement. *Journal of Applied Behavior Analysis, 3,* 123–132.

Glynn, E. L., Thomas, J. D., & Shee, S. M. (1973). Behavioral self-control of on-task behavior in an elementary classroom. *Journal of Applied Behavior Analysis, 6,* 105–113.

Gordon, D. E. (1990). Formal operational thinking: The role of cognitive-developmental processes in adolescent decision-making about pregnancy and contraception. *American Journal of Orthopsychiatry, 60,* 346–356.

Graham, S., & Freeman, S. (1986). Strategy training and teacher- vs. student-controlled study conditions: Effects on LD students' spelling performance. *Learning Disability Quarterly, 9,* 15–22.

Greer, R. D. (1994). A systems analysis of the behaviors of schooling. *Journal of Behavioral Education, 4,* 255–264.

Greer, R. D. (1996). Acting to save our schools (1984–1994). In W. Ishaq & J. Cautela (Eds.), *Contemporary issues in behavior therapy: Improving the human condition* (pp. 137–158). New York: Plenum.

Greer, R. D., & McDonough, S. H. (1999). Is the learn unit a fundamental measure of pedagogy? *Behavior Analyst, 1,* 5–16.

Gregson-Paxton, J., & John, D. R. (1995). Are young children adaptive decision-makers? A study of age differences in information search behavior. *Journal of Consumer Research, 21,* 567–580.

Haaga, D. A., & Davison, G. C. (1986). Cognitive change methods. In F. H. Kanfer & A. P. Goldstein (Eds.), *Helping people change* (pp. 236–282). New York: Pergamon Press.

Haley, J. (1976). *Problem solving therapy.* San Francisco: Jossey-Bass.

Hanley, G. P., Piazza, C. C., Fisher, W. W., Contrucci, S. A., & Maglieri, K. A. (1997). Evaluation of client preferences for function-based treatment packages. *Journal of Applied Behavior Analysis, 30*(3), 459–473.

Haring, N. G., & Schiefelbusch, R. L. (Eds.). (1976). *Teaching special children.* New York: McGraw-Hill.

Hickson, L., & Khemka, I. (1999). Decision-making and mental retardation. *International Review of Research in Mental Retardation, 22,* 227–265.

Hickson, L., Golden, H., Khemka, I., Urv, T., & Yamusah, S. (1998). A closer look at interpersonal decision-making in adults with and without mental retardation. *American Journal on Mental Retardation, 103*(3), 209–224.

Hogarth, R. M. (1980). *Judgement and choice: The psychology of decision.* New York: John Wiley & Sons.

Horner, C. M. (1987). Homework: A way to teach problem solving. *Academic Therapy, 22*(3), 239–244.

Janis, I. L., & Mann, L. (1977). *Decision making: A psychological analysis of conflict, choice, and commitment.* New York: Free Press.

Kaser-Boyd, N., Adelmann, H. S., & Taylor, L. (1985). Minors' ability to identify risks and benefits of therapy. *Professional Psychology: Research and Practice, 16,* 411–417.

Lent, R. W., Bron, S. P., & Larkin, K. C. (1984). Relationship of self-efficacy expectations to academic achievement and persistence. *Journal of Counseling Psychology, 31,* 356–362.

Lewis, C. C. (1981). How adolescents approach decisions: Changes over grades seven to twelve and policy implications. *Child Development, 52,* 538–544.

Licht, B. G. (1983). Cognitive-motivational factors that contribute to the achievement of learning-disabled children. *Journal of Learning Disabilities, 16*(8), 483–490.

Lindsley, O. R. (1964). Direct measurement and prosthesis of retarded behavior. *Journal of Education, 147,* 62–81.

Lochman, J. E., & Curry, J. F. (1986). Effects of social problem-solving training and self-instruction training with aggressive boys. *Journal of Clinical Child Psychology, 15*(2), 159–164.

Lochman, J. E., & Lampron, L. B. (1986). Situational social problem-solving skills and self-esteem of aggressive and nonaggressive boys. *Journal of Abnormal Child Psychology, 14*(4), 605–617.

Loper, A. B., Hallahan, D. P., & Ianna, S. O. (1982). Meta-attention in learning disabled and normal students. *Learning Disability Quarterly, 5,* 29–36.

Lovitt, T. C. (1967). Assessment of children with learning disabilities. *Exceptional Children, 34*(4), 233–239.

Lovitt, T. C., & Curtiss, K. A. (1969). Academic response rate as a function of teacher and self-imposed contingencies. *Journal of Applied Behavior Analysis, 2,* 49–53.

Mann, L., Harmoni, R., & Power, C. (1989). Adolescent decision-making: The development of competence. *Journal of Adolescence, 12,* 265–278.

McFall, R. M., & Dodge, K. A. (1983). Self-management and interpersonal skills learning. In P. Karoly & F. H. Kanfer (Eds.), *Self-management and behavior change: From theory to practice* (pp. 353–392). New York: Pergamon Press.

McGinnis, E., Sauerbry, L., & Nichols, P. (1985, Spring). Skill-streaming: Teaching social skills to children with behavioral disorders. *Teaching Exceptional Children,* pp. 160–167.

Miller, D. L., & Kelley, M. L. (1994). The use of goal setting and contingency contracting for improving children's homework performance. *Journal of Applied Behavior Analysis, 27*(1), 73–84.

Mithaug, D. E. (1993). *Self-regulation theory: How optimal adjustment maximizes gain*. Westport, CT: Praeger.

Mithaug, D. E. (2000). *Learning to theorize: A four-step strategy*. Thousand Oaks, CA: Sage.

Mithaug, D. E., & Hanawalt, D. A. (1978). The validation of procedures to assess prevocational task preferences in three severely retarded young adults. *Journal of Applied Behavior Analysis, 11*, 153–162.

Mithaug, D. E., & Mar, D. (1980). The relation between choosing and working prevocational tasks in two severely retarded young adults. *Journal of Applied Behavior Analysis, 13*, 177–192.

Mithaug, D. E., Martin, J. E., & Agran, M. (1987). Adaptability instruction: The goal of transitional programming. *Exceptional Children, 53*, 500–505.

Olympia, D. E., Sheridan, S. M., Jenson, W. R., & Andrews, D. (1994). Using student-managed interventions to increase homework completion and accuracy. *Journal of Applied Behavior Analysis, 27*(1), 85–99.

Paris, S. G., Lipson, M. Y., & Wixson, K. K. (1983). Becoming a strategic reader. *Contemporary Educational Psychology, 8*, 293–316.

Parsons, M. B., Reid, D. H., Reynolds, J., & Bumgardner, M. (1990). Effects of chosen versus assigned jobs on the work performance of persons with severe handicaps. *Journal of Applied Behavior Analysis, 23*, 253–258.

Phillips, P. (1990). A self-advocacy plan for high school students with learning disabilities: A comparative case study analysis of students', teachers', and parents' perceptions of program effects. *Journal of Learning Disabilities, 23*, 466–471.

Pressley, M., Borkowski, J. G., & Schneider, W. (1987). Cognitive strategies: Good strategy users coordinate metacognition and knowledge. In R. Vasta & G. Whitehurst (Eds.), *Annals of child development* (Vol. 5, pp. 89–129). New York: JAI Press.

Pressley, M., Ross, K. A., Levin, J. R., & Ghatala, E. S. (1984). The role of strategy-utility knowledge in children's decision-making. *Journal of Experimental Child Pscyhology, 38*, 491–504.

Reeve, R. A., & Brown, A. L. (1985). Metacognition reconsidered: Implications for intervention research. *Journal of Abnormal Child Psychology, 13*(3), 343–356.

Reyna, V. F., & Ellis, S. C. (1994). Fuzzy-trace theory and framing effects in children's risky decision-making. *Psychological Science, 5*, 275–279.

Rose, S. (1986). Group methods. In F. H. Kanfer & A. P. Goldstein (Eds.), *Helping people change* (pp. 437–469). New York: Pergamon Press.

Ross, D. M., & Ross, S. A. (1978). Cognitive training for EMR children: Choosing the best alternative. *American Journal of Mental Deficiency, 82*, 598–601.

Schloss, P., & Wood, C. E. (1990). Effect of self-monitoring on maintenance and generalization of conversation skills of persons with mental retardation. *Mental Retardation, 218*, 105–113.

Schunk, D. H. (1984). Self-efficacy perspective on achievement behavior. *Educational Psychologist, 19*, 48–58.

Schunk, D. H., & Cox, P. D. (1986). Strategy training and attributional feedback with learning disabled students. *Journal of Educational Psychology, 78*(3), 201–209.

Schunk, D. H., & Swartz, C. W. (1993). Goals and progress feedback: Effects of self-efficacy and writing achievement. *Contemporary Educational Psychology, 18*, 337–354.

Sidman, M. (1960). *Tactics of scientific research*. New York: Basic Books.

Sowers, J., Verdi, M., Bourbeau, P., & Sheehan, M. (1985). Teaching job independence and flexibility to mentally retarded students through the use of a self-control package. *Journal of Applied Behavior Analysis, 18*, 81–85.

Spivack, G., Platt, J. J., & Shure, M. B. (1976). *The problem-solving approach to adjustment*. San Francisco: Jossey-Bass.

Spivack, G., & Shure, M. B. (1974). *Social adjustment of young children: A cognitive approach to solving real-life problems.* San Francisco: Jossey-Bass.

Stark, K. D., Reynolds, M., & Kaslow, N. J. (1987). A comparison of the relative efficacy of self-control therapy and a behavioral problem-solving therapy for depression in children. *Journal of Abnormal Child Psychology, 15*(1), 91–113.

Stevenson, H. C., & Fantuzzo, J. W. (1984). Application of the "generalization map" to a self-control intervention with school-aged children. *Journal of Applied Behavior Analysis, 17,* 203–212.

Stevenson, H. C., & Fantuzzo, J. W. (1986). The generality of social validity of a competency-based self-control training intervention for underachieving students. *Journal of Applied Behavior Analysis, 19,* 269–276.

Tawney, J. W., & Gast, D. L. (1984). *Single subject research in special education.* Columbus, OH: Charles E. Merrill.

Taylor, L., Adelman, H. S., & Kaser-Boyd, N. (1983). Perspectives of children regarding their participation in psychoeducational decisions. *Professional Psychology: Research and Practice, 14,* 882–894.

Taylor, L., Adelman, H. S., & Kaser-Boyd, N. (1985). Minors' attitudes and competence toward participation in psychoeducational decisions. *Professional Psychology: Research and Practice, 16,* 226–235.

Thomas, A., & Pashley, B. (1982). Effects of classroom training on LD students' task persistence and attributions. *Learning Disability Quarterly, 5,* 133–144.

Tymchuk, A. J., Andron, L., & Rahbar, B. (1988). Effective decision-making/problem-solving training with mothers who have mental retardation. *American Journal on Mental Retardation, 92,* 510–516.

Tymchuk, A. J., Yokota, A., & Rahbar, B. (1990). Decision-making abilities of mothers with mental retardation. *Research in Developmental Disabilities, 11,* 97–109.

Valett, R. (1986). Developing thinking skills. *Academic Therapy, 11*(2), 187–198.

Wang, M. C., & Stiles, B. (1976). An investigation of children's concept of responsibility for their school learning. *American Educational Research Journal, 13,* 159–179.

Wehmeyer, M. L., & Kelchner, K. (1996). Perceptions of classroom environment, locus of control and academic attributions of adolescents with and without cognitive disabilities. *Career Development for Exceptional Individuals, 19*(1), 15–30.

Wehmeyer, M. L., & Lawrence, M. (1995). Whose future is it anyway? Promoting student involvement in transition planning. *Career Development for Exceptional Individuals, 18,* 69–83.

Weinstein, C. E., & Meyer, R. E. (1986). The teaching of learning strategies. In M. C. Wittrock (Eds.), *Handbook of research on teaching* (3rd ed., pp. 315–327). New York: Macmillan.

Weithorn, L. A., & Campbell, S. B. (1982). The competency of children and adolescents to make informed decisions. *Child Development, 53,* 1589–1598.

Whitman, T. L. (1990). Self-regulation and mental retardation. *American Journal on Mental Retardation, 94*(4), 347–362.

Whitman, T. L., Burgio, L., & Johnston, M. B. (1984). Cognitive behavior therapy with the mentally retarded. In A. Meyers & E. Craighead (Eds.), *Cognitive behavior therapy with children* (pp. 193–227). New York: Plenum Press.

Wong, B. Y. L. (1980). Activating the inactive learner: Use of questions/prompts to enhance comprehension and retention of implied information in learning disabled children. *Learning Disability Quarterly, 3,* 28–37.

Wong, B. Y. L., & Jones, W. (1982). Increasing metacomprehension in learning disabled and normally achieving students through self-questioning training. *Learning Disabilities Quarterly, 5,* 228–240.

Yu, P., Harris, G. E., Solovitz, B. L., & Franklin, J. L. (1986). A social problem-solving intervention for children at high risk for later psychopathology. *Journal of Clinical Child Psychology, 15*(1), 30–40.

Zimmerman, B. J. (1985). The development of "intrinsic" motivation: A social learning analysis. *Annals of Child Development, 2,* 117–160.

Zimmerman, B. J. (1990). Self-regulated learning and academic achievement: An overview. *Educational Psychologist, 25*(1), 3–17.

Zimmerman, B. J., & Martinez-Pons, M. (1986). Development of a structured interview for assessing student use of self-regulated learning strategies. *American Educational Research Journal, 23,* 614–628.

Zimmerman, B. J., Bonner, S., & Kovach, R. (1996). *Developing self-regulated learners: Beyond achievement to self-efficacy.* Washington DC: American Psychological Association.

II

PREDICTION VERIFICATION

4

Assessing Self-Determination Prospects Among Students With and Without Disabilities

Dennis E. Mithaug
Peggie L. Campeau
Jean M. Wolman

This chapter investigates the prediction derived from self-determined learning theory that achievement and self-determination are positively correlated. The reasoning for this prediction is as follows. If people who are self-determined learners know how to optimize learning challenges to maximize their learning, they will be high in achievement. And if those people also know how to optimize their adjustments to meet self-determined goals, they will be high in self-determination. Therefore people high in achievement will be high in self-determination. Hence achievement and self-determination should correlate.

According to self-determined learning theory and self-determination theory, the capacity to regulate adjustments to new opportunities affects learning and prospects for self-determination (Mithaug, 1993, 1996a, 1996b, in press). Hence any decrement in achievement or in self-determination prospects can be traced to inadequate adjustment capabilities. Table 4.1 applies these predictions to students who have been identified as low achievers. The first argument claims that their low achievement is due to inadequate adjustments to learning opportunities and that students in special education are likely to exhibit this difficulty. The second argument claims that self-determination prospects are also affected by adjustment inadequacies. Therefore, students in special education should have lower prospects for self-determination than do students in general education.

The study reported in this chapter tested whether students in special education reported lowered prospects for self-determination due to this inability to adjust to opportunities for gain. The study compared prospects for self-determination of students enrolled in special and general ed-

TABLE 4.1
Explanations for the Effects of Adjustment
on Achievement and Self-Determination

---

1. School achievement is a function of adjustments to opportunities for learning gain.
   a. Underachievement is due to inadequate adjustment to opportunities to learn.
   b. Many students in special education underachieve.
   c. Therefore these students adjust inadequately to opportunities to learn.
2. Self-determination prospects are a function of adjustments to opportunities for self-determined gain.
   a. People who adjust inadequately to opportunities for self-determined gain have lower prospects for self-determination than do people who adjust adequately to those opportunities.
   b. Many students in special education adjust inadequately to opportunities for self-determined gain.
   c. Therefore these students are likely to have lower prospects for self-determination than are students who adjust adequately to opportunities for self-determined gain.

---

ucation by asking teachers and students to report on their capacities and opportunities to self-determine in school and at home. The study tested predictions about those ratings based on the arguments in Table 4.1. First, it tested the prediction that respondents would rate prospects for self-determination lower for students in special education than for students in general education. Second, it tested the claim that participants would rate capacities to self-determine lower for students in special education than for students in general education. Third, it tested whether respondents would rate the self-regulated adjustments lower for students in special education than for students in general education. Last, the study determined whether respondents would rate school opportunities higher and home opportunities lower for students in special education than for students in general education. The reasoning behind this prediction was that students in special education would rate their school opportunities higher because they received individualized instruction, which tends to optimize opportunities at school but not at home. Therefore, they would rate those opportunities less favorably. The following hypotheses reflect these predictions.

1. Teachers rate self-determination prospects of students in general education higher than they rate self-determination prospects of students in special education.
2. Teachers and students report higher capacities to self-determine for students in general education than for students in special education.
3. Students in general education receive higher self-regulation ratings than do students in special education.

4. Teachers and students report more favorable school opportunities to self-determine for students in special education than for students in general education.

5. Teachers and students report more favorable home opportunities to self-determine for students in general education than for students in special education.

THE AIR SELF-DETERMINATION STUDY

The study that tested these predictions was part of a project conducted by the American Institutes for Research and Teachers College Columbia University to develop the AIR Self-Determination Scale, which was used to assess students' prospects for self-determination (Wolman, Campeau, DuBois, Mithaug, & Stolarski, 1994).[1] The theory driving the development of that instrument was that adaptive capacity and environmental opportunity affect prospects for self-determination (Mithaug, 1993). As a student's capacity to adjust to a circumstance increases and as opportunities for gain by changing that situation become more favorable, engagement in self-determined pursuits becomes more likely. Hence, prospects for self-determination improve. The instrument was designed to measure students' capacity to adjust to opportunity for meeting self-set goals and opportunities at school and home for engaging in opportunities for personal gain.

The AIR Self-Determination Scale

The AIR Self-Determination Scale (see Table 4.2) was developed to assess students' capacity to adjust to opportunities for self-determined gain. It assessed students' adjustment capability by measuring how well they connected beliefs about what they needed, wanted, and could do with their expectations, choices, actions, and results. It assessed opportunities for self-determined engagement by determining the extent to which circumstances at school and home allowed students to engage and control events to produce the gain they wanted. The assumption was that when students knew how to regulate events that affected their needs and wants, and when they had frequent opportunities to engage in those regulatory behaviors, then self-determination would increase. In other words, the greater the students' capacity and opportunity to self-determine, the greater would be their prospects for self-determination.

---

[1]This project, Self-Determination for Students with Disabilities, was funded by the U.S. Department of Education, Office of Special Education Programs, under cooperative agreement HO23J200005.

TABLE 4.2
Sample Educator and Student Items of the AIR Self-Determination Scale

Educator Items for Students' "Ability to Perform Self-Determined Behaviors" (1 of 3 AIR Scales)	Student Items for "Things I Do" (1 of 2 AIR Scales)
Capacity to Self-Determine	Capacity to Self-Determine
1. Student expresses own interests, needs, and abilities.	1. I know what I need, what I like, and what I'm good at.
2. Student sets expectations and goals that will satisfy own interests, needs, and wants.	2. I set goals to get what I want or need. I think about what I am good at when I do this.
3. Student makes choices, decisions, and plans to meet own goals and expectations.	3. I figure out how to meet my goals. I make plans and decide what I should do.
4. Student initiates actions on own choices and plans.	4. I begin working on my plans to meet my goals as soon as possible.
5. Student gathers information on results of actions.	5. I check how I'm doing when I'm working on my plan. If I need to, I ask others what they think of how I'm doing.
6. Student changes own actions or plans to satisfy expectations and goals, if necessary.	6. If my plan doesn't work, I try another one to meet my goals.
School Opportunities to Self-Determine	School Opportunities to Self-Determine
1. Student has opportunities at school to explore, express, and feel good about own needs, interests, and abilities.	1. People at school listen to me when I talk about what I want, what I need, or what I'm good at.
2. Student has opportunities at school to identify goals and expectations that will meet his or her needs, interests, and abilities; to set these goals; and to feel good about them.	2. People at school let me know that I can set my own goals to get what I want or need.
3. Student has opportunities at school to learn about making choices and plans, to make them, and to feel good about them.	3. At school, I have learned how to make plans to meet my goals and to feel good about them.
4. Student has opportunities at school to initiate actions to meet expectations and goals.	4. People at school encourage me to start working on my plans right away.
5. Student has opportunities at school to get results of actions taken to meet own plans.	5. I have someone at school who can tell me if I am meeting my goals.
6. Student has opportunities at school to change actions and plans to satisfy own expectations.	6. People at school understand when I have to change my plan to meet my goal. They offer advice and encourage me when I'm doing this.

(Continued)

TABLE 4.2
(Continued)

Educator Items for Students' "Ability to Perform Self-Determined Behaviors" (1 of 3 AIR Scales)	Student Items for "Things I Do" (1 of 2 AIR Scales)
Home Opportunities to Self-Determine	Home Opportunities to Self-Determine
1. Student has opportunities at home to explore, express, and feel good about own needs, interests, and abilities.	1. People at home listen to me when I talk about what I want, what I need, or what I'm good at.
2. Student has opportunities at home to identify goals and expectations that will meet his or her needs, interests, and abilities; to set these goals; and to feel good about them.	2. People at home let me know that I can set my own goals to get what I want or need.
3. Student has opportunities at home to learn about making choices and plans, to make them, and to feel good about them.	3. At home, I have learned how to make plans to meet my goals and to feel good about them.
4. Student has opportunities at home to initiate actions to meet expectations and goals.	4. People at home encourage me to start working on my plans right away.
5. Student has opportunities at home to get results of actions taken to meet own plans.	5. I have someone at home who can tell me if I am meeting my goals.
6. Student has opportunities at home to change actions and plans to satisfy own expectations.	6. People at home understand when I ·have to change my plan to meet my goal. They offer advice and encourage me when I'm doing this.

The AIR Scale for teachers had three scales to rate student capacity to self-determine (knowledge, ability, and perceptions), and two scales to rate their opportunities to self-determine. The AIR Scale for students had two scales to rate capacity to self-determine (What I Think and How I Feel) and two scales to rate their opportunities to self-determine. The capacity scales included questions in six regulatory domains: awareness of abilities and interests (question 1), setting expectations and goals (question 2), making choices, decisions, and plans (question 3), taking actions (question 4), evaluating results (question 5), and adjusting actions and plans (question 6). The opportunity indicators consisted of the parallel set of six questions for opportunities at school and six questions for opportunities at home. Each assessment item was scored on a 5-point Likert scale to indicate how frequently they engaged in a behavior: *never, almost never, sometimes, almost always,* and *always.* Table 4.2 lists sample items from the ability scale for teachers and the "Things I Do" scale for students.

The Test Population

The AIR Self-Determination Scale was fielded tested in 72 schools and programs in San Jose, California, and New York City, New York. Educators, including special education teachers, resource specialists, and regular classroom teachers, assessed more than 450 students with and without disabilities. The educator ages ranged from 20 to 67 years with the majority being between 25 and 49 years of age. They identified themselves as general education teachers (11%), resource-room teachers (6%), self-contained special education teachers (33%), transition teachers (29%), student teachers and aides (11%), and other school-related personnel (10%).

The population of assessed students was 39% female and 61% male. Thirty-three percent were African-American, 39% Hispanic, 22% White, 3% Asian or Pacific Islander, and 3% other groups. Nearly all the students (91.9%) came from schools in the city, with the remainder coming from schools in suburbs (7.8%) and small towns (0.2%). The most frequently used languages in the homes of students were English (58.5%) and Spanish (33.0%). The ages of students ranged from 6 to 25 years, with 12% between 6 and 9 years, 17% between 10 and 12 years, 12% between 13 and 15 years, 24% between 16 and 18 years, 35% between 19 and 21 years, and 0.4% between 22 and 25 years. Students also varied in economic status, with 72% enrolled in free lunch programs. Finally, 82% of the students were enrolled in special education and 18% were enrolled in general education. Table 4.3 summarizes the disability characteristics of the test population.

Instrument Reliability and Validity

The authors of the *AIR Self-Determination Scale and User Guide* (Wolman et al., 1994) reported reliability results using an alternative-item correlation for item consistency, a split-half test of the internal consistency of the instrument, and a test–retest measure of stability of instrument assessments over time. A field-test version of the scale included duplicate items for each of the six questions comprising the capacity component of the assessment. These components covered students' ability to know and express needs, interest, and abilities; to set expectations and goals; to make choices

TABLE 4.3
Percent of Participants by Disability Group

No Disability	1 Mild/Moderate Mental Retardation	2 Learning Disability	3 Emotional and Behavior Disorder	4 Physical & Health Impairment
16.4	11.1	30.6	7.6	34.3

and plans; to act on plans; to evaluate results of actions; and to alter plans and actions to meet goals more effectively. The alternative-item tests produced correlation coefficients that ranged from .91 to .98. The split-half test for internal consistency compared even-numbered items of the instrument with odd-numbered items. It yielded a correlation of .95. The test–retest measure of consistency was conducted over a period of 3 months and yielded a correlation of .74.

The instrument was also validated by an analysis that examined the constructs used in its construction: the capacity and opportunity to self-determine. Results of a factor analysis indicated the presence of four factors, which explained 74% of the variance of the 30-item instrument. Factor 1, the capacity to self-determine factor, explained 42.4% of the variance. Factor 2, the home-school factor, explained 17.2% of the variance. Factor 3, the opportunity factor, explained 10.3% of the variance. Factor 4, the knowledge–ability–perception factor used to differentiate student's capacity to self-determine, explained 4.1% of the variance. Overall, the four factors explained most of the variance in the item scores, which supported the claim that the instrument reflected the conceptual constructs of capacity and opportunity. In other words, the instrument measured what it was purported to measure — students' capacity and opportunity to self-determine.

RESULTS OF THE STUDY

The results indicated that there were no significant differences on levels of self-determination among students by gender, ethnicity, or age. Male and female students scored similarly on measures of their levels of self-determination, which combined capacity and opportunity components, as did students from different ethnic and age groups. As indicated in Table 4.4, students enrolled in general education received significantly higher self-determination ratings than students enrolled in special education.

TABLE 4.4
Comparison of Self-Determination Levels
by School Placement and Economic Status

School Placement		Economic Status	
Special Education	General Education	Free Lunch	No Free Lunch
99.2	111.2	99.0	106.5
	$p = .000$		$p = .006$

Also, students enrolled in the free lunch program received significantly lower ratings than students not enrolled in those programs.

Hypothesis 1 Results

Figure 4.1 presents data comparing teacher ratings of students' prospects for self-determination. As indicated in the figure, teachers rated students without disabilities significantly higher ($p < .001$) than they rated students with disabilities. Of that group, students with other disabilities received the highest AIR score (101.4) and students with behavior disorders received the lowest score (93). But all of the scores for students with disabilities were lower than the average for students without disabilities (112). These results are consistent with Hypothesis 1 from the beginning of the chapter claiming that teachers would report higher self-determination prospects for students in general education than for student in special education.

Hypothesis 2 Results

Figure 4.2 presents data comparing teacher and student ratings on students' capacity to self-determine. As indicated in the figure, both teachers and students rated the two groups similarly in that students without disabilities received significantly higher capacity ratings than did students with disabilities ($p < .001$). There is agreement between the two groups that students without disabilities have greater capacity to self-determine. These results are consistent with Hypothesis 2 that claims teachers and students would rate the capacity for self-determination of students in gen-

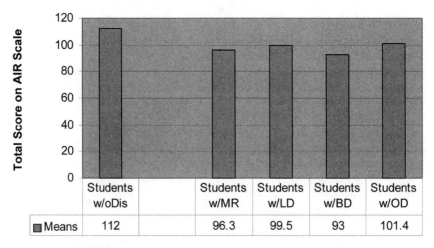

FIG. 4.1. Teacher ratings of students' prospects for self-determination.

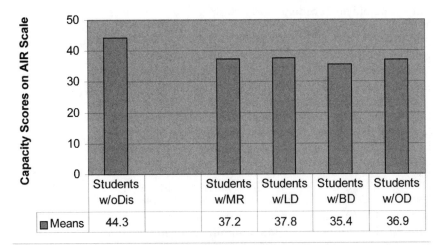

Teacher Ratings of Capacity to Self-Determine

	Students w/oDis		Students w/MR	Students w/LD	Students w/BD	Students w/OD
■Means	44.3		37.2	37.8	35.4	36.9

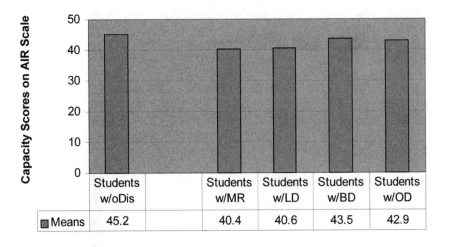

Student Ratings of Capacity to Self-Determine

	Students w/oDis		Students w/MR	Students w/LD	Students w/BD	Students w/OD
■Means	45.2		40.4	40.6	43.5	42.9

FIG. 4.2. Teacher and student ratings on students' capacity to self-determine.

eral education higher than they would rate the capacity for self-determination of students in special education.

Another finding is that although general education teachers and students produced similar capacity ratings (44.3 vs. 45.2, respectively), special educators and students did not. Special education teachers rated students in special education consistently lower than the students rated themsleves. The discrepancy averaged 5 points (36.8 vs. 41.9). It was an 8.1-point discrepacy for students with behavior disorders, a 6-point discrepancy for students with other disabilities, a 3.2-point discrepancy for students with mental retardation, and a 2.8-point discrepancy for students with learning disabilities.

Hypothesis 3 Results

Figure 4.3 presents data comparing combined teacher–student assessments of how well students regulated their expectations, choices, actions, results to satisfy their needs and interests (items 1–6 in the second column of Table 4.1). Again, the results present a consistent pattern of students without disabilities being rated significantly higher than students with disabilities ($p < .001$). The differences were present across all self-regulation categories. On average, students without disabilities were rated 8 to 9 points higher in each self-regulation categories than were students with disabilities. These findings are consistent with the hypothesis that students in general education would receive higher self-regulation ratings than would students in special education.

Hypothesis 4 Results

Figure 4.4 presents data on teacher and student assessments of their opportunities to self-determine at school. The results indicate that both teachers and students rated school opportunities for students without disabilities significantly lower than they rated school opportunities for students with disabilities. These differences were significant for the teacher ratings of students with behavior disorders (w/BD) and their ratings of students with other disabilities (w/OD) ($p < .15$). They were also significant for student ratings of those two groups ($p < .05$). Again differences between teacher and student ratings were present as well, with teacher ratings of school opportunities for self-determination 7 to 9 points higher than student ratings of those opportunities.

Hypothesis 5 Results

Figure 4.5 presents data on teacher and student assessments of student opportunities to self-determine at home. The results indicate that both

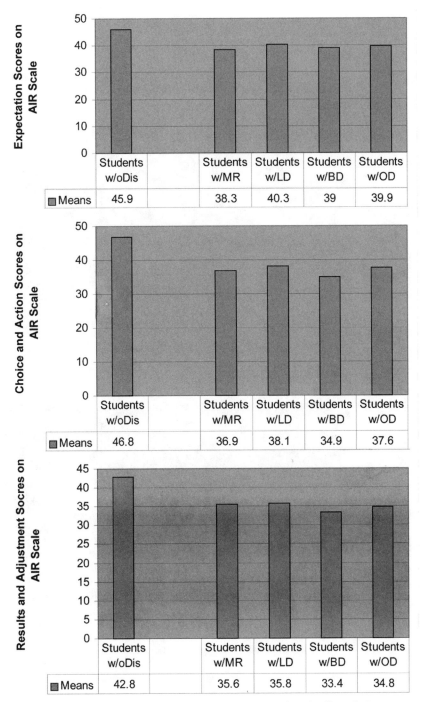

FIG. 4.3. Combined teacher–student ratings on students' self-regulation skills.

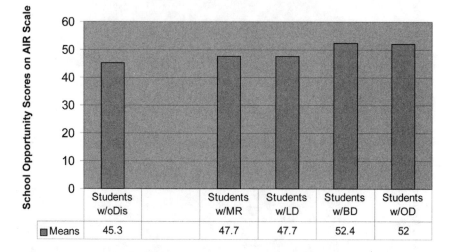

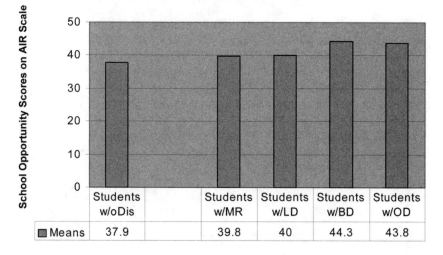

FIG. 4.4. Teacher and student ratings on school opportunities to self-determine.

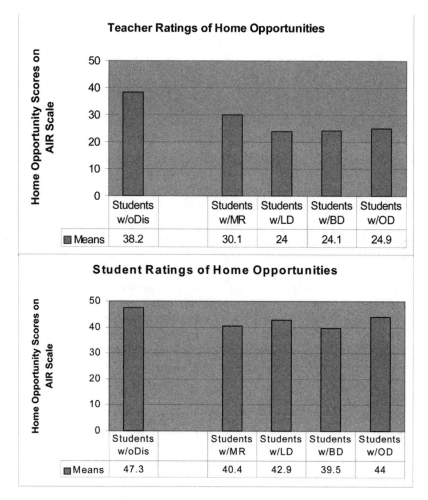

FIG. 4.5. Teacher and student ratings of home opportunities to self-determine.

teachers and students rated home opportunities lower for students with disabilities than for students without disabilities. They support the hypothesis that teachers and students will rate home opportunities higher for students in general education than for students in special education. These predicted differences were significant for teacher ratings of students with behavior disorders (w/BD) and for teacher ratings of students with other disabilities (w/OD) ($p < .05$). They were also significant for student ratings of those same groups ($p < .05$). Again, teachers and students rated the magnitude of those differences very differently. General education raters judged home opportunities for students without disabilities to

be 9 points lower than did general education student raters of those opportunities. Special education teachers judged home opportunities for
students with disabilities to be 10 (students w/MR) to 19 (students
w/OD) points lower than did students in special education.

DISCUSSION

This study provided indirect evidence to support the claim that self-
determination and achievement are correlated because both are a function
of the ability to adjust to challenging circumstances. Figure 4.6 illustrates
the causal sequence we believe is responsible for the association. According to self-determined learning theory, the opportunity to learn from a
challenge and the adjustment to that opportunity affect learning and
achievement. And according to self-determination theory, the opportunity for self-determined gain and the adjustment to that opportunity affect
prospects for self-determination. The factor common to the two theories is
the ability to adjust to challenging opportunities. Hence, achievement
does not cause self-determination to increase or decrease, nor does self-
determination cause achievement to increase or decrease. Self-regulated
adjustments to challenging opportunities cause them to increase or decrease, which yields the correlation between them. Hence, groups that differ on that factor are likely to experience parallel effects on learning,
achievement, and self-determination.

We tested this claim by measuring levels of self-determination of students whose achievement differences were indicated by their placements
in general and special education classes. The prediction was that students
in special education classes would have lowered prospects for self-determination and that this would be due to their lowered capacity to regulate
adjustments to opportunities for self-determined gain. Test comparisons
between students in special and general education supported this prediction. Students in special education classes had lower prospects for self-
determination, which was due to their lowered capacity to adjust to opportunities for self-determined gain. The data were consistent with various predictions of this claim. Teachers and students consistently reported
higher prospects for self-determination, higher capacities to self-determine, and greater regulatory capacity to adjust for students in general education classes than for students in special education classes. Teachers
and students also reported consistently higher opportunities to self-determine at school and lower opportunities to self-determine at home for students in special education classes.

Still, the findings are equivocal as to whether these differences were
due to a disability effect on adjustment capability or to a socioeconomic ef-

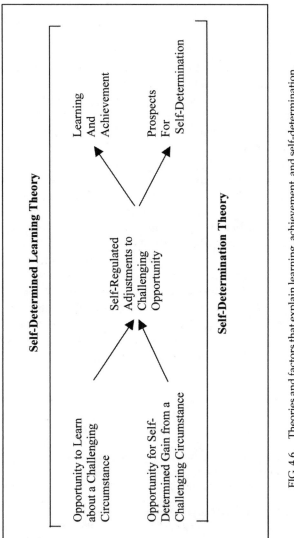

FIG. 4.6. Theories and factors that explain learning, achievement, and self-determination.

fect on adjustment capability that was also associated with placements in special education classes. The fact that both disability and low-income status were more frequent among students in special education means that either or both factors could be responsible for the lower self-determination scores. This possibility does not jeopardize the credibility of the explanations in Table 4.1, however, because either way the mediating factor is still adjustment capability and its effects on learning and self-determination. Whether poverty or disability lowers adjustment capability does not alter the claim that underachievement and lowered prospects for self-determination are adversely affected by the common factor, which is adjustment capability.

Nonetheless, this alternative explanation has implications for predicting future outcomes for the two groups because if socioeconomic factors are responsible for poor adjustments and lowered self-determination prospects, then a change in those circumstances — for example, by getting a college degree — should ameliorate group differences on self-determination prospects. The presence of a disabling condition for members of one group but not another group should not adversely affect those prospects. On the other hand, if disability turns out to be adversely affecting adjustments to challenge, then a change in socioeconomic circumstances would not eliminate group differences on self-determination.

One way to test this possibility is to conduct a follow-up study of adults with and without disabilities who have graduated from college and determine whether there are group differences on self-determination that can be attributed to disability and not these equalized socioeconomic circumstances. This was the approach used for chapter 5.

REFERENCES

Mithaug, D. E. (1993). *Self-regulation theory: How optimal adjustment maximizes gain*. Westport, CT: Praeger.

Mithaug, D. E. (1996a). *Equal opportunity theory*. Thousand Oaks, CA: Sage.

Mithaug, D. E. (1996b). The optimal prospects principle: A theoretical basis for rethinking instructional practices for self-determination. In S. J. Sands & M. L. Wehmeyer (Eds.), *Self-determination across the life span: Independence and choice for people with disabilities* (pp. 147–165). Baltimore, MD: Paul H. Brookes.

Mithaug, D. E. (in press). Evaluating credibility and worth of self-determination theory. In M. L. Wehmeyer, B. Abery, D. E. Mithaug, L. E. Powers, & R. J. Stancliffe (Eds.), *Theory in self-determination: Foundations of educational practice*. Springfield, IL: Charles C. Thomas.

Wolman, J. M, Campeau, P. L., DuBois, P. A., Mithaug, D. E., & Stolarski, V. S. (1994). *AIR self-determination scale and user guide*. Palo Alto, CA: American Institutes for Research.

5

Assessing Prospects for Self-Determination Among College Graduates With and Without Disabilities

Sherrel Powell
Dennis E. Mithaug

The study in this chapter reports on the adjustments of adults with and without disabilities who recently graduated from a community college. The study is notable in that previous follow-ups of former special education students found uniformly dismal outcomes (Affleck, Edgar, Levine, & Kortering, 1990; Hasazi, Gordon, & Roe, 1985; Mithaug & Horiuchi, 1983; Mithaug, Horiuchi, & Fanning, 1985; Mithaug, Hoiruchi, & McNulty, 1987; Neel, Meadows, Levine, & Edgar, 1988; Scuccimarra & Speece, 1990). Indeed, the conclusion from much of that research was that prospects for youth with disabilities would decline rather than improve as students matured (Chadsey-Rusch, Rusch, & O'Reilly, 1991; Wehmeyer, 1996).

One of the recommendations to avert this dire prediction was to prepare students to be more self-determined during their school years. Indeed, much of the 1990s research and demonstrations on school-to-work transition for this population reflected the assumption that prospects for leading a decent life after school could be enhanced if students learned to control the content and direction of their lives while in school. Although the assumed connection between instruction, learning, and self-determination had yet to be demonstrated at the time, many believed such instruction would increase students' self-determination and hence improve their chances of living a decent life after school (Agran, 1997; Sands & Wehmeyer, 1996; Wehmeyer & Sands, 1998).

Subsequently, this claim was supported empirically by Wehmeyer and colleagues in follow-up studies examining the association between self-

77

determination and the outcomes experienced by special education graduates with cognitive disabilities. Wehmeyer and Schwartz (1997) measured the self-determination of 80 students with cognitive disabilities in their final year of high school. One year after leaving school, these young people completed a questionnaire concerning their lives and activities at that time. By controlling for differences in intelligence among these respondents, Wehmeyer and Schwartz (1997) were able to show that students who were more self-determined were more independent overall, and were significantly more likely to be working for pay and at a higher hourly wage. Subsequently, Wehmeyer and Palmer (2001) found that three years after graduation, outcomes were more positive for 94 students with mental retardation and learning disabilities who scored higher on a self-determination measure. Self-determined learning theory explains these findings by claiming that students who are self-determined do better after leaving school because they know how to adjust to challenging circumstances to get what they need and want in life.

These findings and those of the previous chapter suggest that students with disabilities are less prepared for adult life than they could be because they rate their prospects for self-determination lower than do students without disabilities. However, there was a problem with that finding in that a socioeconomic explanation for group differences was also possible. According to that account, the disproportionate number of students with disabilities who were also enrolled in free lunch programs experienced unusual social and economic hardship at home and hence believed they were less capable of pursuing their own goals in life. This possibility is important because the theorizing in previous chapters suggested that disability affects adjustments and hence learning and self-determination prospects (Arnold & Clement, 1981; Graham, Harris, & Reid, 1992; Whitman, 1990).

The present study deals with this potential confound by controlling for socioeconomic circumstances so any difference in self-determination prospects among community college graduates with and without disabilities can be attributed to disability alone. The following hypotheses reflect this expectation that when socioeconomic conditions are held constant, there will be an association between disability and lowered adjustment ratings on measures of self-determination.

1. College students with and without disabilities report similar opportunities to self-determine at school.
2. College students with disabilities report lower capacities to self-determine than do college students without disabilities.
3. College students with disabilities report lower prospects for self-determination than do college students without disabilities.

COMPARING SELF-DETERMINATION PROSPECTS OF COMMUNITY COLLEGE GRADUATES WITH AND WITHOUT DISABILITIES

This study was part of dissertation research conducted by the first author. It took place in a community college at a large northeastern city where the first author was a faculty member. The first author worked with officials at the college's office for students with disabilities to select participant names and addresses and to mail out questionnaires requesting information about their background characteristics, success at college, and self-determination ratings.

Participant Characteristics

The 203 graduates who responded to the follow-up survey attended college between 1993 to 1999 and had graduated from college with an associate's degree. They included 117 graduates without disabilities and 86 graduates with disabilities. The background characteristics of the two groups are presented in Tables 5.1–5.4. Tables 5.1–5.3 present data showing similarities between the groups, and Table 5.4 reports data on differences between them.

Group Similarities. As indicated in Table 5.1, there were no significant differences between the two groups on mean age, gender, or college major. Nor were there significant differences on changes in major or in the frequency or amount of time taken off from school. The groups were also similar on the number of previous colleges attended, whether they viewed faculty as supportive, whether they experienced problems in school, and whether they were ever placed on probation. Finally, there was no disability effect on choice of major by members of the group with disabilities.

Table 5.2 presents data on the social and economic characteristics of the two groups. These results indicate that there were no significant group differences on ethnicity, parent education, status among family members' educational achievements, or financial status in college.

Table 5.3 compares college level achievements of the two groups, their rates of progress toward graduation, and other accomplishments since graduation. Again the groups were similar. There were no significant differences in the two groups of participants on their reported grade point accumulations during college, in the year they began college, or in the number of other accomplishments they reported since graduation.

Group Differences. There were, however, several significant differences between groups, as indicated in Table 5.4. One was that college graduates with disabilities were more likely to have received special edu-

TABLE 5.1
Background of Community College Graduates

	Community College Graduates Without Disabilities n = 117	Community College Graduates With Disabilities n = 86	Significance p < .05
Mean age	30 years	31 years	ns
Gender			
Female	.78	.77	ns
Male	.22	.23	
Major			
Occupational therapy	.57	.44	ns
Physical therapy	.06	.07	
Human development	.22	.17	
Liberal arts	.07	.13	
Business	.02	.02	
Computers	.01	.05	
Nursing	.05	.15	
Changed major? No	.70	.67	ns
Took time off from school? No	.76	.65	ns
How much time off?			
1–6 months	.16	.10	ns
7–12 months	.04	.10	
1–2 years	.04	.10	
>2 years	.03	.02	
Attend other colleges?			
No	.51	.59	ns
One	.30	.28	
Two	.11	.08	
Three	.05	.03	
Four/+	.01	.02	
Faculty supportive? Yes	.38	.33	ns
Experienced problems? No	.74	.33	ns
Ever on probation? No	.97	.89	ns
Disability affected major? Yes	.00	.03	ns

cation services during their elementary and secondary school years. Although 94% of graduates without disabilities reported that they had never received special education services, only 24% of graduates with disabilities reported never receiving services. And although 48% of graduates with disabilities had been in resource rooms during school, only 2% of the graduates without disabilities reported resource-room experiences. A second finding was that graduates without disabilities were more likely to report that their parents expected them to attend college, or that their parents were influential in making that decision. The third finding was that graduates with disabilities were more likely to have graduated in 1998

TABLE 5.2
Social and Economic Characteristics of Graduates

	Community College Graduates Without Disabilities n = 117	Community College Graduates With Disabilities n = 86	Significance p < .05
Ethnicity (%)			
White	.18	.24	ns
Hispanic	.25	.29	
Black	.38	.29	
Asian/Pacific-Islander	.01	.11	
Other	.08	.07	
Parents' education			
Less than high school	.11	.14	ns
High school	.51	.55	
2-Year college	.14	.08	
4-Year college	.19	.15	
Graduate school	.05	.08	
First to attend college? Yes	.67	.40	ns
Tuition support?			
Scholarship	.22	.24	ns
Loan	.12	.13	
Parent resources	.05	.05	
Own resources	.61	.58	

TABLE 5.3
Mean Accomplishments Reported by Graduates

	Community College Graduates Without Disabilities n = 117	Community College Graduates With Disabilities n = 86	Significance p < .05
Grade point average			
1.5	.01	.01	ns
2.0	.00	.01	
2.0–2.5	.09	.20	
2.6–3.0	.20	.22	
3.1–3.5	.32	.25	
3.6–4.0	.38	.31	
Year started college			
1998	.03	.06	ns
1997	.19	.19	
1996	.38	.35	
1995	.18	.13	
1994	.12	.10	
1993	.04	.07	
<1993	.06	.10	
Recent accomplishments	.97	.92	ns
Nonaccomplishments	.76	.65	ns

TABLE 5.4
Special Education Background Characteristics of Graduates

	Community College Graduates Without Disabilities $n = 117$	Community College Graduates With Disabilities $n = 86$	Significance
Special education background			
None	.90	.24	$p < .001$
Speech	.05	.10	
Occupational therapy	.02	.04	
Physical therapy	.01	.02	
Resource room	.02	.48	
Counseling	.00	.03	
Self-contained class	.00	.02	
Parents expect college? No	.19	.35	$p < .01$
Influenced by?			
Teachers	.08	.07	$p < .03$
Parents	.38	.17	
Counselor	.05	.07	
Friends	.13	.17	
Others	.37	.51	
Year graduated			
1998	.30	.53	$p < .05$
1999	.70	.47	

than were graduates without disabilities, who were more likely to have graduated a year later in 1999.

Self-Determination Indicators

The question of whether the two groups differed on indicators of self-determination was addressed by asking respondents to rate their opportunities to self-determine at college and beyond and their capacity to self-determine during those opportunities. Table 5.5 presents items for opportunities to self-determine, and Table 5.6 presents items on capacity to adjust in order to self-determine to those opportunities. All items were derived from the AIR Self-Determination Scales used in chapter 4 (Wolman, Campeau, DuBois, Mithaug, & Stolarski, 1994). Respondents rated each item using a 5-point Likert rating scale. Scores for opportunities to self-determine were the sum of these ratings for the 12 items in Table 5.5, and scores for capacity to self-determine were the sum of the ratings for the 12 items in Table 5.6. The score for prospects for self-determination was the sum of the opportunity and capacity scores.

TABLE 5.5
Items for Opportunities to Self-Determine

What happens at the college
1. Faculty and staff listen to me when I talk.
2. Faculty and staff support me in setting my own goals to get what I want or need.
3. At my college, I have learned how to make plans to meet my goals.
4. Faculty and staff at my college encourage me to start working on my plans right away.
5. I have resources at my college where I can go to get feedback regarding whether I am meeting my goals.
6. People at my college understand when I have to change my plans to meet my goal. They offer advice and support when I am doing this.

What happens outside college
1. My family and friends listen to me when I talk about what I want, what I need, or what I am good at.
2. My family and friends tell me that I am able to set my own goals to get what I want and need.
3. At home, I was taught how to make plans and to feel good about them.
4. Family and friends encourage me to begin working on my plans right away.
5. My family and friends can give me feedback about whether or not I am meeting my goals.
6. My family and friends understand when I have to change my goals. They offer help and support when I do this.

TABLE 5.6
Capacity to Self-Determine Questions

How I get what I want
1. I know what I need with regard to my academic studies.
2. I set goals to get what I want or need. I think about what I am good at when I do this.
3. I figure out how to meet my goals. I make plans and decide what I should do.
4. I begin working on my plans to meet my goals as soon as possible.
5. I monitor myself when I am working on my plans. If necessary, I ask others for feedback.
6. If my plan doesn't work, I try another one to meet my goals.

How I feel about getting what I want
1. I feel confident about what I like, want, and what I do well.
2. I believe that I can set goals to get what I want.
3. I enjoy making plans to meet my goals.
4. I like to begin working on my plans right away.
5. I like to check on how well I'm doing in meeting my goals.
6. I am willing to try another way if it helps me to meet my goals.

RESULTS

Tables 5.1–5.3 reveal that the two groups were similar in all factors that might affect self-determination ratings. Table 5.1 showed the groups to be similar in age, gender, college major, frequency of changing majors, time taken off from school, number of other colleges attended, whether faculty were supportive, whether they experienced problems at school, and whether disability affected their major. Table 5.2 showed that the groups were similar on ethnic background, educational achievement of parents, whether they were the first to go to college, and whether they received tuition support during school. Finally, Table 5.3 showed that the groups experienced similar success while in college and after. They reported similar enrollment dates for college, similar grade point averages during college, and similar accomplishments since graduation.

The three significant differences between groups were on enrollment in special education, parental expectations and support for college, and the year they graduated from college. Graduates with disabilities were, as expected, more likely to have received special education services, and, perhaps as a consequence, less likely to have parents who expected them to attend college or who influenced their decision to go. The third significant difference was that graduates with disabilities were more likely to have graduated in 1998 than in 1999 when graduates without disabilities graduated. None of these data suggest that one group would be more likely to rate their prospects for self-determination higher or lower than the other group.

The data in Table 5.7 show, however, that there were significant group differences on two of the self-determination indicators. The first row of data shows that although the mean rating for opportunities to self-determine was higher for graduates without disabilities than for graduates with disabilities, that difference was not significant. These data support Hypothesis 1, that there would be no differences in graduates' ratings on opportunities for self-determination. The second row of data in the table shows that the ratings for capacity to self-determine were significantly

TABLE 5.7
Self-Determination Levels of Community College Graduates

	Community College Graduates Without Disabilities $n = 117$	Community College Graduates With Disabilities $n = 86$	Significance
Opportunity to self-determine	45.2	43.5	n.s.
Capacity to self-determine	50.0	47.4	$p < .02$
Prospects for self-determination	95.4	90.6	$p < .05$

different for the two groups. In the third row the combined capacity and opportunity ratings yielded significantly different prospects for self-determination for the two groups. Graduates without disabilities reported significantly higher prospects for self-determination than did graduates with disabilities. These results were consistent with Hypotheses 2 and 3, that graduates without disabilities would report higher capacities and prospects for self-determination than would graduates with disabilities.

CONCLUSION

These results narrow the possible explanations for group differences on self-determination. Indeed, they tend to rule out the socioeconomic explanation that group differences on self-determination are due to background characteristics unrelated to disability. The only background characteristics that differentiated the groups were enrollment in special education, parental expectations and influences about going to college, and graduation dates. None of these was likely to relate to socioeconomic status. Enrollment in special education is related to disability. Parental expectations and influences about going to college are probably related to disability as well. And the college graduation date is unlikely to correlate with self-determination ratings in that it would favor students with disabilities who graduated earlier. Moreover, if graduation date were a proxy for economic hardship, then we would expect the group with lower prospects for self-determination to graduate later. This was not the case. College graduates with disabilities graduated significantly earlier than did graduates without disabilities.

This returns us to the original explanation for differences in self-determination. Disability tends to constrain adaptive capacity, which in turn reduces prospects for self-determination. In chapter 4, we argued that both underachievement and lowered self-determination prospects were due to poor adjustments to challenging opportunities. Students who do not know how to adjust in order to learn will also have difficulty knowing how to adjust in order to pursue their self-determined goals in life. Hence, they will report lowered prospects for self-determination as adults. The results of this study were consistent with that prediction. College graduates with disabilities rated their capacity to self-determine significantly lower than did college graduates without disabilities, the same finding reported in the previous chapter for elementary and secondary students with and without disabilities.

The explanation afforded by self-determined learning theory is that poor adjustment capability impedes learning and lowers prospects for self-determination. When students' capacity to adjust to new challenges is constrained or underdeveloped, learning prospects are negatively affected by adjustments, as are prospects for self-determination. Table 5.8 presents this reasoning again to highlight the connection between adjustment, achievement, and self-determination. If disability constrains one's capacity to adjust, then learning, achievement, and prospects for self-determination should be affected.

Of course, this does not mean all persons with disabilities are poor adapters and hence lacking in self-determination, because this is certainly not the case. Instead it suggests that people with disabilities *who underachieve* are probably poor adjusters, which will negatively affect their prospects for self-determination. This is a wise stipulation because even this study produced a contradiction to the generalization that disability constrains both achievement and self-determination. Consider Prediction 2c in Table 5.8, that students with disabilities underachieve and experience lowered prospects for self-determination. This prediction was supported for self-determination but not for achievement. The two groups proved to be equal on that outcome.

Perhaps this inconsistency can be explained by the self-determination ratings themselves, which are expressions of *beliefs* about prospects for self-determination and hence are a product of years of adjusting to challenges in life. The fact that graduates with disabilities succeeded at college but still held more modest beliefs about self-determination prospects than did graduates without disabilities reveals this retrospective function of beliefs. They are based on an accumulation of accomplishment and failure rather than a few episodes. Hence, a background of difficulty adjusting and achieving as well as being placed in special education classes can explain why graduates with disabilities held less robust beliefs about prospects for self-determination than did graduates without disabilities.

TABLE 5.8
Explanations for the Effects of Adjustment
on Achievement and Self-Determination

---

1. School achievement is a function of adjustments to opportunities for learning gain.
   a. Underachievement is due to inadequate adjustment to opportunities for learning gain.
   b. Many students with disabilities underachieve.
   c. Therefore students with disabilities adjust inadequately to opportunities for learning gain.
2. Self-determination prospects are a function of adjustments to opportunities for self-determined gain.
   a. People who adjust inadequately to opportunities for gain have lower prospects for self-determination than do people who adjust adequately to those opportunities.
   b. Many students with disabilities adjust inadequately to opportunities for gain.
   c. Therefore students with disabilities are likely to have lower prospects for self-determination than are students without disabilities.

A final factor to take into account in attempting to explain differences in the experience of freedom and self-determination is this country's cultural emphasis on the self-determined pursuit. Perhaps we are so consumed with the ideal of individual initiative and powerful action that any uncertainty about our ability to adjust in order to get what we want in life amplifies feelings and beliefs of inadequacy. Indeed, an overemphasis on individualism may encourage us to judge our capability based on the ability to engage challenges fully independently, and to judge prospects for success on this alone. Perhaps in countries with less emphasis on personal power and control, beliefs about prospects for living the self-determined life do not vary much among groups with significantly different adjustment experiences. We investigate this possibility in the next chapter by determining whether the self-determination differences among students with and without disabilities reported in the last two chapters are present in a country with a different culture of self-determination.

REFERENCES

Affleck, J. Q., Edgar, E., Levine, P., & Kortering, L. (1990). Postschool status of students classified as mildly mentally retarded, learning disabled, or nonhandicapped: Does it get better with time? *Education and Training in Mental Retardation, 25*, 315–324.

Agran, M. (1997). *Student directed learning: Teaching self-determination skills.* Pacific Grove, CA: Brooks/Cole.

Arnold, J. H., & Clement, P. W. (1981). Temporal generalization of self-regulation effects in under-controlled children. *Child Behavior Therapy, 3*(4), 43–67.

Chadsey-Rusch, J., Rusch, F., & O'Reilly, M. F. (1991). Transition from school to integrated communities. *Remedial and Special Education, 12*, 23–33.

Graham, S., Harris, K. R., & Reid, R. (1992). Developing self-regulated learners. *Focus on Exceptional Children, 24*(6), 1–16.

Hasazi, S. B., Gordon, L. R., & Roe, C. A. (1985). Factors associated with employment status of handicapped youth exiting high school from 1979–1983. *Exceptional Children, 51*, 455–469.

Mithaug, D. E., & Horiuchi, C. N. (1983). *Colorado statewide follow-up survey of special education students.* Denver, CO: Colorado Department of Education.

Mithaug, D. E., Horiuchi, C. N., & Fanning, P. N. (1985). A report on the Colorado statewide follow-up survey of special education students. *Exceptional Children, 51*, 397–404.

Mithaug, D. E., Horiuchi, C. N., & McNulty, B. A. (1987). *Parent reports on the transitions of students graduating from Colorado special education programs in 1978 and 1979.* Denver, CO: Colorado Department of Education.

Neel, R. S., Meadows, N., Levine, P., & Edgar, E. B. (1988). What happens after special education: A statewide follow-up study of secondary students who have behavioral disorders. *Behavioral Disorders, 13*, 209–216.

Sands, D. J., & Wehmeyer, M. L. (1996). *Self-determination across the life span: Independence and choice for people with disabilities.* Baltimore, MD: Paul H. Brookes.

Scuccimarra, D. K., & Speece, D. L. (1990). Employment outcomes and social integration of students with mild handicaps: The quality of life two years after high school. *Journal of Learning Disabilities, 23*, 213–219.

Wehmeyer, M. L. (1996). Self-determination in youth with severe cognitive disabilities: From theory to practice. In L. Powers, G. H. S. Singer, & J. Sowers (Eds.), *On the road to autonomy: Promoting self-competence in children and youth with disabilities* (pp. 115–133). Baltimore, MD: Paul H. Brookes.

Wehmeyer, M. L., & Palmer, S. B. (2001). *Adult outcomes for students with cognitive disabilities three years after high school: The impact of self-determination.* Unpublished manuscript.

Wehmeyer, M. L., & Sands, D. J. (Eds.). (1998). *Making it happen: Student involvement in education planning, decision making, and instruction.* Baltimore, MD: Paul Brookes.

Wehmeyer, M. L., & Schwartz, M. (1997). Self-determination and positive adult outcomes: A follow-up study of youth with mental retardation or learning disabilities. *Exceptional Children, 63,* 245–255.

Whitman, T. L. (1990). Self-regulation and mental retardation. *American Journal on Mental Retardation, 94*(4), 347–362.

Wolman, J. M., Campeau, P. L., DuBois, P. A., Mithaug, D. E., & Stolarski, V. S. (1994). *AIR self-determination scale and user guide.* Palo Alto, CA: American Institutes for Research.

6

Assessing Self-Determination Prospects of Students With and Without Disabilities in The Gambia, West Africa

Amadou Sohna Kebbeh
Dennis E. Mithaug

One of the first educators to recognize the importance of preparing young people for life in a free society was John Dewey. He argued nearly a century ago that every child should learn to adapt to unpredictable change and, while adjusting, to learn to control and shape that change.

> The ethical responsibility of the school on the social side must be interpreted in the broadest and freest spirit; it is equivalent to that training of the child which will give him such possession of himself that he may *take charge of himself; may not only adapt himself to the changes that are going on, but have power to shape and direct them.* (Dewey, 1909/1975, p. 11, italics added)

Dewey anchored his prescription in progressive education, which he claimed was well suited for the free society. Its purpose was to develop the "power of self-direction and power of directing others." In the language of this book, progressive education would help all children become self-determined in their learning and their lives.

> Moreover, the society of which the child is to be a member is, in the United States, a democratic and progressive society. The child must be educated for leadership as well as for obedience. He must have power of self-direction and power of directing others, power of administration, ability to assume positions of responsibility. (Dewey, 1909/1975, p. 10)

Today, this view is as pervasive as ever. Adult educators claim that in the free society adult learners must control their own learning. They must have "a coherent and robust set of personal values and beliefs that give consistency . . . to life" (Candy, 1991, p. 125). They must be self-directed by their own ability to conceive of goals and plans, to exercise freedom of choice, to use their capacity for rational reflection, to exhibit the willpower to follow through, to exercise self-restraint and self-discipline, and to view themselves as autonomous agents. In other words, adults must become self-determined learners and achievers in the free society.

The question we want answered is whether these prescriptions for success through self-determined pursuits are culture bound. Have they been shaped by the freedom condition such that one mode of adjustment is valued over all others? Does this encourage people to adapt in order to gain personal control over their circumstances and pursuits? And does this in turn encourage them to evaluate themselves according to their ability to engage such pursuits successfully? Finally, do countries with less emphasis on individual initiative encourage adaptations that focus more on fitting into the group than on leading or changing it to satisfy the individual's needs and interests?

This chapter investigates the cultural relativity hypothesis by assessing prospects for self-determination among students with and without disabilities in The Gambia, West Africa, a country with an economic, social, religious, and freedom experience that is very different from that of this country. Our view is that the group differences reported in previous chapters will be present among similarly situated groups in The Gambia. This is because we believe disability, not culture, affects adjustment and self-determination ratings. Hence, all groups who differ on this factor will vary in their prospects for self-determination. A country's emphasis on individual freedom will not alter these differences in adjustments and self-determination prospects. The following hypotheses reflect this view.

1. In The Gambia, West Africa, middle school students without disabilities report higher prospects for self-determination than do middle school students with disabilities.
2. In The Gambia, West Africa, middle school students without disabilities report higher capacities to self-determine than do middle school students with disabilities.
3. In The Gambia, West Africa, middle school students without disabilities report more opportunities to self-determine than do students with disabilities.
4. In The Gambia, West Africa, community elders report higher self-determination levels for students without disabilities than students with disabilities report for themselves.

PROSPECTS FOR SELF-DETERMINATION AMONG STUDENTS IN THE GAMBIA

This study tested the cultural relativity hypothesis by investigating self-determination prospects of students in a country with a relatively brief history of individual freedom. The Gambia gained its independence from Britain in 1965, whereas the United States declared its independence from Britain 189 years earlier, in 1776. Practically speaking, The Gambia has had significantly less time to establish the value of equal freedom for all. Therefore, this value should be less influential in selecting self-determined patterns of adjustment over other-determined adjustment patterns. Indeed, there is evidence that freedom is not universally experienced in the country because, according to the first author, elite groups have taken control of the government to advance their interests at the expense of the interests of the citizenry.

> Independence and self-determination meant political independence with the local elite taking over governance of the country from the colonial masters. Ordinary people became caught up in a cycle of dependency because the elite perpetuated a system of governance that was similar to that of the colonialists and equally detrimental to the development of individuals and communities. The elite used their knowledge to disenfranchise the great majority of the people in order to empower themselves. Corruption, nepotism, and excessive bureaucracy characterized the modus operandi of the elite. It was simply governance of exclusion. Evidence of that form of governance of exclusion was manifested in the appalling standards of living of ordinary citizens. They experienced abject poverty, economic hardship, disease, and malnutrition among other things.
>
> Education services have also been affected. Public school infrastructure was grossly neglected and there was mass production for so-called trained teachers. There were limited number of secondary schools; high drop out rates at the primary and secondary school levels; irrelevant curricula aspects; high unemployment rates among secondary school graduates and rising crime rates. Independence for The Gambia was therefore political and primarily served the interests of the few to the determinant of the many. (Kebbeh, 2000, p. 25)

Setting

The study was conducted in one of six regional education administrative units of the country. The site was selected because of the high proportion of female students with disabilities in schools there. The 10 participating middle schools in the district were located in Banjul and Kmobo St. Mary.

They included four city middle schools, four suburban middle schools, and two rural middle schools located within 10 km of Banjul. The schools had average enrollments of between 45 and 55 students per classroom and were fully staffed by teachers and administrators.

Participants

The participants included 43 community elders, 40 students without disabilities, and 40 students with disabilities. The students with disabilities represented a full range of physical, mental, emotional, and behavioral conditions. The two student groups were drawn in equal proportions from the 10 schools. Four students with disabilities and four students without disabilities were drawn from each city middle school. Four students with disabilities and four students without disabilities were drawn from each suburban middle school. And four students with and without disabilities were drawn from the two rural middle schools. Forty-three adults living in the communities of each school were randomly selected to serve as elder respondents. In The Gambia, an elder is an informal leader of the community.

Table 6.1 lists the gender and age characteristics of the sample. There were more male than female students and more male than female elders. The mean age of the elders was 45 years and the mean age of students was 16 years.

Procedures

All participants completed a 36-item questionnaire that assessed students' prospects, capacity, and opportunities for self-determination. The questionnaire was derived from the AIR Self-Determination Scale (Wolman, Campeau, DuBois, Mithaug, & Stolarski, 1994). The community elders completed one version and students completed the other version. Both instruments contained capacity and opportunity components. The capacity component assessed students' ability to self-regulate in order to meet self-

TABLE 6.1
Gender and Age of Participants

Gender and Age Characteristics	Community Elders (n = 43)	Students without Disabilities (n = 40)	Students with Disabilities (n = 40)
Male	27	22	26
Female	16	18	14
Male mean age	46.5	15.6	16.0
Female mean age	44.2	15.7	16.0

determined needs and interests. The opportunity component assessed opportunities at school and in religion, tradition, human rights, and economic activity to engage in self-determined pursuits. Respondents completed the questionnaire by circling rating numbers on a 5-point Likert scale for the capacity and opportunity items.

Items on Capacity to Self-Determine. This component duplicated the "Things I Do" questionnaire of the AIR Self-Determination Scale. Table 6.2 lists those items. The AIR Self-Determination Scale was also adapted so community elders could rate prospects for middle school students without disabilities in the same areas. Table 6.3 lists those items. All respondents circled numbers on a 5-point scale indicating the extent of their agreement with statements.

Opportunities to Self-Determine in The Gambia. The questionnaire also included an opportunity component that rated various community opportunities for self-determined pursuits. In the AIR Self-Determination Scale there were components for rating school and home opportunities for

TABLE 6.2
Student Assessment Items on Their Capacity to Self-Determine

1. I know what I need, what I like, and what I'm good at.
2. I set goals to get what I want or need. I think about what I am good at when I do this.
3. I figure out how to meet my goals. I make plans and decide what I should do.
4. I begin working on my plans to meet my goals as soon as possible.
5. I check how I'm doing when I'm working on a plan. If I need to, I ask others what they think of how I'm doing.
6. If my plan doesn't work, I try another one to meet my goals.

TABLE 6.3
Elders' Assessment Items on Student Capacity to Self-Determine

1. Middle school students in my community ask about things that affect them or others.
2. Middle school students in my community set goals to get what they want. They think about what they are good at when setting their goals.
3. Middle school students in my community make plans or figure out how to meet their goals.
4. Middle school students in my community begin to work on their plans to meet their goals as soon as they set their goals.
5. Middle school students in my community check on how they are doing with their plans to meet goals and ask others in the community about how they are doing with their plans.
6. Middle school students in my community try other plans to meet goals if their original plans do not work to achieve their goals.

self-determination. This questionnaire matched those opportunity items. It also included items to assess community opportunities for self-determination in economic life, human rights, religion, and tradition. The first author constructed those items to represent the social conditions in The Gambia. Table 6.4 lists these question items in the five opportunity categories. Table 6.5 lists the question items in those five opportunity categories that were used to assess elders' judgments of opportunities for middle school students without disabilities. All participants answered items by circling numbers on 5-point Likert scales indicating agreement or disagreement with statements.

RESULTS

The results are presented in Figs. 6.1–6.3. Figure 6.1 presents average ratings for each group on prospects for self-determination, capacity to self-determine, and opportunities for self-determination. Figure 6.2 presents mean ratings for each group on school and religious opportunities to self-determine. And Fig. 6.3 presents average ratings for each group on opportunities for self-determination in human rights, traditional activities, and economic activities. Table 6.6 presents average self-determination ratings by the gender of respondents in each group, and Table 6.7 presents average self-determination ratings by the age of respondents in each group.

Hypothesis 1: Prospects for Self-Determination

Students' prospects for self-determination were the sum of their capacity and opportunity scores. The first set of bar graphs in Fig. 6.1 presents these data. As indicated in the chart, community elders rated prospects for middle school students at 46.2, students without disabilities rated their prospects at 45, and students with disabilities rated their prospects at 36. The ratings by students with disabilities were significantly lower than the ratings by community elders and by students without disabilities ($p < .05$). This finding is consistent with Hypothesis 1 that in The Gambia students without disabilities would rate their prospects for self-determination higher than would students with disabilities.

Hypothesis 2: Capacity to Self-Determine

The student capacity ratings were based on questions 1–6 of the student instrument in Table 6.3 and the community elders instrument in Table 6.4. The second set of bar graphs in Fig. 6.1 presents those results. The mean capacity ratings by community elders and students without disabilities were similar.

TABLE 6.4
Student Assessment Items of Their Opportunity to Self-Determine

Economic activity
1. I talk to my friends and family members about the trade or business I am interested in doing when I graduate.
2. I plan to open my own store, kiosk, or workshop when I graduate from school.
3. I will learn about the steps to take in order to start my own store, kiosk, or workshop.
4. I will carefully follow the rules I will make when I open my own store, kiosk, or workshop.
5. I will seek advice from successful local store, kiosk, or workshop owners in my community.
6. I will change the way I do things if my store, kiosk, or workshop is not doing well.

Human rights
1. I let my family members know what I want to eat, wear, or say even if they do not agree with me.
2. I eat, sleep, and have a bath every day at home.
3. I can attend school every day regardless of my background or sex.
4. I can get treatment when I get sick or hurt from a health care facility without any difficulty.
5. I work for somebody else to support myself.
6. I am forced to do things that I do not want to do.

Religion
1. People in my community listen to me when I talk about the different religions practiced in my community.
2. The imam or priest in my community talks to me about what I want to do and how I think I can do it.
3. I make plans to learn about the different religions practiced in my community.
4. I am free to worship in a church, mosque, or idol shrine whenever I want.
5. The imam or priest and my family use religious teaching to tell me what they think and about my progress on goals I am working on.
6. The imam or priest in my community is willing to give me advice to change my plans on what I am doing when necessary.

School
1. People at school listen to me when I talk to them about what I want, what I need, or what I am good at.
2. I set my own goals at school to get what I want or need.
3. I make plans to meet my goals at school and feel good about them.
4. People at school encourage me to start working on my plans to meet my goals.
5. People at school are interested in knowing how I am doing on my goals.
6. People at school understand when I have to change my plans to meet my goals. They offer me advice and encourage me to change my plans when necessary.

Tradition
1. My parents and other family members tell me stories, folk tales, and proverbs that teach me to express how I feel about things that affect others and me.
2. Circumcision, naming and marriage ceremonies, and learning family trades are initiation rites that prepare people for life in my culture. These practices teach me to set goals and pursue them to get what I want.
3. Community members including my parents and extended family members teach me how to make plans to meet my goals as part of my upbringing.
4. My parents, extended family members, or other community elders feel good about encouraging me to start working on my plans.
5. My parents, extended family members, or other elders in the community are interested in what I am doing. They ask me how I am going on my plans.
6. My parents, extended family members, and other community elders are willing to offer me advice to change my plans to meet my goals when necessary.

TABLE 6.5
Elders' Assessment Items of Student Opportunity to Self-Determine

Economic activity

1. Middle school students in my community talk about business and family trades they want to do when they graduate from school.
2. Middle school students in my community are interested in opening their own stores, kiosks, or workshops in the future and talk about ways of figuring it out.
3. Middle school students in my community express interests in learning about steps to take to open their own stores, kiosks, and workshops in the future.
4. Local business people in my community will be willing to teach middle school students rules to follow when they open stores, kiosks, or workshops in the future.
5. Middle school students seek advice from community leaders on whatever they will do when they open their own store, kiosk, or workshop.
6. Elders and local business people in my community will emphasize the importance of changing the ways of doing business to middle school students if a shop, kiosk, or workshop is not doing well.

Human rights

1. Middle school students in my community express how they feel about what they want to eat and wear and how those things affect them and others.
2. Middle school students in my community eat, sleep, and have a bath every day at home.
3. Middle school students in my community can attend school regardless of whether they are disabled or not or whether they are male or female.
4. Middle school students in my community get treatment whenever they get sick or hurt, regardless of whether they are disabled or not or whether they are male or female.
5. Middle school students in my community work to support themselves.
6. Middle school students in my community are forced to do things they do not want to do.

Religion

1. Middle school students in my community can learn about and express their feelings about different religions practiced in the community.
2. Religious organizations in my community use religious teachings to teach middle school students to set goals to get what they want.
3. Imams, priests, and parents in my community talk to middle school students about their plans to meet their goals based on religious teachings.
4. Middle school students in my community are free to worship in a church, mosque, or idol shrine of their choice.
5. Religious organizations in my community are concerned about progress made by students on goals they pursue.
6. Imams, priests, and parents in my community give advice to students to change their plans to meet their goals based on religious teachings.

School

1. Middle school students in my community talk about what they want, need, or are good at in school and are listened to when they do so.
2. Middle school students in my community set their own goals in school to get what they want.
3. Middle school students in my community make plans to meet their goals and feel good about that.
4. Middle school students in my community are encouraged by people at school to start working on their goals as soon as possible.
5. Middle school students in my community are monitored at school in order to determine if they are meeting goals they set.
6. Middle school students in my community are advised by teachers and others in school to change plans to meet goals when necessary.

(Continued)

TABLE 6.5
(Continued)

Tradition

1. Traditional practices in my community including storytelling, folk tales, and proverbs teach children and youth to express how they feel about things that affect them and others.
2. Initiation rites in my community including naming and marriage ceremonies, circumcision, and family trades teach children and youth to set goals to get what they want in life.
3. Elders in my community use traditional practices to encourage children and youth to make plans to meet their goals.
4. Elders in my community feel good about encouraging children and youth to start working on their plans to meet their goals.
5. Elders in my community show interest in what children and youth are doing about their plans to meet their goals.
6. Elders in my community are willing to help children and youth change their plans when necessary to meet their goals.

Community elders rated middle school students' capacity for self-determination at 25.2, whereas students without disabilities rated their capacity for self-determination at 24. Students with disabilities in contrast rated their capacity for self-determination at 18, which was significantly lower than those ratings ($p < .05$). These data support Hypothesis 2 that in The Gambia students without disabilities would rate their capacity to self-determine significantly higher than would students with disabilities.

Hypothesis 3: Opportunity to Self-Determine

The opportunity ratings were based on responses to 30 items covering economic activity (6 items), human rights (6 items), religious activities (6 items), school activities (6 items), and traditions (6 items). The last three bar graphs in Fig. 6.1 summarize these results. They present average ratings for the three groups across the five opportunity categories. As indicated in the figure, community elders and students without disabilities rated opportunities to self-determine for students without disabilities at 21, which was significantly higher than the 18 average rating by students with disabilities ($p < .05$). Figures 6.2 and 6.3 present mean ratings by the three groups for the five opportunity categories. Figure 6.2 shows that the ratings by students with and without disabilities on school and religious opportunities were similar, but significantly different than the ratings by community elders ($p < .05$). Figure 6.3, on the other hand, shows that the ratings by students without disabilities on economic activity, human rights, and traditional activities were significantly higher than ratings for those activities by students with disabilities ($p < .05$). The same ratings by community elders for middle school students without disabilities were significantly higher than the ratings that students with disabilities gave themselves ($p < .05$). There were also significant differences in ratings by

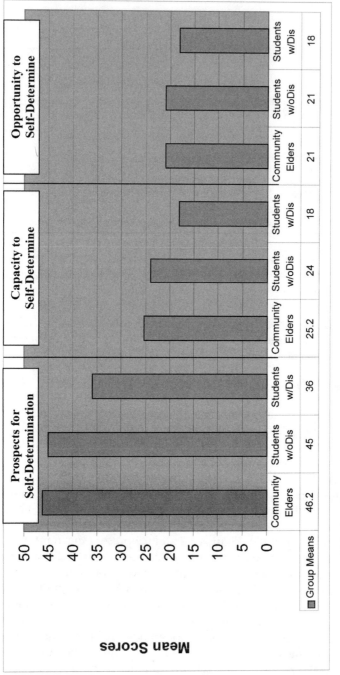

FIG. 6.1. Ratings by community elders, students without disabilities, and students with disabilities on students' prospects, capacity, and opportunity to self-determine.

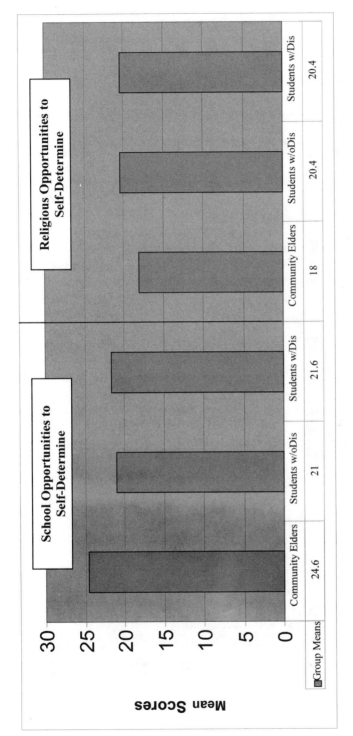

FIG. 6.2. School and religious opportunity ratings by community elders, students without disabilities, and students with disabilities.

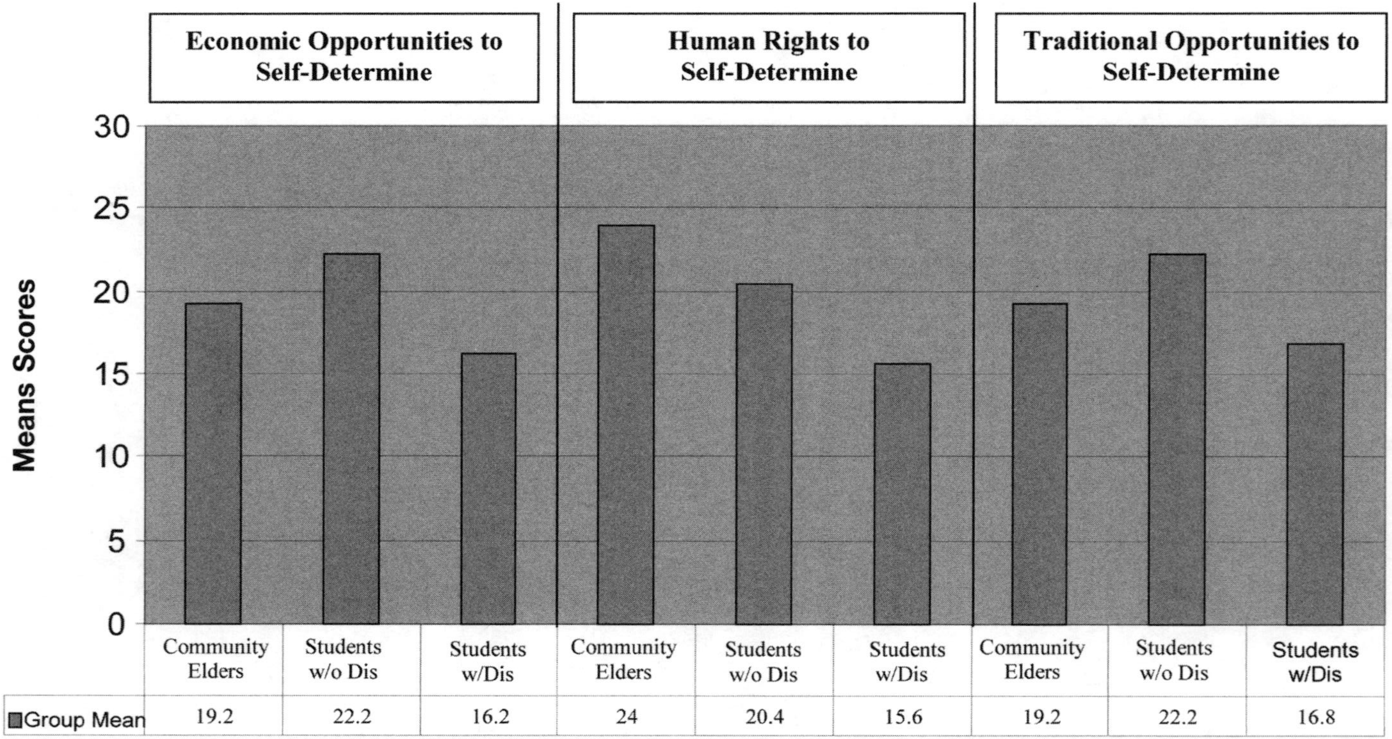

FIG. 6.3. Economic, human rights, and traditional opportunity ratings by community elders, students without disabilities, and students with disabilities.

	Economic Opportunities to Self-Determine			Human Rights to Self-Determine			Traditional Opportunities to Self-Determine		
	Community Elders	Students w/o Dis	Students w/Dis	Community Elders	Students w/o Dis	Students w/Dis	Community Elders	Students w/o Dis	Students w/Dis
Group Mean	19.2	22.2	16.2	24	20.4	15.6	19.2	22.2	16.8

TABLE 6.6
Mean Capacity and Opportunity Ratings
for Each Group by Gender of Respondents

	Community Elders		Students without Disabilities		Students with Disabilities	
	Male	Female	Male	Female	Male	Female
Capacity	24.6	25.8	24.0	24.0	18.6	16.8
Opportunity	21.0	21.6	21.0	21.0	18.6	16.2
Economic activity	20.4	18.6	22.2	22.2	16.2	15.6
Human rights	24.0	24.0	19.8	20.4	16.2	15.0
Religion	16.8	22.8*	21.0	19.8	21.0	19.8
School	25.2	24.0	21.0	20.4	21.0	22.2
Tradition	20.4	19.2	21.6	22.2	18.0	15.0

*$p < .05$.

TABLE 6.7
Mean Capacity and Opportunity Ratings
for Each Group by Age of Respondents

	Community Elders		Students Without Disabilities		Students With Disabilities	
	23–43 years	44–108 years	13–15 years	16–21 years	12–15 years	16–21 years
Capacity	24.6	25.2	23.4	24.6	17.4	18.6
Opportunity	21	21	21	21.6	17.4	19.8
Economic activity	19.2	20.4	22.8	22.2	15.6	16.8
Human rights	24	24	19.8	20.4	16.8	19.8*
Religion	18	18	20.4	19.8	19.8	19.8
School	24.6	24.6	21	22.8	21	22.8
Tradition	19.2	19.2	22.2	21.6	15	18.6*

*$p < .05$.

community elders and students without disabilities. They rated opportunities for economic and traditional activities significantly lower and human rights significantly higher than did students without disabilities ($p <$
.05). These findings are consistent with the claim in Hypothesis 3 that students without disabilities would rate community opportunities to self-
determine higher than would students with disabilities.

Hypothesis 4: Elders' Self-Determination Ratings

The data on ratings by community elders were also consistent with Hypothesis 4 that they would rate self-determination indicators for students
without disabilities higher than students with disabilities would rate

those opportunities for themselves. Figure 6.1 showed this consistent pattern. Ratings by elders and students without disabilities were significantly higher than the ratings by students with disabilities on prospects, capacity, and opportunities for self-determination ($p < .05$). There were, nonetheless, variations in those ratings on the opportunity indicators. In Fig. 6.2 elders rated opportunities at school higher and in religion lower than did either student group ($p < .05$). However, as illustrated in Fig. 6.3, their opportunity ratings were similar to those made by students without disabilities in that they were significantly higher than were ratings by students with disabilities ($p < .05$).

Gender and Age Effects

The only gender difference in the self-determination ratings was among elders for religious opportunities for middle school students without disabilities. Female elders rated religious opportunities for middle school students significantly higher than did male elders ($p < .05$). Table 6.6 lists the mean ratings for gender for the three self-determination variables. An analysis of age differences indicated that older students with disabilities rated human rights opportunities and traditional activities significantly higher than did younger students with disabilities ($p < .05$). Table 6.7 lists these data on age.

DISCUSSION

The findings of this study support our claim that the group differences on self-determination reported for students with and without disabilities in the United States are due to disability, not culture. They showed that even though the participants of this study lived in a very different cultural and historical setting, similar differences obtained. Not only did students differentiate prospects, capacities, and opportunities for self-determination according to their membership in disability and nondisability groups, but ratings by community elders were similar. They were significantly higher for students without disabilities than for students with disabilities. In the survey described in chapter 4, educators also rated prospects higher for students without disabilities than for students with disabilities.

Although these findings challenge the culture relativity hypothesis, they cannot rule it out completely, if only because the freedom ideal is present to some extent in every country of the world. Recall that from 1948 to the present the United Nations has advanced the Universal Declaration of Human rights doctrine, which argues for universal freedom. Indeed, Article 1 of the document states that "All human beings are born free and equal in dignity and rights; They are endowed with reason and conscience and should act toward one another in a spirit of brotherhood." And Article 2 states that "Everyone is entitled to all the rights and freedoms set forth in this Declaration, without distinction of any kind, such as race, colour, sex, language, religion, political or other opinion, national or social origin, property, birth or other status" (Humana, 1992, p. 382). Given this, it is probably unrealistic to expect members of any community or country in the world to be immune to the freedom ideal and unaffected by the types of adjustments it encourages. There may be no way of fully untangling cultural effects from disability effects.

Another approach to determining whether disability affects adjustment and self-determination is to examine whether variation in this factor alone yields differences in adjustment and prospect ratings. We can do this by comparing groups of people with different disabilities to determine whether that variation is associated with differences in prospects for self-determination. This is the approach used in the next chapter.

REFERENCES

Candy, P. C. (1991). *Self-direction for lifelong learning: A comprehensive guide to theory and practice.* San Francisco: Jossey-Bass.

Dewey, J. (1975). *Moral principles in education.* London: Feffer & Sons. (Original work published 1909)

Humana, C. (1992). *World human rights guide.* New York: Oxford University Press.

Kebbeh, A. S. (2000). *Self-determination: Prospects for secondary school students with and without disabilities in The Gambia.* Unpublished doctoral dissertation, Teachers College, Columbia University, New York.

Wolman, J. M., Campeau, P. L., DuBois, P. A., Mithaug, D. E., & Stolarski, V. S. (1994). *AIR self-determination scale and user guide.* Palo Alto, CA: American Institutes for Research.

7

Assessing Self-Determination Prospects of Students With Different Sensory Impairments

Susan Lipkowitz
Dennis E. Mithaug

Our explanation for why students with disabilities report lower levels of self-determination is that their disabling conditions affect their beliefs about whether a circumstance is an obstacle or an opportunity for gain and whether they can adjust in order to gain from it. These beliefs about opportunities and capabilities in turn affect their prospects for self-determination. The study described in chapter 4 supported this view in that comparisons between students with disabilities reported lower adjustment and self-determination ratings than did students without disabilities. The studies described in chapters 5 and 6 supported similar differences among adult learners with and without disabilities and among students with and without disabilities in another country.

Another way of investigating this hypothesis about disability effects on adjustment capability is to test for differences among persons who vary on disability alone. This would test the disability-effect hypothesis more directly because there is no reason to believe different disabilities have the same effect on adjustments and prospects for self-determination. Indeed, in chapter 4, teacher ratings of the adjustment capabilities of students with mental retardation and learning disabilities were higher than their adjustment ratings for students with behavior disorders and other disabilities. The problem with this finding was that these ratings were inconsistent with ratings by students on themselves. Students with behavior disorders and other disabilities rated their adjustment capacities higher than did students with mental retardation and learning disabilities.

So although it is reasonable to expect variation in disability to correlate with self-determination ratings, the results reported in chapter 4 did not support this view unequivocally. This raises the possibility that other factors associated with disability may affect adjustment capability and prospects for self-determination. Chapter 6 ruled out the possibility that cultural factors related to self-determination are responsible, but did not rule out social factors like group identity. Perhaps some students with disabilities feel isolated from mainstream activity and this is responsible for their lower adjustment and self-determination ratings. According to the group-identity hypothesis, students with strong group identities have higher self-determination ratings than do students with weak group identities. The following argument makes this claim.

1. Students who lack a strong group identity have lower self-determination ratings than do students who have a strong group identity.
2. Students with disabilities who lack a strong group identity have lower self-determination ratings than do students with disabilities who have a strong group identity score.
3. Therefore, prospects for self-determination are positively correlated with group identity but not with level or type of disability.

This chapter reports findings from a study that tested the disability-effect and group-identity hypotheses by comparing adjustment and self-determination ratings among students with different sensory disabilities. The participants were students with blindness and visual impairment and students with deafness and hearing impairment.

The rationale for claiming a disability effect on adjustment is based on data presented in the previous chapters showing that students with disabilities received lower adjustment ratings than did students without disabilities. Based on this, we would expect that variation in disability to produce corresponding variation in adjustment ratings. Fortunately, the participants in this study varied markedly on this factor. One group of participants was deaf and hence would have learned to adjust to the communication demands imposed by a hearing world, and the other group of participants was blind and would have learned to adjust to the navigation challenges posed by the sighted world. Because the two adjustments are different, we could expect adjustment ratings by the two groups to be different as well — if the disability-effect hypothesis is supported, that is.

The rationale for claiming a group-identity effect on adjustment and self-determination comes from the literature on Deaf culture that suggests students who are deaf tend to identify with Deaf communities and as a result prefer to be educated with students who are deaf (Corker, 1998). That strong group identity may enhance their beliefs about adjustment capability and self-determination. The absence of comparable group identity for students who are blind permits a comparison to test whether there is a group-identity difference between the groups and if so whether that difference is associated with adjustment and self-determination ratings, as claimed by the group-identity hypothesis.

The two groups also presented an opportunity to test a third prediction based on self-determined learning theory—that adjustment and learning correlate. This test was possible because the two groups received different types of special education instruction. Some participants received instruction in resource rooms, some received instruction in special classes, and other participants received instruction in special schools. To the extent that the locus of instruction matched participants' learning needs, we would expect ratings on adjustment capabilities to correspond with the place of instruction. Students receiving instruction in resource rooms would rate their adjustments higher than would students receiving instruction in special classes or special schools, for example. Also, we would expect students in resource rooms to have higher math, reading, and self-esteem scores than students in special classes or special schools.

The following hypotheses reflect this belief that disability and not group identity is associated with group differences on adjustment, self-determination, special education placement, self-esteem, and achievement.

1. Students with different sensory impairments report similar inclusion preferences and group-identity ratings, but they report different levels of self-determination, capacities to self-determine, and self-esteem levels, and they have different achievement levels.

2. Students with sensory impairment report lower self-esteem and capacities to self-determine when they are in special schools than when they are in resource rooms.

3. Students with sensory impairment report lower group identity and higher inclusion preferences when they are in resource rooms than when they are in special schools.

4. There are no correlations between group-identity scores and adjustment or achievement scores for students with sensory impairments, but there are positive correlations between inclusion preference and those indicators.

ADJUSTMENT CORRELATES
OF SENSORY IMPAIRMENT

The study was part of the first author's dissertation (Lipkowitz, 2000) and was conducted in schools located in a northeastern city. The schools served ethnically diverse populations of students with disabilities whose families resided in various regions of the state.

Student Respondents

The participating students included 109 males and 100 females, representing a full range of ages, grade levels, and ethnic backgrounds. Table 7.1 presents their age and grade level distributions.

The participants included 21 students with blindness, 63 students with visual impairment, 83 students with hearing impairment, and 42 students with deafness. Table 7.2 presents the special education placements for these groups at the time of the study. As indicated in row totals, most students were enrolled in resource rooms and self-contained classes. However, as indicated by the column totals, students with blindness and visual impairment were more likely to be in resource rooms and students who were deaf and hard of hearing were more likely to be in self-contained classes and special schools.

Assessment Instruments

Data were collected from two sources: student files that provided grade levels in reading and math and a questionnaire that the students completed. The questionnaire included questions on students' gender, age, grade level, and school type. It asked questions about students' disability experience, identification with their disability group, capacity to self-

TABLE 7.1
Proportionate Age and Grade Distribution of Student Respondents

12 years	13 years	14 years	15 years	16 years	17 years	18–21 years
.01	.12	.09	.21	.15	.22	.18

Grade 6	Grade 7	Grade 8	Grade 9	Grade 10	Grade 11	Grade 12
.01	.11	.10	.22	.21	.20	.14

TABLE 7.2
Distribution of Student Participants
by Disability and Special Education Placement

Special Education Placement	Students With Blindness	Students With Visual Impairment	Students With Hearing Impairment	Students With Deafness	Total
Resource room	16	44	20	5	85
Self-contained class	3	15	61	10	89
Special school class	2	4	2	27	35
Total	21	63	83	42	209

determine, opportunity to self-determine, self-concept, and preference for inclusive learning. Tables 7.3–7.8 list questions for each variable of study.

Disability Experience. The purpose of this first set of yes–no questions was to describe students' family background, and to assess whether that was evident in their language or reading habits. Students with deafness and hearing impairment received a version focusing on language habits and students with blindness and visual impairment received a question set that focused on reading habits. Table 7.3 lists those questions.

Disability Group Identity. The second set of yes–no questions focused on whether students learned about their disability group in class instruction and whether they identified with their group. Again, there was a question version for students with deafness and hearing impairment and a question version for students with blindness and visual impairment. Table 7.4 lists those two question sets.

Self-Determination. Another set of questions assessed students' levels of self-determination. The first component assessed students' capacity to self-determine by asking questions about what students did and how they felt during the process of adjusting to a self-determined pursuit. These questions were taken from the student version of the AIR Self-Determination Scale used in previous chapters. Students answered each

TABLE 7.3
Questions on Participants' Disability Background and Experience

---

For students who are deaf and hard of hearing
1. Have you always been deaf?
2. Have you always been hard of hearing?
3. Is your mother or father deaf?
4. Is anyone else in your family deaf or hard of hearing?
5. Do you have friends who are deaf or hard of hearing?
6. Did you use English when you were growing up?
   If not, what language did you use?
7. Do you use English as your main language now?
8. Do you use American Sign Language?
For students who are blind and visually impaired
1. Have you always been blind?
2. Have you always been visually impaired?
3. Is your mother or father blind?
4. Is anyone else in your family blind or visually impaired?
5. Do you have friends who are blind or visually impaired?
6. Did you use Braille when you were growing up?
   If not, what method of reading did you use?
7. Do you use English as your main reading method now?
8. Do you use Braille or assistive technology?

---

question by circling a number on a 5-point Likert scale, with a 5 indicating the statement they were answering was always the case and 1 indicating it was never the case. Table 7.5 lists those items.

A second set of 12 questions assessed students' opportunities to self-determine at home and at school. Using the same six-item question format for those opportunities, students responded to the same 5-point Likert

TABLE 7.4

Questions on Participants' Knowledge
of and Identity with a Disability Group

For students who are deaf and hard of hearing
1. Do you learn about the deaf as a special group of people?
2. Do you learn about famous people who are deaf?
3. Do you learn about being proud of yourself as a deaf person?
4. Do you think that the deaf are a special group?
5. Do you think that you belong to this group?
6. Do you feel proud to be a person who is deaf or hard of hearing?
7. Do you like to be with people who are deaf more than with people who are hearing?
8. Do you go to special events for deaf people?
For students who are blind and visually impaired
1. Do you learn about the blind as a special group of people?
2. Do you learn about famous people who are blind?
3. Do you learn about being proud of yourself as a blind/visually impaired person?
4. Do you think that people who are blind are a special group?
5. Do you think that you belong to this group?
6. Do you feel proud to be a person who is blind or visually impaired?
7. Do you like to be with people who are blind more than with people who are sighted?
8. Do you go to special events for people who are blind and visually impaired?

TABLE 7.5

AIR Self-Determination Items on Students' Capacity to Self-Determine

Things I do:
1. I know what I need, what I like, and what I'm good at.
2. I set goals to get what I want or need. I think about what I am good at when I do this.
3. I figure out how to meet my goals. I make plans and decide what I should do.
4. I begin working on my plans to meet my goals as soon as possible.
5. I check how I'm doing when I'm working on a plan. If I need to, I ask others what they think of how I'm doing.
6. If my plan doesn't work, I try another one to meet my goals.
How I feel:
1. I feel good about what I like, what I want, and what I do well.
2. I believe that I can set goals to get what I want.
3. I like to make plans to meet my goals.
4. I like to begin working on my plans right away.
5. I like to check on how well I'm doing in meeting my goals.
6. I am willing to try another way if it helps me to meet my goals.

TABLE 7.6
AIR Self-Determination Scale Items
on Students' Opportunities to Self-Determine

What happens at home
1. People at home listen to me when I talk about what I want, what I need, or what I'm good at.
2. People at home let me know that I can set my own goals to get what I want or what I need.
3. At home, I have learned how to make plans to meet my goals and feel good about them.
4. People at home encourage me to start working on my plans right away.
5. I have someone at home who can tell me if I am meeting my goals.
6. People at home understand when I have to change my plans to meet my goal. They offer help and encourage me when I'm doing this.
What happens at school
1. People at school listen to me when I talk about what I want, what I need, or what I'm good at.
2. People at school let me know that I can set my own goals to get what I want or need.
3. At school, I have learned how to make plans to meet my goals and to feel good about them.
4. People at school encourage me to start working on my plans right away.
5. I have someone at school who can tell me if I am meeting my goals.
6. People at school understand when I have to change my plan to meet my goal. They offer advice and encourage me when I'm doing this.

---

scale indicating how closely the statement described their opportunities to engage self-determined pursuits. Table 7.6 lists those items.

Student responses to the questions in Tables 7.5 yielded a score for their capacity to self-determine, and the responses to questions in Table 7.6 yielded a score for their opportunity to self-determine. The total for items in the two tables yielded their prospects for self-determination score.

Self-Concept. The student questionnaire also included the 30 yes–no items in Table 7.7 to assess self-concept. These items are from the Culture Free Self-Esteem Inventory developed by Battle (1990).

Inclusive Learning Preference. The student questionnaire also assessed students' preferences for inclusive learning by asking whether they preferred regular classes with non-disabled peers (item 1 in Table 7.8), separate classes with only students who have similar disabilities (item 2 in Table 7.8), or some of each (item 3 in Table 7.8). Students responded by circling *yes* (3), *sometimes* (2), or *no* (1).

RESULTS

Analysis of background characteristics of the two groups indicated that there were no significant gender or age differences on self-determination prospects, self-concept, disability experiences, group identity, or inclusive

TABLE 7.7
Self-Concept Question Items

1. I wish I were younger.
2. Boys and girls like to play with me.
3. I usually quit when my schoolwork is too hard.
4. My parents never get angry at me.
5. I only have a few friends.
6. I have lots of fun with my friends.
7. I like being a boy/I like being a girl.
8. I am a failure at school.
9. My parents make me feel that I am not good enough.
10. I usually fail when I try to do important things.
11. I am happy most of the time.
12. I have never taken anything that did not belong to me.
13. I often feel ashamed of myself.
14. Most boys and girls play games better than I do.
15. I often feel that I am no good at all.
16. Most boys and girls are smarter than I am.
17. My parents dislike me because I am not good enough.
18. I like everyone I know.
19. I am as happy as most boys and girls.
20. Most boys and girls are better than I am.
21. I like to play with children younger than I am.
22. I often feel like quitting school.
23. I can do things as well as other boys and girls.
24. I would change many things about myself if I could.
25. There are many times when I would like to run away from home.
26. I never worry about anything.
27. I always tell the truth.
28. My teacher feels that I am not good enough.
29. My parents think that I am a failure.
30. I worry a lot.

TABLE 7.8
Question Items on Preference for Inclusive Schooling

1. Do you like to be in regular classes with students who are hearing/sighted?
2. Do you like to be in separate classes for students who are deaf-hard of hearing/blind-visually impaired?
3. Do you like to be in some separate and some regular classes?

learning preference. There was a significant difference on self-concept scores by grade level, however. Students in Grades 10–12 scored 19.2 on the self-concept measure, whereas students in Grades 6–9 scored an average of 17.5 on the scale. Also, there was a significant relationship between disability and school placement. Students who were blind and visually impaired were more likely to be in resource rooms and students who were deaf and hard of hearing were more likely to be self-contained or special schools.

Hypothesis 1 Results

Figure 7.1 presents group averages for students' self-determination prospects, capacity to self-determine, and self-esteem ratings. The group averages for all adjustment indicators were significantly different. The mean ratings on prospects for self-determination were 99.2 for students with blindness and visual impairment (BVD) and 85.5 for students with deafness and hearing impairment (DHH) ($p < .05$). The mean ratings on capacity to self-determine were 46.9 for students with blindness and visual impairment and 43.7 for students with deafness and hearing impairment ($p < .05$). The mean ratings on opportunities to self-determine were 51.7 for students with blindness and visual impairment and 41.8 for students with deafness and hearing impairment ($p < .05$). The average ratings on self-esteem were 19 for students with blindness and visual impairment and 17.3 for students with deafness and hearing impairment ($p < .05$).

Figure 7.2 presents group averages for reading and math scores, which were also significantly different. Students with blindness and visual impairment were at a 7.3-year reading level and students with deafness and hearing impairment were at a 5.0 reading level ($p < .05$). On math students with blindness and visual impairment were at a 7.0 level ($p < .05$) and students with deafness and hearing impairment were at a 5.6 level ($p < .05$).

However, there were no significant differences between the groups on their inclusion preference ratings or on their disability group identity ratings. The average ratings on inclusion preferences were 6.5 for students with blindness and visual impairment and 6.1 for students with deafness and hearing impairment. The average ratings on group identity were 6.0 for students with blindness and visual impairment and 5.7 for students with deafness and hearing impairment. These findings support Hypothesis 1 that students with different sensory impairments will have different prospects for self-determination, capacities to self-determine, self-esteem ratings, and levels of achievement but their inclusion preferences or group identity ratings will be similar.

Hypothesis 2 Results

Figure 7.3 presents data on self-determination capacity and self-esteem ratings for students enrolled in resource rooms, self-contained classes, and special schools. There were differences in the ratings for both indicators. The average capacity rating for students in resource rooms was 48.4, which was significantly higher than the average rating of 46.2 by students

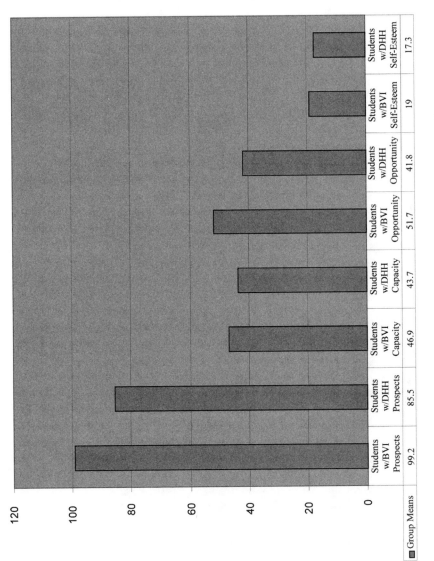

FIG. 7.1. Group averages for student ratings on self-determination prospects, capacity to self-determine, and self-esteem.

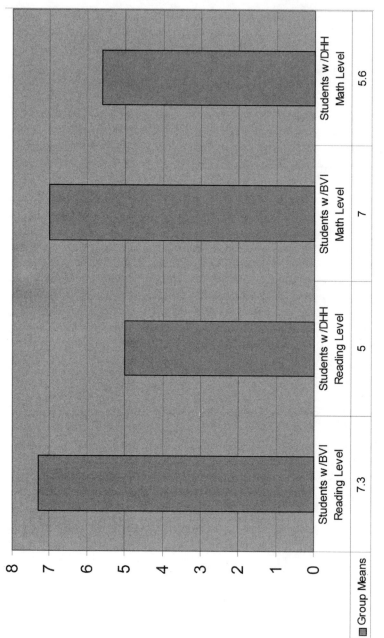

FIG. 7.2. Average reading and math grade levels for the two groups.

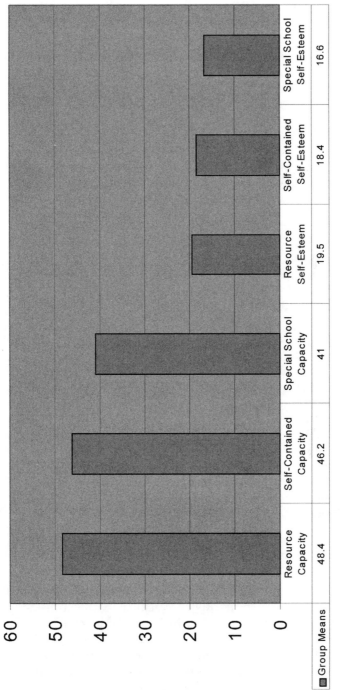

FIG. 7.3. Mean ratings on self-determination, capacity, and self-esteem for students enrolled in resource rooms, self-contained classes, and special schools.

115

in self-contained classes which in turn was significantly higher than the average rating of 41 by students in special school classes ($p < .05$). A similar pattern emerged for self-esteem ratings. The average self-esteem rating for students in resource rooms was 19.5, which was significantly higher than the average rating of 18.4 by students in self-contained classes, which in turn was significantly higher than the average rating of 16.6 by students in special school classes ($p < .05$).

These results support Hypothesis 2, that students with sensory impairments who are in special schools will report lower capacities to self-determine and lower self-esteem levels than will students with sensory impairments who are in resource rooms.

Hypothesis 3 Results

Figure 7.4 presents inclusion preference and group identity ratings for students enrolled in resource rooms, self-contained classes, and special schools. As indicated in the chart, preferences for integrated instruction declined as group identity increased across the three placements. Students in resource rooms and self-contained classes expressed significant higher preferences for inclusive instruction than did students in special schools ($p < .05$). Conversely, students in special schools rated group identity significantly higher than did students enrolled in special or resource classes ($p < .05$). These data support Hypothesis 3, that students with sensory impairments will report lower group identity ratings and higher inclusion preference ratings when they are placed in resource rooms than when they are placed in special schools. In other words, group identity was as much a function of separate placements as inclusion preference was a function of being in inclusive environments. Apparently, the instructional environment, not disability, was associated with group identity and inclusion preference.

Hypothesis 4 Results

Table 7.9 presents data on the last hypothesis, that for students with sensory disabilities, there are positive correlations between the adjustment and achievement indicators and inclusion preferences, but not between those indicators and group identity. The results supported the hypothesis. They showed that adjustment and achievement indicators correlated positively with inclusion preferences but not with group identity. This was prominent for students with deafness and hard of hearing. For this group, there was a significant negative correlation between academic achievement and group identity, whereas for students with blindness and visual

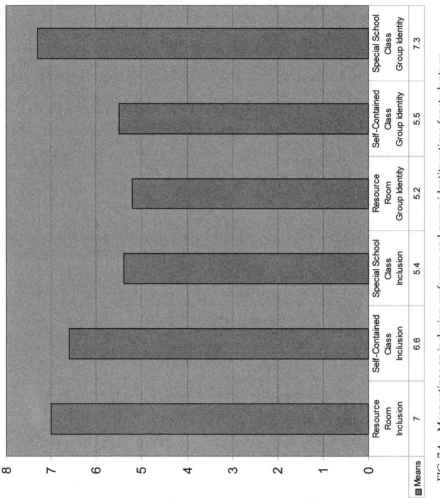

FIG. 7.4. Mean ratings on inclusion preference and group identity ratings for students en-rolled in resource rooms, self-contained classes, and special schools.

117

TABLE 7.9
Correlations Between Adjustment and Achievement Indicators
and Students' Inclusion Preference and Group Identity Scores

	Inclusion Preference		Group Identity	
	DHH	BVI	DHH	BVI
Adjustment indicators				
Prospects for self-determination	.27*	.04	.06	.01
Capacity to self-determine	.37*	.10	.05	.13
Opportunity to self-determine	.075	.02	.04	.16
Self-esteem	.27*	.24*	.04	.00
Achievement indicators				
Reading	.40*	−.02	−.27*	.04
Math	.41*	−.04	−.20*	.04

Note. Disability group: DHH, deaf/hard of hearing; BVI, blind/visually impaired.
*$p < .05$.

impairment there were no significant correlations between those indicators and group identity.

These findings are interesting in that although there were no group differences on the group identity ratings, that variable did correlate negatively with achievement for one of those groups—students with deafness and hard of hearing. Conversely, the inclusion variable correlated positively with five of the adjustment variables for that group: prospects for self-determination (.27), capacity to self-determine (.37), self-esteem (.27), reading achievement (.40), and math (.41). The results support the hypothesis that for students with sensory impairments, there will be positive correlations between self-determination prospects, capacities, opportunities, self-esteem, achievement, and inclusion preferences, but not between those adjustment and achievement indicators and group identity.

DISCUSSION

The results of this study showed that self-determination prospects correlate with disability and educational placement but not with group identity. They showed that there were no significant group differences on group identity or inclusion preference but that there were significant group differences on prospects for self-determination, opportunities to self-determine, capacity to self-determine, self-esteem, and achievement. Hence, the results tended to rule against the social-factor explanation for group differences on adjustments and self-determination prospects. The correlations between educational placement and student ratings on self-determined adjustments did as well. Students in more restrictive special education placements tended to rate their adjustment capabilities lower than did students in more inclusive settings, which was consistent with the disability-effect hypothesis.

The findings were less clear on why students with blindness and visual impairment rated their self-determined adjustment capabilities significantly higher than did students with deafness and hearing impairment. Perhaps blindness provokes unique adaptive challenges in that success in meeting them bolsters beliefs about being able to deal with new circumstances effectively. And perhaps students with deafness who live in deaf-only communities have fewer challenges demanding the development of new adaptations in order to succeed, and hence their beliefs about what they can do are less robust.

Given this account, we would expect adjustment ratings by the two groups to cover different circumstances. Hence, the correlations between adjustment and achievements for the groups might be different as well. Table 7.10 presents these data, which show that students with blindness and visual impairment rated their adjustments differently than did students who were deaf and hard of hearing. For the latter group, the correlation between adjustment and reading was significant at .20 and between adjustment and math significant at .25. But for students with blindness and visual impairment there were no significant correlations between those ratings and achievement. Indeed, for reading the correlation with adjustment was −.03 and for math it was −.01. At the same time, ratings for opportunities to self-determine were similar for the two groups. Apparently the adjustment ratings by students with blindness and visual impairment reflected activities and challenges that were very different from those required for academic achievement.

This raises questions about the claim by self-determined learning theory that adjustment and learning are functionally related. According to the data in Table 7.10, adjustment ratings correlated with achievement scores for students who were deaf and hard of hearing but not for stu-

TABLE 7.10

Correlations Between Self-Determination Scores and Reading and Math Scores for Students with Deafness and Hard of Hearing (DHH) and for Students with Blindness and Visual Impairment (BVI)

Self-Determination	Reading Scores		Math Scores	
	DHH	BVI	DHH	BVI
Prospects	.20*	.20	.25*	.18
Capacity	.20*	−.03	.25*	−.01
Opportunity	.18*	.24*	.19*	.22

*p < .05.

dents who were blind or visually impaired. Does this mean that adjustment ratings are not functionally related to learning as claimed by the theory? We think not, if only because those ratings reflected students' *beliefs* about their adjustment capability and hence could be based on experience with challenging circumstances that has little to do with achievement experienced in reading and math.

Still, the question remains as to how to demonstrate this predicted association between adjustment and learning. Because even with the favorable interpretation of results of this study, there is only an inference that the association exists. To get direct support, we need a different methodology, one that produces data on students' actual adjustments to different opportunities for gain. This is the approach used in the next chapter.

REFERENCES

Battle, J. (1990). *Culture free self-esteem inventories* (2nd ed.), Form A and B. Austin, TX: ProEd.
Corker, M. (1998). *Deaf and disabled or deafness disabled?* Philadelphia, PA: Open University Press.
Lipkowitz, S. (2000). *The relationship between sensory disabilities and self-determination, self-esteem, cultural/disability identification, inclusion and academic achievement.* Unpublished dissertation, Teachers College, Columbia University, New York.

8

Assessing Adjustment Gains by Students in General and Special Education

Dennis E. Mithaug
Deirdre K. Mithaug

The studies described in chapters 4–6 found that students with disabilities *believed* they had lower capacities to adjust to opportunities for self-determined gain than did students without disabilities. And the study described in chapter 7 found that students with blindness and visual impairment believed they had greater capacity to adjust to opportunities for self-determined gain than did students with deafness and hearing impairment. These findings are consistent with the prediction that differences in adjustment capabilities correlate with disability. The following argument from chapter 4 made this claim for students in special education. It linked their known histories of learning difficulty with ineffective adjustment and that adjustment with lowered prospects for self-determination.

1. School achievement is a function of adjustments to opportunities for learning gain.
    a. Underachievement is due to inadequate adjustment to opportunities for learning gain.
    b. Many students in special education underachieve.
    c. Therefore these students adjust inadequately to opportunities for learning gain.
2. Self-determination prospects are a function of adjustments to opportunities for self-determined gain.
    a. People who adjust inadequately to opportunities for gain have lower prospects for self-determination than do people who adjust adequately to those opportunities.

  b. Many students in special education adjust inadequately to op-
     portunities for gain.
  c. Therefore these students are likely to have lower prospects for
     self-determination than are students who adjust adequately to
     opportunities for gain.

Another way of interpreting the findings of the previous chapters of
course is to claim that because they were derived from *ratings* of capability
and opportunity, they reflected *beliefs about what students could do to get
what they needed or wanted from new situations.* Therefore, it is not a student's disability that constrains self-determination prospects per se. It is
negative beliefs about that capability. If students were to improve their beliefs about adjustment capability, they would be more likely to engage
and succeed at self-determined pursuits.

The problem with this interpretation is that it assumes beliefs can be
significantly discrepant from the adjustments they provoke, which is contrary to the causal model of adjustment presented in previous chapters.
According to that model, beliefs, expectations, choices, actions, and results function interdependently. A change in beliefs will affect the regulation of adjustments, and the regulation of adjustments will affect beliefs.
Hence, beliefs that are significantly discrepant from adjustments will provoke regulatory behavior to restore the match between them and those
adjustments. This means that students' beliefs about their adjustment capacity *are* accurate reflections of actual capability.

Given that the causal model we developed is itself under investigation
in this book, we probably should not be using it to argue for the present
claim that is also in question. This leaves that question open, unless of
course we can measure adjustments directly during different opportunities for gain to show that students with disabilities do in fact adjust less effectively to opportunities than do students without disabilities. Then we
would have also evidence to support our claim that beliefs, opportunities,
and adjustments correspond, whether they are assessed using student ratings of adjustment or are measured directly.

The study we report in this chapter uses this approach. It measures self-
regulated adjustments of students with and without disabilities directly.
Hence it allows us to determine whether students in special and general
education who have significantly different reading and math scores also
made significantly different adjustments to equally challenging opportunities of gain. The study also provides an opportunity to test the main
claim of self-determined learning theory directly that both optimal opportunities and optimal adjustments maximize gain.

Table 8.1 presents these predictions. The reasoning behind them is that
if opportunities and adjustments affect gain maximization, then groups

TABLE 8.1
Predicted Gain by Students Making Suboptimal and Optimal
Adjustments during Suboptimal and Optimal Opportunities for Gain

Predicted Adjustments	Suboptimal Opportunities for Gain	Optimal Opportunities for Gain
Suboptimal adjustments by students in special education	1. Low gain	2. Moderate gain
Optimal adjustments by students in general education	3. Moderate gain	4. High gain

differing in their adjustment capabilities will differ in the gain they produce during different opportunities. The cells of the table make four such predictions. The rows of the table list groups according to their predicted differences on adjustment capability. Students in special education are represented in the first row of the table and are predicted to produce suboptimal adjustments. Students in general education are represented in the second row and are predicted to produce optimal adjustments. The columns represent the experimental conditions both groups experienced: suboptimal choice opportunities during the first eight sessions of the experiment and optimal choice opportunities during the second eight sessions of the experiment. The four cells representing various combinations of suboptimal and optimal adjustments and opportunities yield four gain predictions by the theory. In cell 1 the students in special education are predicted to respond to the suboptimal opportunity condition with suboptimal adjustments to produce minimum gain. In cell 2 the same group of students is predicted to adjust similarly to the optimal opportunity condition to produce moderate gain. In cell 3, students in general education are predicted to respond to the suboptimal opportunity condition with optimal adjustments to produce moderate gain. And in cell 4 they are predicted to respond similarly to the optimal opportunity condition to produce maximum gain.

The following hypotheses reflect these predictions, which are based on the assumption that students in special and general education differ in their ability to self-regulate effectively to adjust optimally during different opportunities for gain. The first hypothesis predicts that when opportunities for gain change from suboptimal to optimal, both groups will increase gain production. A comparison between gain produced in cell 1 with gain produced in cell 2 tests this hypothesis for students in special education. A comparison between gain produced in cell 3 with gain produced in cell 4 tests the hypothesis for students in general education. The second hypothesis predicts that for both suboptimal and optimal opportunity conditions, students in general education will produce more gain than will students in special education. The comparison between gain produced in cell 1 by students in special education with gain in cell 3 produced by students in general education tests this hypothesis for the suboptimal opportunity condition. A comparison between gain in cell 2 produced by students in special education with gain in cell 4 produced by students in general education tests the hypothesis for the optimal opportunity condition.

Hypotheses 3 and 4 predict that the two groups are in fact different in their adjustments and self-regulatory behavior. Hypothesis 3 predicts that the adjustments produced by students in special education will be less effective than the adjustments produced by students in general education during both opportunity conditions. Hypothesis 4 predicts the same for their self-regulation, which will be less effective for students in special education than for students in general education.

1. Students in general and special education are more productive during optimal choice opportunities than during suboptimal choice opportunities.
2. Students in general education are more productive than are students in special education in both suboptimal and optimal choice opportunities.
3. Students in general education adjust more effectively than do students in special education during both suboptimal and optimal choice opportunities.
4. Students in general education regulate their expectations, choices, actions, and results more effectively than do students in special education during both suboptimal and optimal choice opportunities.

ASSESSING SELF-REGULATED ADJUSTMENTS DURING SUBOPTIMAL AND OPTIMAL OPPORTUNITIES

The study compared self-regulation and gain differences of students in general and special education by using computer-generated adjustment problems presented during different opportunities for gain. The simulation measured self-regulated adjustments during recursive problem solving to meet self-set goals (Mithaug, 1993). Each adjustment episode presented options for completing tasks and producing points in a fixed amount of time and with a fixed number of mouse clicks. The program simulated the problem of figuring out how to use time and resources optimally to maximize gain under conditions of uncertainty. It gave students repeated opportunities to solve the problem, which required that they set goals for the point gain they expected, choose a task to produce points, work at a task to produce points, and then monitor progress toward meeting goals *exactly*. The reward contingency was that they only earned points accumulated during five adjustment episodes that *exactly* matched the goal set for that session. Each session gave students five adjustment episodes to solve the problem, which required setting a goal that could be met exactly with the point clicks and time allotted. The program simulated self-regulated problem solving to meet self-set goals. It recorded student responses to generate the points they believed they could produce to match their goals.

Participants.   The participants were 40 elementary students enrolled in general and special education programs at a suburban and a city school. They included 10 suburban students in special education, 10 suburban students in general education, and two groups of 10 city students in general education. Table 8.2 indicates that 24 were female and 16 were male. Their average age was 12.2 years and average score on the Wechsler Individual Achievement Test (WIAT) was 124.2. The table also shows that the groups differed significantly in age, reading, and math. City students were significantly older than suburban students, and scored significantly higher on the WIAT than suburban students. Suburban students in general education also scored significantly higher on the WIAT than did the suburban students in special education.

The Adjustment Simulation.   The students completed two 50-minute periods of eight sessions by working a Macintosh adjustment simulation.[1] During each period, they completed eight successive sessions of setting goals for point gain, choosing a task to produce points, working the task to produce points, and monitoring results. Each session consisted of five 1-minute episodes of attempting to meet a self-set goal by choosing tasks, working tasks, and checking results. The first 50-minute period presented a more difficult set of task options than did the second 50-minute period. It was a *suboptimal opportunity* because students had to discover the task option that was most favorable for producing point gain. The second 50-minute period was an *optimal opportunity* because any choice made would produce the same gain. A comparison of students' self-regulation, adjustments, and gain production during the two opportunity conditions tested the four hypotheses.

---

[1]This program was developed by Eva Frazier from the University of Colorado at Colorado Springs.

TABLE 8.2
Characteristics of the 40 Students Who Participated
in the Adjustment Assessment Study

Background	Suburban Special Ed Group n = 10	Suburban General Ed Group n = 10	City General Ed Group n = 10	City General Ed Group n = 10	Total/ Mean
Female	6	5	7	8	26
Male	4	5	3	2	14
Age	11.1	11.2	12.7**	13.9***	12.2
WIAT Total	93.1	122.0*	140.2**	141.4**	124.2

*$p < .05$ for SubSpEd vs. SubGenEd. **$p < .05$ for CityGenEd vs. SubSpec and SubGenEd.

Students used six page views or screens on the computer to complete each 5-minute adjustment session. Page 1, the home page, listed all of the pages and provided buttons to click to move to other screens. Page 2, the goal page, allowed students to specify the number of points they expected to produce by the end of the five-episode session. Page 3, the options page, listed the three tasks and buttons to click to find the ratio of mouse clicks to points for each task. Page 4, the choice page, provided a button to click to select a task to work for that episode. Page 5, the work screen, presented the wall construction task to complete to produce a point. The screen presented a small square that expanded with mouse clicks to fill the screen completely when the wall was completed. For the task option with a 1:1 ratio, the wall was completed with a single click. For the task option with the 2:1 ratio, the wall was completed to produce a point after two mouse clicks. For task option with the 3:1 ratio, the wall was completed to produce a point after three clicks. Page 6, the results screen, presented two thermometer-like charts comparing points accumulated for the session with points required to meet the session goal.

All functions on the screens required mouse clicks. Moving from screen to screen required a click, setting session goals required clicks, checking on task options to reveal their ratios required clicks, choosing a task to work on required a click, building a wall to produce points required clicks, and viewing point accumulations and progress toward the session goal required a click. The challenge was to complete each adjustment episode by using as many mouse clicks as possible to produce as many points as possible. To do this, students had to set session goals as high as possible and then to choose the task that they could complete with the mouse clicks available to produce that amount of gain exactly. If they produced too many or too few points compared to what was specified in their session goal, they earned zero points for the session. The limitation of available mouse clicks and time challenged their ability to regulate optimally to produce the most gain possible during each session. The simulation's eight-session periods allowed students to improve this capability over time. And the two-period experimental design allowed students to demonstrate this adaptive capability during different opportunity conditions, with the first eight-session period being less favorable than the second eight-session period.

Procedures.   Prior to the study, each participant received an hour of instruction on how to work the computer simulation. During these sessions, the experimenter followed a training script consisting of 48 instructional cues, questions, and response opportunities that guided students through the simulation. Also, students were asked about each function of the six page views and then were required to perform the function. By the end of the instruction, all students demonstrated the requisite skills of moving from screen to screen, setting expectations, reviewing options, making choices, working at the task, and checking results. Every session of the study began with the experimenter providing the following instructions:

Try to make as many points as you can.

You are on your own.

You will have 5 one-minute trials to meet each goal exactly.

You will have only 10 clicks and 60 seconds for each period.

After each one-minute period, there will be a short break.

You have 8 sessions to produce as many points as you can that exactly match your goals.

Conditions.   The first eight-session period was the suboptimal choice opportunity condition because it presented three task options with randomly different click-to-point ratios of 1:1, 2:1, or 3:1. This made finding the best task difficult to manage and hence less than optimal for producing the most gain possible. To act on this opportunity optimally, students had to use some of their clicks to find the task that yielded the best ratio. Not doing this meant that they could choose a less efficient task, which would produce fewer points and would be less accurate in meeting the points set for session goal. The second eight-session period was the optimal choice opportunity condition because it presented the same 1:1 click-to-point ratio for all three tasks. Hence, students who discovered this change could avoid using mouse clicks to view any of the task options and instead go directly to the third page to choose a task at random and commence completing it to produce points. This condition allowed them to spend more time and clicks on task completion and point gain. Of course, they would have to increase their point goal for the session to earn more of the points possible. Only the suburban groups experienced this condition. Both eight-session periods were suboptimal for the city groups.

Indicators of Self-Regulation, Adjustment, and Gain.   The program recorded mouse clicks for each page to provide data on self-regulation, adjustments, and point gain. The indicators of *self-regulation* were goals set (expectations), task choices (choices), tasks completed (actions), and points produced (results) The *adjustment optimality* was the product of the optimality scores for goals, task choices, task completions, and points produced. The *gain in points* was the number of points earned for the session that exactly matched the number of points expected for the session goal.

Self-regulation effectiveness was the optimality of students' expectations, choices, actions, and results during a five-episode adjustment. For point expectations specified in session goals, the percent optimal was the number of points set for the session goal divided by the number of points that could be produced in a five-epsosde session if all mouse clicks were used to find and complete the best task available. For choices, the percent optimal was the point production possible from the task selected divided by the point production possible from the most efficient task (e.g., the one yielding the 1:1 click to point ratio). For actions, the percent optimal was the mouse clicks used to complete tasks divided by the clicks available when the minimum was used to set goals and make choices. For results, the percent optimal was the session point total divided by that total plus the discrepancy between the total and the number for the session goal.

Adjustment optimality was the product of the optimalities for expectations, choices, actions, and results. Hence for each session the adjustment optimality was the expectation optimality multiplied by the choice optimality multiplied by the action optimality multiplied by the result optimality. When all four factors were 1, or 100% optimal, the adjustment optimality was also 1, or 100% optimal.

Points gained per session were the numbers of points accumulated during a session that exactly matched the points specified in the session goal. Point accumulations that exceeded or fell short of the goal were not earned and yielded zero gain for the session. Students only gained the points that matched their goal.

In sum, each adjustment variable was a percent of the optimal. Hence, problems in self-regulation or adjustment were simply deviations from 100%. A 10% optimality for expectations meant that students set session goals that were 90% lower or higher than the amount possible given the clicks and time available. A 10% choice optimality meant that students selected tasks that were 90% less efficient than the most productive tasks available. A 10% response optimality meant that students used a fraction of the available mouse clicks for the wall building and point production when clicks were distributed optimally between setting expectations, making choices, and producing points. Finally, 10% result optimality meant that students produced gain that was 90% lower or higher than their goal for the session. For a discussion of these indicators and their relation to gain production, see Mithaug (1993, pp. 129–139).

RESULTS

The results from these adjustment simulation sessions supported the two predictions that students in general and special education produce more gain during optimal choice opportunities and that students in general education produce more gain than do special education students in both conditions (Hypotheses 1 and 2). They also supported the predictions that students in general education are more effective adjusters and self-regulators than are students in special education (Hypotheses 3 and 4).

Hypothesis 1 Results

According to Hypothesis 1, students in general and special education will produce significantly more gain during optimal choice conditions than during suboptimal choice conditions. Figure 8.1 presents the results supporting this hypothesis. The point gains for students in special education increased significantly from a mean of 8.4 points per student in the suboptimal condition to a mean of 19.6 points per student in the optimal condition ($p < .05$). The gain for students in general education also increased significantly from the suboptimal to optimal choice conditions. During the suboptimal condition the mean was 29.6 points per student and during the optimal condition it was 44.4 points per student ($p < .05$).

These data are consistent with Hypothesis 1 that regardless of the self-regulatory differences between groups, both groups would significantly improve their production when choice opportunities become more favorable. The reason for this was that in the optimal condition all tasks yielded the same 1:1 click-to-point ratio, which left additional clicks for students to produce points.

Hypothesis 2 Results

Figure 8.2 compares the four groups during each opportunity condition. During the first eight sessions of suboptimal opportunities, there was a significant difference between the special education group's mean point accumulation rate of 8.4 and the three general education groups' mean accumulation rate of 25.4 ($p < .05$). In the second eight sessions when conditions

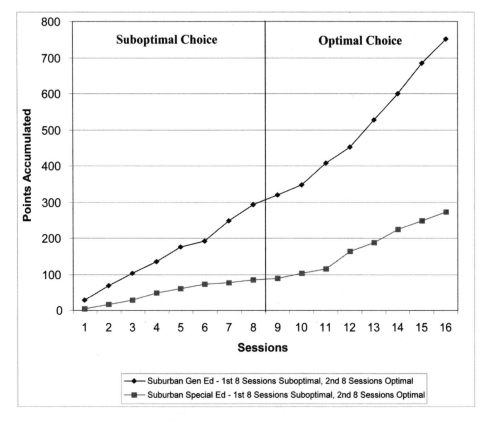

FIG. 8.1. Point accumulations by students in general and special education during suboptimal and optimal choice conditions.

changed to optimal choice opportunities for the suburban special and general education groups, the differences between these two groups maintained. The special education group's mean point accumulation rate of 19.6
was significantly lower than the suburban general education group's mean
rate of 44.4 ($p < .05$). For the two city groups during that second eight-
session period when the suboptimal choice opportunity condition was still
in effect, the average point accumulation rate was 26.8, which was not significantly higher than the rate for the special education group.

These results are consistent with Hypothesis 2, that students in general
education will produce more gain than will students in special education
during suboptimal and optimal choice conditions. The results are also consistent with the expectation that the improvement of opportunities for students in special education but not for students in general education will
equalize gain production for the two groups. This was evident in the comparison between city students in general education who produced gain

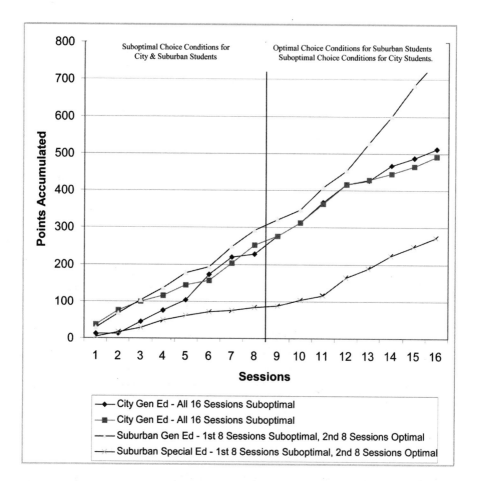

FIG. 8.2.   Gain accumulations for students in general and special education during suboptimal and optimal choice opportunity conditions.

during the suboptimal opportunity condition while suburban students in special education produced gain during the optimal opportunity condition. Here there were no significant gain differences between groups. This supports the view that interventions that optimize opportunities for a less adaptive group will equalize learning gains with a more adaptive group.

Hypothesis 3 Results

Figure 8.3 presents adjustment optimality data for the groups during the two eight-session periods. The adjustment optimality was the percent of students' expectations, choices, actions, and results that were optimal for

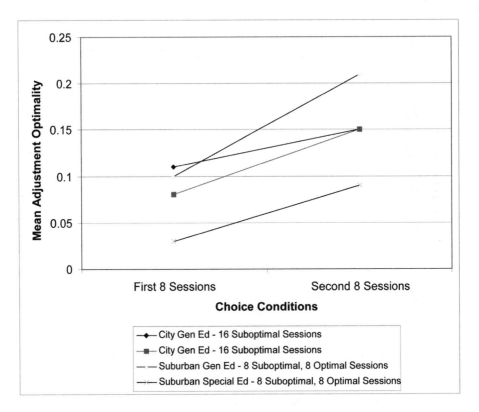

FIG. 8.3.   Mean adjustment optimality scores for students in general and special education during two eight-session choice opportunity conditions.

the sessions. An adjustment was 100% optimal when students set expectations has high as possible, made the best choice of those available, responded as efficiently as possible to produce points, and produced results that exactly matched expectations.

As indicated in Fig. 8.3, the mean adjustment optimality score was lower for students in special education than for students in general education groups during both eight-session periods. For the first eight-session period, the mean optimality score for students in special education was .03, which was significantly lower than the mean optimality score of .10 for the three groups of students in general education ($p < .001$). The results for the second eight sessions were similar. The mean optimality score for students in special education was .09, which was significantly lower than the mean optimal score of .17 for the three groups in general education groups ($p < .05$).

These data support Hypothesis 3, which claimed there would be significant adjustment differences between students in general and special education during both suboptimal and optimal opportunity conditions. Students in general education maintained their adaptive advantage over students in special education throughout the study. Even though students in special education improved their adjustment optimality scores significantly when conditions changed from suboptimal to optimal, they continued to adjust less effectively than did students in general education. More telling perhaps was that adjustment optimality scores for students in special education improved when the optimal opportunity condition was in effect, but were still significantly lower than the scores for city students in general education during their suboptimal opportunity condition of the second period ($p < .05$).

Hypothesis 4 Results

Figures 8.4 and 8.5 chart the four groups' optimality scores for each of the self-regulation variables comprising the adjustment optimality: expectations, choices, actions, and results. The expectation and choice optimality scores are charted in Fig. 8.4 and the action and results optimality scores are charted in Fig. 8.5. These results are consistent with those presented in Fig. 8.3. The students in special education scored significantly lower than students in general education on all four self-regulation variables ($p < .05$). The only exception was the choice optimality score in the second eight-session period when the two suburban groups worked the optimal choice opportunity task (see second chart in Fig. 8.4). Here the choice optimality was 1 for both groups because during that condition all choices were optimal. It did not matter how students chose, as all responses yielded the same press to point ratio of 1:1. Students in special education chose optimally in that condition because that was the only choice available.

Also of interest is the apparent lack of improvement in self-regulation scores by students in special education. Although students in other groups significantly increased their optimality scores from the first to the second eight-session periods, students in special education did not. The suburban students in general education significantly improved their actions and results ($p < .05$), city students in the first general education group significantly improved their expectations and actions ($p < .05$), and city students in the second general education group significantly improved their expectations, choices, and actions ($p < .05$). In contrast, the only improvement exhibited by students in the special education was the change in choice optimality scores due to the condition changes from suboptimal to optimal choice opportunities.

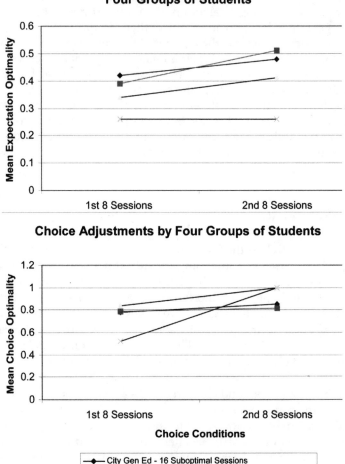

FIG. 8.4.   Expectation and choice adjustments for the four groups during
the first and second eight sessions.

These findings support Hypothesis 4, that there would be significant self-regulation differences between students in general and special education during suboptimal and optimal choice opportunities. The findings reveal that the adjustment difficulties this group of students experienced persisted in both choice opportunity conditions. They also show how this problem affected the gain accumulation differences between the two groups.

Action Adjustments by Four Groups of Students

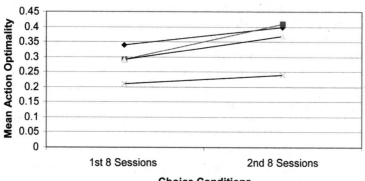

Result Adjustments by Four Groups of Students

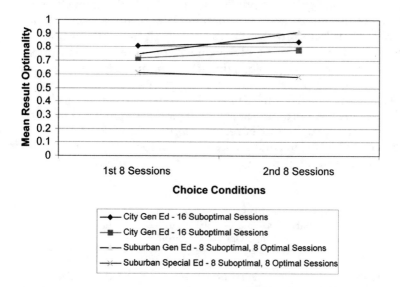
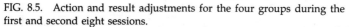

FIG. 8.5. Action and result adjustments for the four groups during the first and second eight sessions.

DISCUSSION

These results are consistent with the prediction by self-determined learning theory that the optimality of a learner's opportunities and adjustments determines the maximization of learning gains. When opportunities and adjustments are optimal, learning maximizes. When either opportunities or adjustments are suboptimal, gain moderates. And when both opportunities and adjustments are suboptimal, gain minimizes. In this study, students in special education were predicted to be suboptimal adjusters when compared with students in general education and hence likely to produce minimum to moderate gain during suboptimal and optimal opportunities. On the other hand, students in general education were predicted to be optimal adjusters and hence producers of moderate to maximum gain during suboptimal and optimal opportunities. Both predictions were confirmed, as Table 8.3 shows.

In cell 1, minimal gain was predicted for students in special education because of their suboptimal adjustments to suboptimal opportunities, and this is what happened. Their average rate of gain was the lowest of the four cells, a mean of 11.9 points per session. In cell 2, moderate gain was predicted for this group of students because of their suboptimal adjustments to optimal opportunities, and this happened too. These students produced an average low to moderate gain rate of 28 points per session. In cell 3, moderate gain was predicted for general education students who made optimal adjustments to suboptimal opportunities, and this also occurred. Their gain production was at a high-moderate average of 36.3 points per session. In cell 4, high gain was predicted for this group of students who made optimal adjustments to optimal opportunities. This too occurred, with a mean gain rate of 63.8 points per session.

This study yielded a near-unequivocal demonstration of the relationships between opportunity, adjustment, and gain predicted by self-determined learning theory. It is reasonable to argue from this that underachievement is due to patterns of self-regulation that produce suboptimal adjustments during both favorable and unfavorable opportunities to learn.

TABLE 8.3
Predictions and Results for Gain Production by Students
With Suboptimal and Optimal Adjustments to Suboptimal
and Optimal Opportunities

Student Adjustments	First Eight Sessions, Suboptimal Opportunities for Gain	Second Eight Sessions, Optimal Opportunities for Gain
	1.	2.
Suboptimal adjustments by 10 students in special education	Prediction: Low rate of gain Result: 11.9 Points gained per session	Prediction: Moderate rate of gain Result: 28.0 Points gained per session
	3.	4.
Optimal adjustments by 10 students in general education	Prediction: Moderate rate of gain Result: 36.3 Points gained per session	Prediction: High rate of gain Result: 63.8 Points gained per session

Students in special education demonstrated this effect in that they were predicted to be poor adjusters to new opportunities for gain, and they were. Moreover, those suboptimal adjustments persisted during both suboptimal and optimal choice opportunities to yield a pattern of gain production characteristic of underachievement.

Of course, these findings were also consistent with results reported in the previous chapters, that students with disabilities tend to rate their capacities to adjust in order to self-determine significantly lower than do students without disabilities. This suggests as well that these self-reports were in fact accurate, at least as compared with the self-reports of students in general education.

The study also revealed an important characteristic of effective learners. They adjust more quickly than do ineffective learners. This was evident in the self-regulation comparisons. The students in general education improved their self-regulation during the 50-minute sessions, whereas students in special education did not. Proposition 2 of self-determined learning theory predicts that when students adjust repeatedly in challenging opportunities like those provided by the 16 adjustment sessions, their expectations become adaptable, their choices become rational, their actions become efficient, and their results become successful. This in turn optimizes their adjustments. Students in general education exhibited these improvements in their self-regulation and adjustments but students in special education did not. This leads us to wonder whether those students would have improved with additional sessions.

However, this was not the purpose of the study, which was to determine whether ineffective self-regulation and suboptimal adjustment were responsible for the underachievement experienced by students in special education. The fact that students in special and general education differed significantly on these factors during both favorable and unfavorable opportunity conditions suggests that the self-regulation variables and the adjustment optimality they produce are responsible. This means, of course, that interventions to improve prospects for learning maximization should focus on improving students' ability to self-regulate to produce optimal adjustments during challenging opportunities for gain. According to self-determined learning theory, this would maximize their learning. Indeed, any intervention that improves the capacity to adjust should improve the ability to learn. The next section of this book examines these approaches to determine whether they increase engagement, adjustment, and learning, as predicted by the theory.

REFERENCES

Mithaug, D. E. (1993). *Self-regulation theory: How optimal adjustmnet maximizes gain.* Westport, CT: Praeger.

III

PRESCRIPTION VERIFICATION

9

The Effects of Choice Opportunities and Self-Regulation Training on the Self-Engagement and Learning of Young Children With Disabilities

Deirdre K. Mithaug
Dennis E. Mithaug

One implication of self-determined learning theory is that when teachers improve students' learning opportunities and adjustment capabilities, students self-engage to maximize learning. This is because according to the theory, favorable learning opportunities provoke engagement, persistent engagement optimizes adjustments, and optimized adjustments maximize learning. Each of the theory's four propositions describes a link in the chain leading to learning. The first proposition claims that the more valuable and doable the opportunity, the more likely is the regulation of expectations, choices, actions, and results to produce gain. The second claims that the more frequent these self-regulated behaviors, the more likely it is that adjustments will optimize as expectations become adaptable, choices become rational, actions efficient, and results become successful. The third claims that as adjustments optimize, learning maximizes. Therefore, the fourth proposition concludes, optimal opportunities maximize learning. From these propositions we deduced the instructional prescription that if teachers improve students' opportunities and adjustments, students will maximize their learning.

The study in chapter 8 examined the claims that support this prescription by measuring the adjustments of two groups of students who regulated their expectations, choices, actions, and results differently in order to produce gain toward their expectations. The results indicated that point gains were highest for the group that experienced optimal opportunities and optimal adjustments and lowest for the group that experienced suboptimal opportunities and suboptimal adjustments, a finding that was consistent with the theory. The results also showed that optimal opportunity on its own was insufficient for maximum gain, as was an optimal adjustment. However, when optimal opportunity was combined with the greater adaptive capability of students in general education, gains maximized.

Although the study was useful for verifying the propositions of the theory, it offered no direct evidence for the prescription for teachers to improve opportunities and adjustments so students will maximize learning. But of course, this was not the purpose of the study, which was to determine whether students with known differences in achievement would exhibit predicted differences in adjustment to opportunities for gain. Indeed, if the study had employed academic rather than computer simulation tasks to test for effects, differences in adjustments between groups could be attributed to students' subject-matter knowledge and skills rather than to their adaptive capability. The fact that the computer tasks required adjustment behaviors rather than academic skills allowed gains to be attributed to adjustment capability and not past academic achievement. This is what happened, because correlations between points earned and test scores in reading, math, and spelling were .05, .28, and .21, respectively, indicating that academic achievement was a poor predictor of group differences in the adjustment simulation. It could only explain 0.3 to 8% of the variance in gain.

Nonetheless, that study suggested that an improvement in opportunities and adjustments could improve academic learning too. The study discussed here tests this claim directly by examining whether independent work on academic tasks would maximize when opportunities and self-regulated adjustments optimized during instruction. The following prescription makes this claim for increasing self-engagement and learning.

Prescription 1: To increase self-engagement and learning, give students a choice about their learning goals, and then give them a method for regulating their expectations, choices, actions, and results to meet those goals.

TESTING PRESCRIPTIONS FOR IMPROVING OPPORTUNITIES AND ADJUSTMENTS

The study was part of the dissertation research conducted by the first author (Mithaug, 1998). It compared the effects of two choice conditions on student use of self-regulation during independent work. During a teacher choice condition, the teacher selected the subjects and tasks for students to complete as they learned to use a card to regulate their expectations, choices, actions, and results. During a student choice condition, students selected the subjects and the number of tasks they would complete as they learned use of the card. We hypothesized that the students would regulate their expectations, choices, actions, and results more effectively during independent work periods that followed student-directed instruction than they would during independent work periods that followed teacher-directed instruction. Indeed, past research has shown student choice to be a more effective opportunity condition for engagement than teacher-choice condition (Dickerson & Creedon, 1981; Fantuzzo & Clement, 1981; Fantuzzo, Polite, Cook, & Quinn, 1988; Fisher, Thompson, Piazza, Crosland, & Gotjen, 1997; Gettinger, 1985; Lovitt & Curtis, 1969; Parsons, Reid, Reynolds, & Bumgarner, 1990; Stevenson & Fantuzzo, 1984, 1986). Consequently, we expected that students would self-regulate more frequently during the independent work that followed student-directed instruction than during the work that followed teacher-directed instruction. Moreover, we expected that the more persistent self-regulation during independent work would lead to better adjustments and greater productivity. In other words, we expected that combining a student-choice opportunity condition with use of a self-regulation card would increase students' engagement and maximize their productivity during independent work.

Participants and Setting

The six students who participated in this study attended a private elementary school in a major metropolitan city in the northeast. They were from diverse ethnic backgrounds and had a variety of disabilities and related learning and behavior problems. Alice was a 5-year-old bilingual Hispanic female diagnosed as having speech/language impairment and a pervasive developmental disorder. Bob, a 6-year-old Hispanic male with a speech and language delay, was described as having autistic-like behaviors. Carter was a 6-year-old Hispanic male identified as having an attention deficit and hyperactivity disorder. Don was a 7-year-old African American male with a developmental delay. Edward was a 6-year-old African American male with behavior problems; Fred was a 6-year-old Hispanic male with speech and language delays, autism, and emotional disorders.

The students were enrolled in a self-contained special education classroom where they received individualized instruction daily from 8:15 to 1:45. Instruction consisted of half-hour periods for math, reading, science, social studies, and writing. Two 20-minute periods scheduled approximately 2 hours apart were allocated for independent work. The staff included a teacher and two assistants. The classroom consisted of a group instruction area and two work-station areas. Instruction on the five academic subjects occurred in the group area. One of the work-station areas was located at the side of the room. The second work-station area was located in an observation room adjacent to the classroom. Both areas included tables, bookcases, chairs, and folders containing materials for the five academic subjects covered during group instruction. A clipboard with a self-regulation card hung from a hook on each student's workstation table.

Materials

The work-station materials included five color-coded folders designating work in math, reading, science, social studies, and writing. Each folder contained two worksheets for that subject. Math folders contained worksheets requiring dot-to-dot connections, addition and subtraction, grouping sets, and solutions to word problems. Reading folders contained worksheets on matching, identifying letters, and spelling. Science and social studies folders contained worksheets on topics from the themes of study for the week. Writing folders contained worksheets on penmanship.

The students also had a self-regulation card in their work-station materials. The teacher and students used it to choose subjects to work on, select the number of worksheets to complete for each subject, record completed worksheets, evaluate assignment completions, and determine reinforcement. The card was a legal-size piece of paper divided into four columns. The column on the left listed pictures from top to bottom signifying the subject area for each row. Students chose a subject to work by circling its picture in the column. The second column, labeled "What I Will Do," consisted of five rows of line spaces for writing the number of worksheets that would be completed for each circled subject area. The third column, labeled "What I Did," consisted of rows of line spaces to be completed by writing the number of worksheets completed for each circled subject. The last column on the right side of the sheet was for "Completed Assignments." It consisted of five rows with the words "Yes" and "No." Circling a "Yes" on the row of a circled subject meant that the number written in the "What I Did" column matched the number written in the "What I Will Do" column for that subject.

During the instructional conditions, a circled "Yes" was an occasion for reinforcement, which consisted of the student choosing an item from a prize box located on a file cabinet at the edge of the workstation area of the room. The items included pencils, posters, stickers, buttons, stamps, bookmarks, and mazes. Students received a prize-selection opportunity for each correctly circled "Yes" on their self-regulation card.

Adjustment and Gain Definitions and Measures

Three self-regulation behaviors were required to complete the self-regulation card: goal setting, self-monitoring, and self-evaluation. During goal setting, students chose the subjects (math, reading, science, social studies, and writing) and the amount of work they planned to complete per subject (number of worksheets). During self-monitoring they recorded the amount of work they completed for each subject. During self-evaluation they indicated whether they met the work goal for each subject.

Students set goals by circling subject pictures on the self-regulation sheet and by writing the number of worksheets they planned to complete for those selections in the "What I Will Do" column. They self-monitored by writing the number of worksheets they completed for each subject in the "What I Did" column. They self-evaluated by circling a "Yes" or a "No" in the "Completed Assignments" column to indicate whether there was a match between assigned tasks and completed work.

The following measures were derived from data collected on use of the self-regulation card: accurate self-regulation, adaptive expectations, rational choice making, efficient responding, successful results, adjustment optimality, and learning production. They were used to verify the prescription that optimizing students' opportunities and adjustments will maximize engagement and academic production.

Accurate Self-Regulation. Accurate self-regulation was defined as correct responses to the self-regulation card. Responses were accurate (correct) when they satisfied three criteria:

1. The number of completed worksheets recorded in the "What I Did" column exactly matched the number assigned in the "What I Will Do" column on the self-regulation card (accurate goal setting).
2. The number of assignments recorded in the "What I Did" column of the self-regulation card exactly matched the number of assignments completed (accurate self-monitoring).
3. The *Yes* and *No* terms circled in the "Completed Assignment" column correctly represented a match or a mismatch between worksheets assigned for each subject in the "What I Will Do" column and the completed worksheets recorded for that subject in the "What I Did" column (accurate self-evaluation).

Adaptive Expectations. Student expectations for work completed during 20 sessions were adaptive to the extent they matched the total they were capable of completing in that time. Given that each student had previously completed at least 10 assignments (2 per subject) during 20-minute periods, the optimal or adaptive level completed work was defined as 10 per independent work session. Percent of optimal expectations was the number of goals set during each work session divided by 10.

Rational Choice Making.   Students were rational in choice making when they used information about their completed work to draw accurate conclusions about whether they met their goals. The indicators of rational selection and use of information were correct self-monitoring and correct self-evaluation. Correct self-monitoring occurred when the work students recorded as completed reflected the work actually completed. Correct self-evaluation occurred when the conclusion about whether the goals were met matched goals actually met. In other words, students concluded with a *Yes* that they met their goal only when there was a match between the recorded number for the goal and the recorded number for completed work. Percent of optimal choosing was the number of correct self-monitorings and self-evaluations divided by 10, which was the total possible for a session (5 self-monitorings and 5 self-evaluations).

Efficient Responding.   Students were efficient during independent work to the extent that they spent their time engaged in on-task behaviors, which were defined as the number of times a student's eyes and/or head were directed toward a worksheet when observed by the teacher during scheduled observations. Recorded beeps from a tape recorder cued the teacher to observe and record students' on-task behavior. On hearing a beep, the teacher observed two students at a time and recorded whether they were attending to the worksheet at that moment. The teacher made six observations of on-task behavior per student during 18 minutes of each 20-minute independent work session. The percent optimal on-task responding was the number of observed on-task behaviors divided by 6.

Successful Results.   Results were successful to the extent that work completed exactly matched goals set for each subject. During the independent work sessions, students set goals in five subjects and hence were free to complete all or none of that work and still meet goals exactly. A "5" could mean that students successfully met all their goals, whether they had set the goal to complete 0, 1, or 2 worksheets for each subject. Students produced a successful result when they did exactly what they said they would do in their goals on the self-regulation card. The percent of optimal results was the number of sheets completed divided by the total completed plus the difference between that total and the number set in their goal.

Adjustment Optimality.   Adjustments were effective or optimal to the extent the four self-regulation indicators were optimal. Hence, it was the product of those four measures: expectation optimality × choice optimality × work optimality × result optimality. When all four indicators were 1 (100%), the adjustment optimality was 1, or 100%, too.

Learning Production. The learning production was the total number of worksheets completed during the 11:10 a.m. independent work sessions. There was a total of 10 worksheets in student folders each period (2 per subject). Productivity was the number of worksheets with appropriate pencil marks on at least 90% of the sheet's items. Percent maximum gain in learning production was the number of sheets with appropriate pencil marks divided by 10.

Procedures

Individualized instruction on use of the self-regulation card occurred from 9:00 to 9:20 a.m. daily when students were at their workstations. It included a baseline, teacher-directed instruction, student-directed instruction, and a second baseline. During the 10:40 to 11:10 a.m. writing periods that also occurred daily, the teacher provided group instruction from 11:00 to 11:10 a.m. on use of the self-regulation card. During those periods, students sat in a semicircle in front of the teacher as she demonstrated how to complete the card with the following instructions.

> The first thing you need to do is write your name at the top of your self-record card. Then go through and circle the subjects you want to work today. After you circle your subjects, open your folders, look at the worksheets, and choose how many worksheets you want to complete in each subject and write this number next to the line "What I will do." When you have finished your work you must go back and fill in the number of worksheets you completed next to the line "What I Did." If you did exactly what you wrote you were going to do, circle "Yes" under the completed assignment section. If you did not, for example, if the number next to the line "What I Did" does not match the number next to the line "What I Will Do," you must circle "No" under the completed assignments section.

Daily 11:10 to 11:30 a.m. independent work sessions followed. The teacher introduced them saying, "It is time for work stations. Go do what you need to do." The students went to their work-station areas and worked on their own for 20 minutes. For 3 days a week they worked at work stations in the classroom and for 2 days a week they worked at their work stations in the observation room. During this period, students were free to complete their self-regulation card to work on math, reading, science, social studies, and writing, or to spend time coloring or playing with sticker books also available. When they needed assistance, they raised their hand and the teacher or an aide provided help at their work stations. Students were also free to sharpen pencils and go to the bathroom as needed. After 20 minutes, the teacher said, "Work stations are over. Do what you need to do." Then she collected work-station materials and prepared self-regulation cards and new worksheets and arranged the folders for the next day's session.

Reliability

Two teacher assistants independently recorded the number of correct responses to the self-regulation card during the 9:00 and 11:10 a.m. sessions, and the number of completed worksheets and on-task behaviors during the 11:10 a.m. independent work sessions. The reliability checks were distributed equally across 50% of the 75 session days of Experiment 1 and across 50% of the 26 session days of Experiment 2.

For Experiment 1, the average percent agreement between the teacher and teacher assistant was 95% for data collected on the number of correct self-regulation responses emitted during the 9:00 a.m. instructional sessions and 94% for data collected on the number of correct self-regulation responses emitted during the 11:10 a.m. independent work sessions. The average agreement for data collected during the 11:10 a.m. independent work sessions was 85% for the number of worksheets they completed and 85% for the number of on-task behaviors that were observed.

For Experiment 2, the average agreement between the teacher and assistant was 98% for data collected on the number of correct self-regulation responses emitted during 9:00 a.m. instruction and 98% for data collected on the number of correct self-regulation responses emitted during the 11:10 a.m. independent work sessions. The average agreement for data collected during the 11:10 a.m. independent work sessions was 95% for the number worksheets they completed and 98% for the number of on-task behaviors that were observed.

EXPERIMENT 1

Procedures

The experimental design was a multiple baseline across subjects with a reversal. For four students, the 9:00–9:20 a.m. instructional sequence was baseline, teacher-directed instruction, student-directed instruction, and baseline. For two students the sequence was baseline, teacher-directed instruction, and then a baseline.

Baseline.   During the 9:00 to 9:20 a.m. baseline conditions, students sat at their work stations and worked on their own. The teacher commenced these sessions with the statement, "Okay, now it is time for work stations. Go do what you need to do." She introduced the 11:10 a.m. independent work sessions with the same instruction. During both periods, students had access to their packets of subject folders, worksheets, and self-regulation cards, but they received no instructions or reinforcement for working on them.

Teacher-Directed Instruction.   When this 9:00 to 9:20 a.m. condition was in effect, the teacher provided instruction on use of the self-regulation card by completing it with students individually. She chose subjects for students to work by circling the subject pictures on the self-regulation card and assigned work by writing the number of assignments to be completed for each circled subject. She varied her assignments between 0, 1, and 2 worksheets per subject, averaging one assigned worksheet per subject per day for the condition. Then she instructed students to work for 15 minutes. After students finished work, she asked them how many assignments they completed, and then showed them how to indicate their answer by writing the number of worksheets they completed for each subject in the "What I Did" column. Next, she asked if they met their goal for each subject, and showed them how to compare the number assigned in the "What I Will Do" column with the number recorded in the "What I Did" column. If the numbers matched, she demonstrated that answer by circling a *Yes* in the "Completed Assignments" column. If the numbers did not match, she demonstrated the correct response for that comparison by circling a *No* in the "Completed Assignments" column. Finally, the teacher provided a reinforcement opportunity for each circled *Yes*. She presented the prize box and allowed students to select one item for each circled *Yes*. Throughout the condition, the teacher provided praise for correct responses to questions about how to complete the self-regulation card and correction procedures for incorrect answers.

Student-Directed Instruction.   During a third 9:00 to 9:20 a.m. condition, the teacher instructed students individually to circle the picture of the subjects they wanted to work and to write the number of worksheets they planned to complete for each subject in the "What I Will Do" column. After they finished work, she instructed them to record the number of worksheets they completed for each subject in the "What I Did" column, and to compare that number with the number they assigned themselves in the "What I Will Do" column. Then she instructed them to circle a *Yes* if the numbers matched and a *No* if they did not in the "Completed Assignments" column. Finally, the teacher provided reinforcement opportunities for every correctly circled *Yes*. She presented the prize box and students selected an item for each circled *Yes*. Throughout the condition, she provided praise for correct responses to the self-regulation card and correction procedures for incorrect responses.

Independent Work Sessions.   During the 11:10 a.m. sessions that followed the 9:00 a.m. instructional sessions, students worked alone at their stations. They were free to complete the self-regulation card and work their worksheets as they wished. Neither the teacher nor teacher assistants gave directions or reinforcement for completed work.

RESULTS

The results indicate that the changes during the 9:00 a.m. instruction on use of the self-regulation card had an effect on self-regulation during 11:10 a.m. independent work. They indicate that for Alice, Bob, and Don, student-directed instruction had a greater effect on correct self-regulation during independent work than did teacher-directed instruction. The results for Carter, Edward, and Fred were insufficient to draw this conclusion. Carter's correct self-regulation during independent work increased after the 9:00 a.m. teacher-directed instruction had been in effect for 18 days and then maintained throughout student-directed instruction. Edward and Fred's correct self-regulation increased precipitously when teacher-directed instruction was introduced following the 9:00 a.m. baseline. These two students never experienced student-directed instruction.

For Alice, the averages were 0.0 when the 9:00 a.m. baseline was in effect, 0.0 when teacher-directed instruction was in effect, 2.7 when student-directed instruction was in effect, and 2.4 when the second baseline was in effect. Bob's averages were 0.0, 0.0, 3.4, and 2.0 for the same sequence. Carter's averages were 0.0, 0.6, 4.7, and 2.5. Don's averages were 0.0, 0.0, 4.5, and 0.8. Edward's 11:10 a.m. averages when the three-condition sequence was in effect at 9:00 a.m. were 0.6 during the baseline, 5.0 during teacher-directed instruction, and 3.4 during the second baseline. Fred's 11:10 a.m. averages when the same sequence was in effect at 9:00 a.m. were 0.2, 3.8, and 0.5.

Still, the results support the prescription derived from self-determined learning theory, that when teachers improve learning opportunities and adjustment capabilities, they self-engage to maximize learning. Self-regulated engagement was more frequent when independent work followed student-directed instruction than when it followed teacher-directed instruction, which supports the claim that optimal opportunities tend to increase self-engagement. The other claims, that increased self-engagement tends to improve adjustments, which in turn increase gain, were supported, too.

Table 9.1 presents these data. It shows that when student-directed instruction preceded independent work, group averages for self-regulated engagement, the adaptability of expectations (goals set), rationality of

TABLE 9.1

Mean Levels of Self-Regulated Engagement, Self-Regulation, Optimal Adjustments, and Gain Maximization During Independent Work Following Baselines, Teacher-Directed Instruction, and Student-Directed Instruction

Self-Determined Learning Variables	Indicators for Self-Regulation, Adjustment Optimality, and Gain Maximization	Predicted Optimality of Opportunity When Students Learned to Use Self-Regulation Card Prior to Independent Work			
		Suboptimal, Baseline	Suboptimal, Teacher-Directed Instruction	Optimal, Student-Directed Instruction[a]	Suboptimal, Baseline
Self-regulated engagement during independent work	Correct self-regulation responses	.03	1.47	3.80	1.9
Adaptability of expectations during independent work	Percent optimal of goals set	.01	.47	.63	.86
Rationality of choice making during independent work	Percent optimal of self-monitoring and self-evaluation	.03	.35	.79	.48
Efficiency of actions during independent work	Percent optimal of on-task behavior	.63	.78	.80	.66
Success of results during independent work	Percent optimal of work completed equaling goals set	.08	.46	.76	.64
Adjustment optimality during independent work	Optimality of expectations × optimality of choices × optimality of actions × optimality of results	.00	.06	.30	.17
Maximization of gain during independent work	Percent of worksheets completed	.50	.57	.71	.55

[a]Data based on the four students who experienced student-directed instruction: Alice, Bob, Carter, and Don.

choices, the efficiency of work, and the optimality of results were highest. This, in turn, yielded the highest adjustment optimality (30% of optimal) and the highest gain (71% of maximum). In other words, when students received an optimal learning opportunity prior to their independent work and when they regulated their expectations, choices, actions, and results by correctly using the self-regulation card, their self-engagement, adjustments, and work completion levels increased during independent work. And when that opportunity condition was discontinued prior to independent work, self-engagement, adjustments, and work completion levels decreased.

The exceptions to this group finding were Carter, who improved in the last two sessions of teacher-directed instruction, and Edward and Fred, who never experienced student-directed instruction at all. So even though the averages in Table 9.1 are consistent with the claims of self-determined learning theory, some of the individual data are not. We conducted a second experiment with a more robust experimental design to test these predictions again.

EXPERIMENT 2

This experiment provided additional data on the comparative effects of teacher- and student-directed instruction on students' independent work. Four students who participated in Experiment 1 were available for this experiment, which was conducted during the summer session of the academic year that ended with Experiment 1. A 1-week vacation period separated the experiments.

Participants and Setting

Alice, Bob, Carter, and Edward participated in this experiment, which took place in the same classroom used for Experiment 1. In that experiment, Alice and Bob exhibited a greater independent work effect when 9:00 a.m. instruction was student-directed than when it was teacher-directed, but Carter and Edward did not. Carter's responses were insufficient to compare the two conditions, and Edward only received teacher-directed instruction.

Procedure

The instructional interventions were administered in a multiple baseline with reversal design across two student pairs who experienced alternate sequences of teacher- and student-directed instruction. One sequence was baseline, teacher-directed instruction, student-directed instruction, and baseline, and the other sequence was baseline, student-directed instruction, teacher-directed instruction, and baseline. Alice and Carter received the first sequence, and Bob and Edward received the second sequence. All other procedures were the same as those used in Experiment 1. Students received training on the self-regulation card from 9:00 to 9:20 a.m. They received group instruction on its use during the 11:00 to 11:10 a.m. period. And they worked alone at their work stations during the 11:10 to 11:30 a.m. independent work sessions.

RESULTS

Table 9.2 presents results for the 11:10 a.m. independent work sessions when these two instructional sequences were in effect. For all students, correct self-regulation responses during the 11:10 a.m. sessions were higher with student-directed instruction in effect at 9:00 a.m. than with teacher-directed instruction in effect at that time. Carter's 11:10 a.m. averages were 1.3 during baseline, 1.0 during teacher-directed instruction, 4.8 during student-directed instruction, and 1.7 during the second baseline. Alice's 11:10 a.m. averages for the same sequence were 0.2, 0.8, 4.2, and 0.0. Bob's 11:10 a.m. averages for the alternated instructional sequence were 1.0 during baseline, 4.8 during student-directed instruction, 0.6 during teacher-directed instruction, and 0.4 during the final baseline. Edward's 11:10 a.m. averages for the same sequence were 3.0, 4.8, 4.2, and 3.0.

These results are consistent with the main finding of Experiment 1 that the optimality of the learning opportunities provided during 9:00 a.m. instruction affected the level and type of engagement that occurred during the 11:10 a.m. independent work sessions. When opportunities were optimal from the students' point of view — when they allowed students to choose what and how much to do — self-regulated engagement persisted during independent work, which is consistent with Proposition 1 of self-determined learning theory, that optimal opportunities increase self-regulated engagement.

The results are also consistent with Proposition 2 of the theory, which claims increased self-engagement leads to improved expectations, choices, actions, and results, and with Proposition 3 claiming that this in turn improves adjustments and maximizes gain. Table 9.2 summarizes these results for the four students. The averages for correct self-regulation, adaptability of expectations, rationality of choices, efficiency of work, and success of results were highest when independent work followed student-directed instruction. These sessions also yielded the highest adjustment

TABLE 9.2

Mean Level of Self-Regulated Engagement, Self-Regulation, Optimal Adjustments, and Gain Maximization During Independent Work Following Baselines, Teacher-Directed Instruction, and Student-Directed Instruction

Self-Determined Learning Variables	Indicators for Self-Regulation, Adjustment Optimality, and Gain Maximization	Predicted Optimality of Opportunity When Students Learned to Use Self-Regulation Card Prior to Independent Work			
		Suboptimal, Baseline	Suboptimal, Teacher-Directed Instruction	Optimal, Student-Directed Instruction	Suboptimal, Baseline
Self-regulated engagement during independent work	Correct self-regulation responses	1.37	1.15	4.65	1.28
Adaptability of expectations during independent work	Percent optimal of goals set	.84	.86	.89	.85
Rationality of choice making during independent work	Percent optimal of self-monitoring and self-evaluation	.33	.41	.92	.30
Efficiency of actions during independent work	Percent optimal of on-task behaviors	.72	.84	.90	.67
Success of results during independent work	Percent optimal of work completed equal-ing goals set	.76	.56	.84	.55
Adjustment optimality during independent work	Optimality of expectations × optimality of choices × optimality of actions × optimality of results	.15	.16	.62	.09
Maximization of gain during independent work	Percent of all worksheets completed	.62	.64	.71	.49

optimality (62% of optimal) and the highest gain (71% of maximum). As in Experiment 1, these levels decreased in the final baseline when independent work no longer followed student-directed instruction.

DISCUSSION

This study, like the one reported in chapter 8, supports the claim that optimal opportunities and adjustments maximize learning. When students are motivated by an optimal opportunity to learn something new and when they know how to set expectations, make choices, take action, and monitor progress toward their expectations, their self-regulation improves as their adjustments optimize to maximize learning. The study demonstrated these relationships by employing a behavioral design to compare different choice opportunity effects on students' self-regulation during independent work. The results were consistent with the prescription posed at the beginning of the chapter. Teachers can increase self-engagement and learning by giving students a choice of learning goals, giving them a method for regulating their expectations, choices, actions, and results to meet those goals, and reinforcing them for meeting those goals exactly.

There is of course an alternative explanation for these findings, which is that students received more reinforcers during student-directed instruction and the amount of reinforcers received during that condition produced the generalized use of the self-regulation card during independent work. But this did not occur. In fact, students received slightly more reinforcers during teacher-directed instruction than during student-directed instruction. Table 9.3 presents these data showing the average reinforcements per day during the three conditions. Note that although reinforcement levels were roughly constant across conditions, self-regulation, adjustments, and learning maximization were not. They were substantially higher during student-directed instruction than during teacher-directed instruction.

Also, reinforcement for matches between goals set and work completed was probably necessary but not sufficient for generalization to occur during independent work. This is because the contingency was in place for teacher-directed instruction but did not produce the generalization effect. Only when it was paired with student-directed instruction did robust generalization effects on self-regulated engagement occur. Based on this, we conclude that when students are encouraged (reinforced) to do what they say they will do and when they know how to self-regulate during independent work, their engagement is likely to persist, their adjustments

TABLE 9.3
Mean Reinforcements During Instruction and Mean Levels of Optimal
Adjustment and Gain Maximization During the Independent Work That
Followed Baselines and Teacher- and Student-Directed Instruction

Experiment	Parameter	Baseline	Teacher-Directed Instruction	Student-Directed Instruction[a]	Baseline
Experiment 1	Reinforcements/student during instruction	0	4.9	4.7	0
n = 6	Percent of optimal adjustment	0%	6%	30%	17%
	Percent of maximum gain	50%	57%	71%	55%
Experiment 2	Reinforcements/student during instruction	0	5.0	4.6	0
n = 4	Percent optimal adjustment	15%	16%	62%	9%
	Percent maximum gain	62%	64%	71%	49%

[a]During Experiment 1 these data were based on the four students who experienced student-directed instruction: Alice, Bob, Carter, and Don. During Experiment 2 these data were based on Alice, Bob, Carter, and Edward.

are likely to optimize, and their learning is likely to maximize. Hence we recommend revising Prescription 1 as follows:

To increase self-engagement and learning, give students a choice of their learning goals, a method for regulating their expectations, choices, actions, and results to meet those goals, *and then reward them for meeting their goals.*

REFERENCES

Dickerson, E. A., & Creedon, C. F. (1981). Self-selection of standards by children: The relative effectiveness of pupil-selected and teacher-selected standards of performance. *Journal of Applied Behavior Analysis, 14,* 425–433.

Fantuzzo, J. W., & Clement, P. W. (1981). Generalization of the effects of teacher and self-administered token reinforcers to nontreated students. *Journal of Applied Behavior Analysis 14,* 435–447.

Fantuzzo, J. W., Polite, K., Cook, D. M., & Quinn, G. (1988). An evaluation of the effectiveness of teacher- vs. student-management classroom interventions. *Psychology in the Schools, 25,* 154–163.

Fisher, W. W., Thompson, R. H., Piazza, C. C., Crosland, K., and Gotjen, D. (1997). On the relative reinforcing effects of choice and differential consequences. *Journal of Applied Behavior Analysis, 30*(3), 423–438.

Gettinger, M. (1985). Effects of teacher-directed versus student-directed instruction and cues versus no cues for improving spelling performance. *Journal of Applied Behavior Analysis, 18*(2), 167–171.

Lovitt, T. C., & Curtiss, K. A. (1969). Academic response rate as a function of teacher and self-imposed contingencies. *Journal of Applied Behavior Analysis, 2,* 49–53.

Mithaug, D. K. (1998). *The generalization effects of choice contingencies on the self-regulated work behavior of young children with behavior disorders.* Unpublished doctoral dissertation, Teachers College, Columbia University, New York.

Parsons, M. B., Reid, D. H., Reynolds, J., & Bumgarner, M. (1990). Effects of chosen vs. assigned jobs on the work behavior of persons with severe handicaps. *Journal of Applied Behavior Analysis, 23,* 253–258.

Stevenson, H. C., & Fantuzzo, J. W. (1984). Application of the "generalization map" to a self-control intervention with school-aged children. *Journal of Applied Behavior Analysis, 17,* 203–212.

Stevenson, H. C., & Fantuzzo, J. W. (1986). The generality of social validity of a competency-based self-control training intervention for underachieving students. *Journal of Applied Behavior Analysis, 19,* 269–276.

10

The Effects of Problem-Solving Instruction on the Self-Determined Learning of Secondary Students With Disabilities

Michael L. Wehmeyer
Martin Agran
Susan B. Palmer
James E. Martin
Dennis E. Mithaug

Although the findings in chapter 9 were consistent with the claim that improvements in opportunities and self-regulatory capacities optimize adjustments and maximize learning during independent work, they did not show how the same conditions promote discovery learning, too. In this chapter we present an instructional model to show this effect. The model presents self-regulation problems that students can solve by reducing the discrepancy between what they know and what they want to know. It contrasts the approach of chapter 9, which encouraged students with disabilities to reduce the discrepancy between what they expected to accomplish during independent work and what they actually accomplished. Both problems are similar nonetheless in that they deal with discrepancies between goal-state expectations and actual-state circumstances.

In chapter 8, students solved these problems by regulating their expectations, choices, actions, and results to reduce the discrepancy between the points expected and points produced; they succeeded to the extent that the points they produced equaled the points they expected. In this chapter, students solve a similar problem by regulating their expectations, choices, actions, and results to reduce the discrepancy between the knowledge they have and the knowledge they want to have. Hence, they also succeed to the extent that the knowledge they acquire equals the knowledge they want to acquire. In both cases the adjustments required to learn depend on the student's ability to self-regulate in order to meet their self-set goals (Mithaug, 1993). We call this self-direction to learn something new *discovery learning*, and we show that students engage it when they are motivated to regulate their expectations, choices, actions, and results to discover what they don't know. The following prescription reflects this instructional approach.

> Prescription 2: To increase discovery learning, teach students to regulate their problem solving to learn what they want to know.

DISCOVERY LEARNING

As discussed in chapter 2, Newell and Simon (1972) provided the foundation for understanding how actors regulate their problem solving to produce new information about unknown circumstances. They tracked the behavior of adult problem solvers who tackled difficult problems of not knowing something. They discovered those learners used a similar strategy to move from an actual state of not knowing something to a goal state of knowing it. This research also showed how interactions between the unknown circumstance and the subjects' self-regulated problem solving incrementally improved their knowledge of the circumstance at the same time as it improved their regulatory capacity to learn from it.

These findings are consistent with self-determined learning theory, which predicts that optimal opportunities and adjustments interact to sustain the self-regulation needed to maximize learning. As learners act on opportunities to learn something they don't know, they alter the optimality of those circumstances and hence make them slightly more favorable for subsequent self-regulated problem solving. This in turn improves their prospects for attempting more learning. The effects of this optimization of circumstances are sustained engagement, repeated adjustment, and maximized learning, as predicted by the theory.

Newell and Simon identified a strategy used in self-regulated problem solving by observing subjects as they thought aloud to solve various problems of not knowing something. They discovered that subjects used the same four-step strategy. First, they identified the discrepancy between the goal state, which was what they wanted to know, and the actual state, which was what they knew. Second, they found an operator to reduce the discrepancy (a procedure that would get them the information they needed). Third, they used that operator to reduce the discrepancy (they acted on that information to solve the problem). Last, they returned to the first step to determine whether the discrepancy was still present and repeated the other steps if it was. When the discrepancy was eliminated, the actual state equaled the goal state and they knew what they wanted to know. Newell and Simon validated the approach by programming a computer to do the same thing, which it did to solve complex problems in chess, memory, learning problems, physics, engineering, education, rule induction, concept formation, perception, and understanding. Simon (1989) described the problem-solving strategy used by the General Problem Solving (GPS) program as follows:

> A problem is defined for GPS by giving it a starting situation and a goal situation (or a test for determining whether the goal has been reached), together with a set of operators that may be used, separately or severally, to transform the starting situation into the goal situation by a sequence of successive applications. Means–ends analysis is the technique used by GPS to decide which operator to apply next:
>
> 1. It compares current situation with goal situation to detect one or more differences between them.
> 2. It retrieves from memory an operator that is associated with the difference it has found (i.e., an operator that has the usual effect of reducing differences of this kind).
> 3. It applies the operator or, if it is not applicable to the current situation, sets up the new goal of creating the conditions that will make it applicable. (p. 36)

The program repeated these steps until the actual state equaled the goal state and the problem was solved. In this sense, then, the GPS program regulated its problem solving using the means–ends strategy similar to the one Newell and Simon (1972) used to get a boy to nursery school. That example also showed how the learning challenge (the opportunity) improved incrementally as Newell moved through the means–ends chain. By step 4, the opportunity was optimal enough to act, which Newell did by calling the repair shop to have a new battery installed in his car. This got him to step 5 and a problem he could solve by driving his son to school.

This illustrates how self-regulated problem solving interacts with circumstances to improve situations and adjustments incrementally until actual states equal goal states. As Newell moved through the means–ends chain, his adjustments improved, as did his chances of producing the goal state: his son at nursery school. By that stage in the process, the suboptimal opportunity of step 1 was now the optimal opportunity of step 5, and Newell could drive his son to school.

Note also that the motivation to problem solve always emanated from a discrepancy between what was wanted and what existed, an inconsistency between an actual state and goal state. Newell's expectation to use his car was inconsistent with the circumstances of having a working car (step 1). This motivated him to construct the next link (step) in the chain, where he discovered yet another discrepancy, his expectation to replace the car's battery with a new one which was discrepant with the actual circumstances of having a battery on hand to replace the dead one (step 2). This motivated him to create another link, where he discovered that his expectation that a repair shop would replace the dead battery was discrepant with the fact that the repair shop was unaware of what he wanted done (step 3). Finally, in step 4 Newell identified a discrepancy he could act on and eliminate, which he did. He called the repair shop to have a new battery installed, which solved this problem and made his circumstances optimal for getting his son to school (step 5). Then he acted on this optimal opportunity by driving his son to school.

This is how discovery learners construct discrepancy conditions (how they define problems) that motivate them to persist in their engagement until they discover what they want to know. Like Newell, they define problems of not knowing something based on *their* expectations and circumstances. Then they search for a means of getting that knowledge and in the process revise and adjust their expectations, choices, and actions until they get results that match their expectations. Discovery learning is the adjusting of expectations, choices, actions, and results in these means–ends sequences leading from what learners know to what they want to know. Each step in these sequences generates new learning, as does the final step that yields the discovery of what they want to know.

ENCOURAGING DISCOVERY LEARNING

This chapter describes the Self-Determined Learning Model of Instruction, which was designed to provoke students with disabilities to learn through discovery and, in so doing, become causal agents in their lives (Mithaug, Wehmeyer, Agran, Martin, & Palmer, 1998; Wehmeyer, Palmer, Agran, Mithaug, & Martin, 2000). Both optimality factors—choice opportunity and self-regulated adjustment—are incorporated in the model's three phases, which are presented in Figs. 10.1–10.3. Each phase poses a problem for students to solve, and a series of questions for them to answer in order to solve it. Although the questions vary, they always comprise the basic steps of self-regulated problem solving. Figure 10.1 depicts the first phase ("Set a Goal"), which provokes students to answer the question "What is my goal?" and then to define a discrepancy between what they know and what they want to know. The questions posed in this phase provoke students to find something they can do to discover what they want to know. The last question in that first phase, "What can I do to make this happen?," provokes students into setting a goal to do something to get the information they need. Figure 10.2 depicts the second phase of the

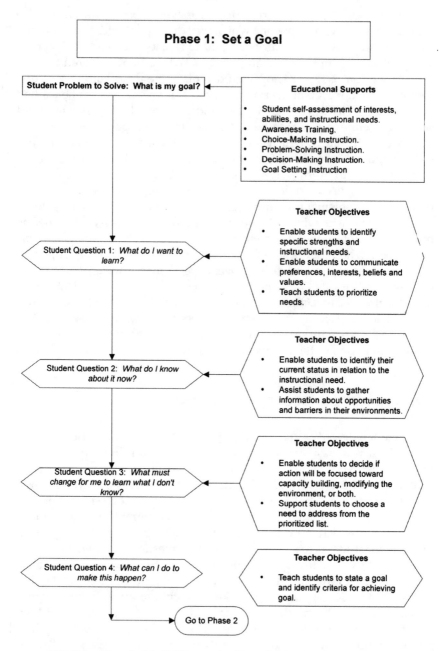

Phase 1: Set a Goal

Student Problem to Solve: What is my goal?

Educational Supports

- Student self-assessment of interests, abilities, and instructional needs.
- Awareness Training.
- Choice-Making Instruction.
- Problem-Solving Instruction.
- Decision-Making Instruction.
- Goal Setting Instruction

Student Question 1: *What do I want to learn?*

Teacher Objectives

- Enable students to identify specific strengths and instructional needs.
- Enable students to communicate preferences, interests, beliefs and values.
- Teach students to prioritize needs.

Student Question 2: *What do I know about it now?*

Teacher Objectives

- Enable students to identify their current status in relation to the instructional need.
- Assist students to gather information about opportunities and barriers in their environments.

Student Question 3: *What must change for me to learn what I don't know?*

Teacher Objectives

- Enable students to decide if action will be focused toward capacity building, modifying the environment, or both.
- Support students to choose a need to address from the prioritized list.

Student Question 4: *What can I do to make this happen?*

Teacher Objectives

- Teach students to state a goal and identify criteria for achieving goal.

Go to Phase 2

FIG. 10.1.   Phase 1 of the Self-Determined Learning Model of Instruction.

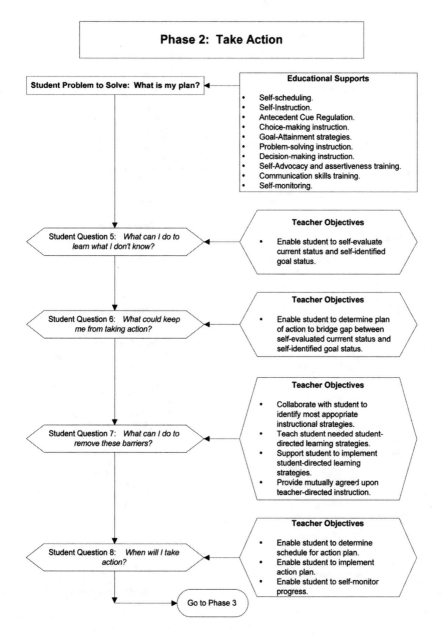

FIG. 10.2. Phase 2 of the Self-Determined Learning Model of Instruction.

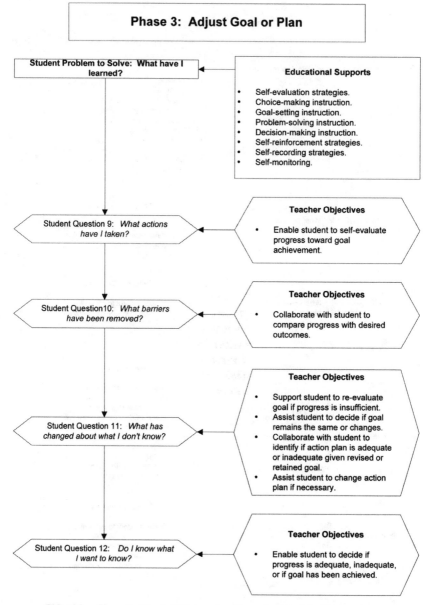

Phase 3: Adjust Goal or Plan

Student Problem to Solve: What have I learned?

Educational Supports

- Self-evaluation strategies.
- Choice-making instruction.
- Goal-setting instruction.
- Problem-solving instruction.
- Decision-making instruction.
- Self-reinforcement strategies.
- Self-recording strategies.
- Self-monitoring.

Student Question 9: *What actions have I taken?*

Teacher Objectives

- Enable student to self-evaluate progress toward goal achievement.

Student Question10: *What barriers have been removed?*

Teacher Objectives

- Collaborate with student to compare progress with desired outcomes.

Student Question 11: *What has changed about what I don't know?*

Teacher Objectives

- Support student to re-evaluate goal if progress is insufficient.
- Assist student to decide if goal remains the same or changes.
- Collaborate with student to identify if action plan is adequate or inadequate given revised or retained goal.
- Assist student to change action plan if necessary.

Student Question 12: *Do I know what I want to know?*

Teacher Objectives

- Enable student to decide if progress is adequate, inadequate, or if goal has been achieved.

FIG. 10.3.   Phase 3 of the Self-Determined Learning Model of Instruction.

model, which solves the problem of knowing how to solve the problem. The question "What is my plan?" provokes students into defining the discrepancy between the action that is necessary to find what they need to know and the action they are capable of taking. This stage in discovery ends with a plan of action reflecting that capability: "When will I take this action?" Figure 10.3 depicts the third and final phase of the model, where a student asks "What have I learned?" and then defines the discrepancy between plans and actions taken on the one hand and what the student expected to learn and actually learned on the other. Here the students are provoked into solving problems that may still be preventing them from getting the information they need or want. Answering these questions may direct them back to phase 2, where they identify new actions to remove obstacles, or take them back to phase 1, where they update the discrepancy between what they want to know and what they know, which may require additional searches and hence continued engagement.

The purpose of the Student Questions is to provoke discussions between teachers and students about how students might solve problems of not knowing something. The Teacher's Objectives in the model guide teachers in providing assistance. The Educational Supports, which are not part of the model per se, identify instructional strategies and educational supports that are likely to help students regulate their problem solving. These methods and tactics come from self-management research, which has proved effective in assisting students with and without disabilities regulate their learning in various settings.

RESEARCH ON THE SELF-DETERMINED LEARNING MODEL OF INSTRUCTION

We tested the model with teachers of elementary (Palmer & Wehmeyer, 2001) and secondary students with disabilities (Agran, Blanchard, & Wehmeyer, 2000; Wehmeyer et al., 2000). This section reviews some of those studies.

Study 1

In one study, Wehmeyer et al. (2000) conducted a field test with 21 teachers and their adolescent students with disabilities who received services in Texas and Wisconsin. Each teacher identified several students to receive instruction using the model. In total, 40 students with mental retardation, learning disabilities, or emotional/behavioral disorders participated. During the model's phase 1 of instruction, the test group selected a total of 43 goals, with three students choosing two goals each. Of this total,

10 goals focused on social skills and knowledge, 13 on such behaviors as compliance to rules, self-control, and adaptive learning, and 20 goals related to academic skills.

The goal attainment efficacy of the students was examined using the Goal Attainment Scaling (GAS) process (Kiresuk & Lund, 1976). This approach has been used with students receiving special education services and, according to Carr (1979), "involves establishing goals and specifying a range of outcomes or behaviors that would indicate progress toward achieving those goals" (p. 89). In this study, GAS scores were attached to each goal identified by students. This was done by having teachers identify five goal attainment outcomes, which ranged from being most favorable to being most unfavorable for attainment. The midpoint of that range was the outcome that teachers considered satisfactory. The other outcome possibilities were assigned values from −2 to +2, from that 0 midpoint.

On completing an instructional activity, teachers used the scale to assess the level of students' goal attainment. They selected an outcome value on the scale for the goal that matched the student's achievement level. These goal rating data were then analyzed using a raw-score conversion key for Goal Attainment Scaling developed by Cardillo (1994). Then raw scores were converted to standardized T-scores (Kiresuk & Lund, 1976), which had a mean of 50 and a standard deviation of 10. This transformation allowed goal attainment comparisons across different subject matter. A T-score value of 50 was an acceptable outcome level in that it was consistent with teacher expectations for achievement in that subject area. Standardized scores of 40 or below were below that expected outcome and scores of 60 and higher were above teacher expectations. GAS scores for students who worked more than one subject area were the averages of the standardized scores for the subject areas covered. Pre- and posttest scores were also collected on students' self-determination using the Arc's Self-Determination Scale (Wehmeyer, 1996), on students' locus of control, and on student reports of their self-regulation using the AIR Self-Determination Scale (Wolman, Campeau, Dubois, Mithaug, & Stolarski, 1994). The six self-regulation items taken from the AIR scale are presented in Table 10.1.

Self-Regulation.   As indicated in Fig. 10.4, there were significant increases in students' self-regulation effectiveness from pre- to posttest sessions. Those increases included goals setting (adaptable expectations), planning, self-monitoring, self-evaluating (rational choosing), and school engagement (efficient action).

Control.   There were also significant differences between pre- and posttest scores on the Arc's Self-Determination Scale and on the locus of control measure. The postintervention scores were significantly higher

TABLE 10.1
Questions Comprising the Self-Regulation Questionnaire

Do you have any interests right now?
Do you have any goals right now?
Do you have any plans for meeting the goal you mentioned?
Do you know when you will meet your goal?
Have you thought about whether your plans are working or not?
Do you have ways at school to reach your goal?

than preintervention scores on both measures. This is consistent with proposition 3 of self-determined learning theory, which claims increased self-regulated engagement will result in a greater sense of control over learning. It is also consistent with the claim that greater control over learning improves prospects for self-determination.

Learning. The field test also showed the model to be effective in provoking students to meet their goals. The mean GAS score for the sample was 49. Twenty-five percent (25%) of the standardized GAS scores equaled 50, and 30% were higher than that, which means that 25% of the goals met teachers expectations for achievement whereas 30% of the goals exceeded expectations. Of the remainder, slightly more than 25% of the GAS scores were between 40 and 49, indicating that they did not meet teacher expectations. In about 20% of the goals, there was no progress.

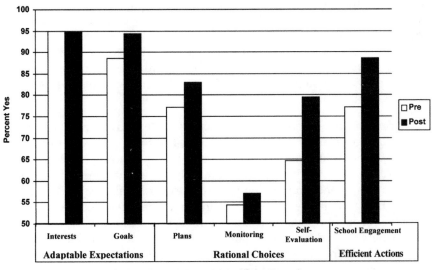

FIG. 10.4. Responses from self-regulation questionnaire.

Study 2

Agran et al. (2000) used the Self-Determined Learning Model of Instruction for students with moderate to severe disabilities. In this study, 19 adolescents received the instruction prescribed by the model in a delayed multiple-baseline across-group design. Students collaborated with their teachers in the first phase of the model to identify their goals, which covered work, social, academic, and community living skills. One student who was visually impaired had a goal to call a bus service, to schedule appointments, and then to be transported to different locations in the community, and another student wanted to learn how to monitor his blood sugar level. Prior to implementing phase 2, teachers and researchers collected baseline data on student progress toward their goals. At staggered intervals following baseline, teachers implemented the model. Data were also collected on goal attainment using the GAS procedure. At the conclusion of the training period, teachers were asked to report details of student progress. Additional data were obtained on responses to worksheets developed to assist implementation of the model. Students responded to these questions: "What has changed?" "Did I do what I said I would do?" "What do I like about it?" Additionally, anecdotal information from students was collected.

Results were positive for all but 2 of the participants. For 17 students, learning gained from baseline to intervention and maintained at high levels thereafter. Also, 12 of the 19 students provided feedback on the model. All of these students indicated that the model helped increase their skills and independence, and 5 students indicated it improved their confidence. This group also reported that they did what they said they would do and that they liked this method of instruction. The reasons given were that they liked problem solving, enjoyed talking with their teachers about themselves, liked making choices, and liked learning skills that were based on those choices.

Sense of Control. Four of the six teachers in the study completed a social validation form for 13 of the students. The forms allowed them to identify factors that helped students complete the three phases of the model. All of these teachers indicated that their students enjoyed the approach, that students were willing to work toward their goals, that they enjoyed being in charge of their learning, and that they liked being responsible for making decisions and taking actions. One teacher thought that teachers should be able to talk with students about the skills they needed to learn in order to promote their self-determination in community employment and adult living. Another teacher suggested that there be time allocated to helping students set goals, as this was difficult for some.

Learning. Again, the students showed that they could reach their goals through problem solving. The mean GAS score for the sample was 60, indicating that on average students exceeded their teachers' expectations for goal attainment. Twenty-one percent (21%) of the standardized GAS scores were 50, indicating that students attained a satisfactory level of achievement. And 68% were higher than 50, indicating that two-thirds of the students exceeded teachers' expectations. Only two students failed to make progress on goals, which meant that 89% of the participants met or exceeded their teachers' expectations.

These finding are consistent with results reported McGlashing, Agran, Sitlington, Cavin, and Wehmeyer (2001), who taught four transition-age students with moderate to severe mental retardation to use a self-regulated problem-solving procedure to enhance their vocational competence. Also, Agran, Cavin, and Wehmeyer (2001) taught three students with mild to moderate learning disabilities who were employed at Pizza Hut and WalMart to use a problem-solving strategy to enhance their job initiation, task completion, and task sequencing skills.

DISCUSSION

The model of instruction described in this chapter was designed to enable teachers to "teach" students to engage in self-regulated problem solving by associating their learning opportunities with their needs and interests and by encouraging goal setting, choice making, action taking, and results monitoring to take advantage of those opportunities. According to self-determined learning theory, this approach was predicted to work because it optimizes opportunities and adjustments. The model guided instruction toward the optimizing of opportunities by connecting learning challenges to students' needs, interests, and choices, and it guided instruction toward optimizing adjustments by encouraging means–ends problem solving as students set expectations, made choices, took actions, and monitored results. Indeed, the test findings were consistent with the theory's predictions and prescriptions. Students became better self-regulators, they felt in control of their learning, and they learned from their self-regulated problem solving.

Unfortunately, most students never feel in control when learning something new. One reason, according to Mithaug (1993), is that these optimal experiences require matches between expectations and performance on the one hand and between learning demands and personal gain on the other. Recall our description from the first chapter of Carey, who never experienced the rewards of overcoming difficult challenges. The reason for her dim prospects was traced to her deficiencies in self-regulated problem solving. She could dream about what she might become when she grew up, but she never acted on her dreams. She never connected them to expectations and expectations to plans or actions. This was evident in how she set goals. She set them so high that no amount of planning or working could meet them, or she set them so low that any amount of planning and working would achieve them. Either way, she never had to alter what she expected, what she chose to do, or how she acted in order to get where she wanted to go. Her poor adjustments at school reflected those difficulties. So did her lack of self-determination.

In the studies reported in this chapter, students like Carey were well represented in that the study participants had a full range of disabilities and had little or no experience with discovery learning. But unlike Carey, these students received instruction on how to regulate their problem solving to discover what they did not know. As a result of this instruction they developed control over their adjustments, produced new learning, and had an enjoyable experience. Indeed, some of these students may have had experiences similar to those Csikszentmihalyi (1990) and others call optimal. Again, these optimal experiences come from gaining control over challenge, which these students defined for themselves when they set their own goals. The control was experienced when they met their own goals.

This raises the possibility that prospects for self-determination can be enhanced directly through similar instruction on problem solving to meet self-set goals. Indeed, we would expect that if students were allowed to choose any goal and then encouraged to solve problems related to its attainment, their prospects for self-determination would increase proportionately. The next chapter examines this possibility by determining whether instruction on self-regulated problem solving improves students' prospects for self-determination.

REFERENCES

Agran, M., Blanchard, C., & Wehmeyer, M. L. (2000). Promoting transition goals and self-determination through student-directed learning: The Self-Determined Learning Model of Instruction. *Education and Training in Mental Retardation and Developmental Disabilities, 35*, 351–364.

Agran, M., Cavin, M., & Wehmeyer, M. L. (2001). *The effects of self-determined learning model of instruction across varied competitive jobs.* Unpublished manuscript.

Cardillo, J. E. (1994). Summary score conversion key. In T. J. Kiresuk, A. Smith, & J. E. Cardillo (Eds.), *Goal attainment scaling: Applications, theory and measurement* (pp. 273–281). Hillsdale, NJ: Lawrence Erlbaum Associates.

Carr, R. W. (1979). Goal attainment scaling as a useful tool for evaluating progress in special education. *Exceptional Children, 46*, 88–95.

Csikzentmihalyi, M. (1990). *Flow: The psychology of optimal experience.* New York: Harper & Row.

Kiresuk, T. J., & Lund, S. H. (1976). Process and measurement using goal attainment scaling. In G. V. Glass (Ed.), *Education Studies Review Manual* (Vol. 1). Beverly Hills, CA: Sage.

McGlashing, J., Agran, M., Sitlington, P., Cavin, M., & Wehmeyer, M. L. (2001). *Enhancing the job performance of youth with moderate to severe cognitive disabilities using the self-determined learning model of instruction.* Unpublished manuscript.

Mithaug, D. E. (1993). *Self-regulation theory. How optimal adjustment maximizes gain.* Westport, CT: Praeger.

Mithaug, D., Wehmeyer, M. L., Agran, M., Martin, J., & Palmer, S. (1998). The self-determined learning model of instruction: Engaging students to solve their learning problems. In M. L. Wehmeyer & D. J. Sands (Eds.), *Making it happen: Student involvement in educational planning, decision-making and instruction* (pp. 299–328). Baltimore, MD: Paul H. Brookes.

Newell, A., & Simon, H. H. (1972). *Human problem solving.* Englewood Cliffs, NJ: Prentice Hall.

Palmer, S., & Wehmeyer, M. L. (2001). *Promoting self-determination in early elementary school: Teaching self-regulated problem-solving and goal setting skills.* Unpublished manuscript.

Simon, H. A. (1989). *Models of thought.* Englewood Cliffs, NJ: Prentice-Hall.

Wehmeyer, M. L. (1996). A self-report measure of self-determination for adolescents with cognitive disabilities. *Education and Training in Mental Retardation and Developmental Disabilities, 31,* 282–293.

Wehmeyer, M. L., Palmer, S., Agran, M., Mithaug, D. E., & Martin, J. (2000). Promoting causal agency: The Self-Determined Learning Model of Instruction. *Exceptional Children, 66,* 439–453.

Wolman, J., Campeau, P., Dubois, P., Mithaug, D., & Stolarski, V. (1994). *AIR self-determination scale and user guide.* Palo Alto, CA: American Institute for Research.

11

The Effects of Self-Regulated Problem-Solving Instruction on the Self-Determination of Secondary Students With Disabilities

MaryAnn Columbus
Dennis E. Mithaug

The studies reported in chapters 4–8 verified a premise of this book, that prospects for self-determination are different for low- and high-achieving students because of differences in their abilities to adjust to new opportunities. Students in special education consistently report lower prospects for self-determination than do students in general education because of their lower capacity to adjust to challenge. The chapter 4 study reported these differences in teacher and student reports on students' capacities and opportunities to self-determine. The chapter 5 study replicated this finding for adults with and without disabilities graduating from a community college. The study reported in chapter 6 found that students with disabilities who were enrolled in secondary schools in the Gambia, West Africa, also rated their capacities to self-determine lower than did students without disabilities enrolled in those schools. And the study in chapter 7 tested whether these differences were related to disability and found a significant disability effect when comparing capacities to self-determine of students with different sensory impairments.

Finally, the study reported in chapter 8 tested for differences in adjustment capability directly by using a computer simulation to measure students' self-regulated adjustments during different opportunity choice conditions. It found that students in special education were less effective self-regulators and hence less optimal adjusters than were students in general education. This difference held during both optimal and suboptimal opportunities to learn from the problems presented by the simulation.

The instructional prescription suggested by these findings was to improve students' adjustments as well as their opportunities for engagement and learning. Chapter 9 tested this prescription with a self-regulation card that improved students' adjustments and a student-directed instruction opportunity that provoked their engagement during independent work. Chapter 10 reported a similar effect through use of a combination of self-regulated problem solving and student choice of learning goals to increase discovery learning of students with disabilities.

Now we return to the original premise about lowered self-determination prospects for students with disabilities and ask whether the capacity-building interventions reported in the previous two chapters will improve their self-determination ratings too. After all, if students with disabilities rate their capacity to self-determine lower than other students because they believe they lack the capacity to self-regulate in order to adjust to get what they want, then an improvement in that capability through problem-solving instruction should improve their ratings. For this chapter, we tested this claim by teaching students to use self-regulated problem solving to meet their own goals. We tested prescription 3, that prospects for self-determination will improve if students learn to regulate their problem solving to meet goals that satisfy their needs and interests:

> Prescription 3: To improve prospects for self-determination, teach problem solving to meet goals that satisfy students' needs and interests.

PROBLEM SOLVING TO SELF-DETERMINE

The study described here was part of the dissertation research conducted by the first author (DeRobertis, 1997). The study included students who were at risk for lowered prospects for self-determination on several counts. First, the school they attended was located in an inner-city neighborhood. Second, the school was self-contained in that it only offered instruction for students with learning disabilities, mental retardation, and emotional disorders. Last, the students had histories of disengagement from learning.

Setting and Participants

The study took place in a special education vocational school for secondary students with disabilities. It was located in an inner-city neighborhood of a major urban center in the east. The first author served as the teacher of one of the school's life-skills program for the two semesters the study was in effect.

The 36 students who participated in the instructional component of the study were adolescents with learning disabilities, mild mental retardation, and emotional and behavioral disorders. The group consisted of 14 females and 22 males. Their average age was 18 years, with a range of 16.8 to 19.8 years. The ethnic backgrounds of the students included African American (21 students), Hispanic (13), Caucasian (1), and Haitian (1). The students' home languages included English (22), Spanish (13), and French (1). The reading levels of the students ranged from 1.0 to 4.5, with 25% of the students reading in the 1.0- to 1.4-range.

The 27 students who did not participate in the instructional component of the study served as a comparison group in that they provided pre- and posttest ratings on the AIR Self-Determination Scale. They consisted of 8 males and 19 females averaging 16.9 years of age, and ranging in age from 15.5 to 19 years. Their ethnic backgrounds included African American (15), Hispanic (10), Caucasian (1), and Cantonese (1). Reading levels were not available for this group.

Study Design

A comparison group design with multiple phases for the treated group was used to compare prospects for self-determination and improvements in problem solving with changes in the instructional intervention. The intervention was delivered in five phases over a period of 8 months that covered two semesters. The conditions included (a) a baseline of 6 days discussing famous people, (b) 8 days of instruction on students' interests, goals, and plans, (c) 7 days of instruction on their actions, evaluations, and adjustments, (d) 5 days on their opportunities at home and school, and (e) 5 days of review. Students received this instruction 2 days a week during regularly scheduled 45-minute periods of life skills.

Baseline. During each day of baseline, the first author (hereafter, instructor) introduced a famous person that the students admired. On day 1 she introduced Michael Jordan, day 2 Eddie Murphy, day 3 Gloria Estefan, day 4 Shaquille O'Neal, day 5 Tina Turner, and on day 6 Oprah Winfrey. Following the introduction, she asked students what they knew about the person, whether they liked and admired him or her, and whether they knew how the person succeeded and became famous. This engaged them in the problem of finding out what they didn't know about the admired person. Next, she introduced information about their early lives that showed how similar they were to the students' lives and that at their age they were not successful or famous either. Then she asked the students to consider what might have happened to cause the famous people to succeed so impressively. She concluded by describing some of the problems these people encountered and what they did to solve them.

Phases 1–4: Problem-Solving Instruction. During these phases, students received instruction on how to regulate their problem-solving activities to meet self-set goals. Each 45-minute class period consisted of a 10-minute presentation by the instructor, a 10–20-minute application of a problem-solving strategy by students, and a 2- to 5-minute summary of the strategy. The sessions ended with students completing a self-report form on their daily use of self-regulated problem solving to meet their goals, which took 5–10 minutes.

During phase 1 (interests, goals, and plans), the instructor introduced strategies for identifying student interests (2 days), setting goals based on those interests (2 days), and making plans to meet goals (4 days). During phase 2 (actions, evaluations, adjustments), she introduced strategies for using a calendar to manage time to complete plans (2 days), using the calendar to evaluate actions and adjust plans (3 days), and thinking positively about taking action on plans (2 days). During phase 3 (opportunities at home and school), the instructor introduced methods for identifying school resources to help students meet goals (1 day), home resources to help them meet goals (1 day), strategies to improve home and school conditions for meeting goals (1 day), and personal strategies for removing obstacles to goal attainment at school and at home (2 days). During phase 4, the last 5 days of the intervention, the instructor used a frequent game-style questioning method to provoke discussion and brainstorming about the use of various strategies to meet their goals.

Self-Regulation Capacity Indicators

At the end of each of the 31 session days of instruction, the 36 students of the study completed a goals questionnaire, a self-report on the self-regulated problem solving they had engaged in recently. Table 11.1 presents the items. Side 1 items asked how frequently students engaged in problem solving related to their interests and goals. Side two asked whether students engaged in those problem-solving behaviors recently, and if so, what they did.

Self-Determination Indicators

A second set of measures assessed student beliefs about their prospects for engaging in self-determined pursuits. The student version of the AIR Self-Determination Scale (Wolman, Campeau, Dubois, Mithaug, & Stolarski, 1994), also employed in the studies in chapters 4–7, was used here. The capacity measure allowed students to express beliefs about their cur-

TABLE 11.1

Item Ratings on Self-Regulated Problem Solving to Meet Self-Set Goals

---

Side 1

1. How often do you think about what *interests* you most?
2. How often do you *set goals* that are interesting to you?
3. How often do you *make plans* to meet your goals?
4. How often do you try *many different* plans to meet your goals?
5. How often do you *finish* each planned activity?
6. How often do you finish each planned activity *on time*?
7. If your plan doesn't work, how often do you find out *why* it didn't work?
8. If your plan doesn't work, how often do you *try another plan*?
9. How often do you look for opportunities at *school* to reach your goal?
10. How often do you look for opportunities at *home* to reach your goal?
11. How often do you try to *improve* your school opportunities to reach your goal?
12. How often do you try to *improve* your home opportunities to reach your goal?

Side 2

1. Do you have any interests right now? Circle: yes/no. If so, what are they?
2. Do you have any goals right now? Circle: yes/no. If so, what are they?
3. Do you have any plans for meeting the goal you checked? Circle: yes/no. If so, what are they?
4. Have you thought about other plans for meeting this goal? Circle: yes/no. If so, what are they?
5. Have you finished any of your plans to reach your goals? Circle: yes/no. If so, what have you done?
6. Do you know when you will meet your goal? Circle: yes/no. If so, when will you meet it?
7. Have you thought about whether your plans are working or not? Circle: yes/no. If so, in what ways did you feel your plans were working or not working?
8. Have you thought about what you would do if your plan does not work? Circle: yes/no. If so, what did you consider?
9. Do you have ways at school to reach your goal? Circle: yes/no. If so, explain what they are.
10. Do you have ways at home to reach your goal? Circle: yes/no. If so, explain what they are.
11. Have you thought about ways you could improve your school opportunities to reach your goal? Circle: yes/no. If so, what did you consider?
12. Have you thought about ways you could improve your home opportunities to reach your goal? Circle: yes/no. If so, what did you consider?

---

rent level of problem solving to meet goals that were consistent with their needs and interests. Table 11.2 lists these assessment items, which were answered by degree of agreement on a 5-point Likert scale. The opportunity measure allowed students to express beliefs about their opportunities at school and home for engaging in problem solving to meet goals that were consistent with their needs and interests. These items were also answered as degree of agreement using a 5-point Likert scale. Table 11.3 presents those items.

TABLE 11.2
Self-Ratings on Capacity to Self-Determine

Self-ratings about knowing how to get what I need and want

1. I know what I need, what I like, and what I'm good at.
2. I decide what I need, what I like, and what I am good at on my own. My teachers, parents, and friends do not decide for me, but I may ask for their help.
3. I set goals to get what I want or need. I think about what I am good at when I do this.
4. I come up with these goals by myself. My teachers, parents, and friends do not set my goals for me, but I may ask for their help.
5. I figure out how to meet my goals. I make plans and decide what I should do.
6. I make plans to meet goals by myself. My parents, teachers, and friends don't make them for me, but I may ask for their help.
7. I begin working on my plans to meet my goals as soon as possible.
8. Once I decide what to do, I get it done.
9. I check how I'm doing when I'm working on my plan. If I need to, I ask others what they think of how I'm doing.
10. When I'm done with a job or task, I wonder if I could have done it another way to meet my goals.
11. If my plan doesn't work, I try another one to meet my goals.
12. I will change my plans again and again until I finally get what I need or want. I will keep on trying.

Self-ratings on how I feel about getting what I need and want

1. I feel good about what I like, what I want, and what I do well.
2. I feel free to talk about what I need, what I like, and what I'm good at, even if other people don't agree with me.
3. I believe that I can set goals to get what I want.
4. I feel free to set my own goals, even if my parents, teachers, or friends want me to do something else.
5. I like to make plans to meet my goals.
6. I feel free to plan how to meet my goals even if other people want me to do something else.
7. I like to begin working on my plans right away.
8. I believe I can carry out my plans to reach my goals.
9. I like to check on how well I'm doing in meeting my goals.
10. I like to have other people tell me how I'm doing because it will help me to meet my goals.
11. I am willing to try another way if it helps me to meet my goals.
12. I don't get discouraged and I want to keep changing my plans as often as I need to to meet my goals.

RESULTS

The data-collection procedures allowed us to assess the effects of instruction on students' use of problem solving to meet goals and satisfy needs and interests, as well as its effects on students' prospects for self-determination. We consider these effects in turn.

TABLE 11.3
Self-Ratings on Opportunities to Self-Determine

Self-ratings on my opportunities to self-determine at school
  1. People at school listen to me when I talk about what I want, what I need, or what I'm good at.
  2. People at school encourage me to talk about what I want, what I need, or what I'm good at.
  3. People at school let me know that I can set my own goals to get what I want or need.
  4. People at school understand my goals and help me if I need it.
  5. At school, I have learned how to make plans to meet my goals and to feel good about them.
  6. People at school help me make plans to meet my goals when I need it.
  7. People at school encourage me to start working on my plans right away.
  8. People at school help me get started on my plans to meet my goals, if I need help.
  9. I have someone at school who can tell me if I am meeting my goals.
  10. I have someone at school who can tell me about other things I could do to meet my goals.
  11. People at school understand when I have to change my plan to meet my goal. They offer advice and encourage me when I'm doing this.
  12. People at school still help me, even if I have to keep changing my plan over and over to meet my goal.

Self-ratings on my opportunities to self-determine at home
  1. People at home listen to me when I talk about what I want, what I need, or what I'm good at.
  2. People at home encourage me to talk about what I want, what I need, or what I'm good at.
  3. People at home let me know that I can set my own goals to get what I want or need.
  4. People at home understand my goals and help me if I need it.
  5. At home, I have learned how to make plans to meet my goals and to feel good about them.
  6. People at home help me make plans to meet my goals when I need it.
  7. People at home encourage me to start working on my plans right away.
  8. People at home help me get started on my plans to meet my goals, if I need help.
  9. I have someone at home who can tell me if I am meeting my goals.
  10. I have someone at home who can tell me about other things I could do to meet my goals.
  11. People at home understand when I have to change my plan to meet my goal. They offer advice and encourage me when I'm doing this.
  12. People at home still help me, even if I have to keep changing my plan over and over to meet my goal.

Effects of Instruction on Problem Solving to Meet Goals and Interests

The effects of instruction on students' self-regulated problem solving were assessed by analyzing the results of student responses to side 1 and side 2 of the goals questionnaire that were completed during each session of the study. On side 1 of the rating form, students used a 5-point Likert scale to indicate how frequently they engaged in behaviors related to meeting their needs and interests, whether they engaged in them at school and at home, and whether they had done so in the last few days. Table 11.4 provides data on the items requesting this information. The highest possible score for each category of self-regulation—(a) interests, goals, plans, (b) actions, evaluations, adjustments, and (c) opportunities at home and school—was 20. Hence, the highest possible score was 60.

Table 11.4 lists the average percentages of the total scores possible for each category and phase of instruction. The ratings were lowest during baseline when the instructor introduced success stories about famous people. The average rating for the group across the three areas was 60.8% of the highest rating possible. However, when instruction commenced in phase 1, the group average increased to 69.9%, which was significantly higher than the baseline level. Then the group average increased to 82% in phase 2, which was also significantly higher than baseline. This level maintained during phase 3. In phase 4, the group level increased again to 85.3%. Each of the three problem-solving areas in the table increased as the total increased. The significant differences here were between baseline and phases 2–4.

Data from sides 1 and 2 of the goals questionnaire were combined to compare average scores prior to instruction with average scores 31 days later, when instruction had ended. The average total raw score during the pretest was 6.28 and the average total raw score during the posttest was 91.8. This difference was also significant ($p < .01$).

TABLE 11.4
Mean Percent Problem-Solving Ratings During Each Phase of Instruction

	Baseline, Stories of Famous People, Days 1–6	Phase 1, Instruction on Interests, Goals, Plans, Days 7–14	Phase 2, Instruction on Act, Evaluate, React, Days 15–21	Phase 3, Instruction on Opportunities at Home and School, Days 22–26	Phase 4, Review Through Games, Days 27–31
Interests, goals, plans	65.0	72.5	84.0*	83.5*	88.0*
Actions, evaluations, adjustments	58.3	66.0	78.8*	76.8*	82.5*
Opportunity at home and school	59.3	71.3	83.5*	81.0*	86.0*
Total problem-solving rating	60.8	69.9*	82.0*	80.3*	85.3*

Note. Percent ratings with different numbers of asterisks are significantly higher than baseline.

These data are consistent with the claim that instruction had the intended effect of increasing students' problem solving to meet goals and satisfy interests. Prior to problem-solving instruction, there was only a 60.8% rating on problems related to goal attainment and needs satisfaction, and after instruction there was an 85.3% rating for working on problems related to those ends. In all, these differences were significant. Also, there were significant differences in rating gains that occurred across all phase changes, except for the change from phase 2, which focused on acting, evaluating, and adjusting, to phase 3, which focused on opportunities at home and school. For these 36 students, the instructional effect was substantial, at least from the students' point of view.

Effects of Instruction on Self-Determination

But did these improvements in problem solving to meet self-set goals just reported increase students' prospects for self-determination? We examined this possibility by comparing pre- and posttest self-determination scores for the 36 students who received instruction and the 27 students who did not. Indeed, an instructional effect would be evident if there was a postinstruction increase in self-determination scores for the instructed group but not for the noninstructed group. This is what happened.

Figure 11.1 compares the pre- and postinstruction test scores for the two groups. The top figure presents the self-determination prospects scores for the two groups, which combines capacity and opportunity ratings. The preinstruction scores were not significantly different for the groups. The mean score was 85.4 for the group that was to receive instruction ($n = 36$) and 83.6 for the comparison group ($n = 23$; missing data for 4 students). The postinstruction scores were very different for the two groups, however. The mean score was 95.0 for the instructed group and 80.0 for the comparison group. This difference was significant ($p < .05$).

A similar pattern was evident for student ratings on their capacity to self-determine. Again there were no significant differences between the groups prior to instruction. The preinstruction capacity scores were 43.5 for the instructed group and 41.5 for the comparison group. Following instruction, those scores changed for the instructed group but not for the comparison group. The mean postinstruction capacity score was 47.8 for the instructed group and 40.7 for the comparison group. This difference was significant ($p < .05$).

The third chart in Fig. 11.1 presents pre- and postinstruction scores on student ratings of their school and home opportunities to self-determine. They reveal the same pattern. There were no differences in preinstruction scores, but there were in postinstruction scores. The mean preinstruction scores for school and home opportunities were the same: 42.0 for the in-

Prospects for Self-Determination

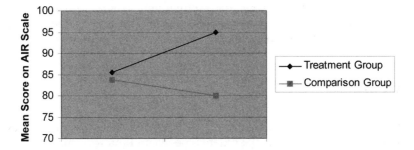

Capacity to Self-Determine

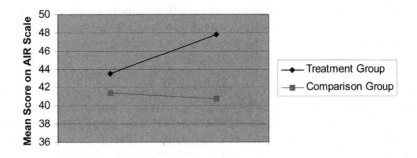

Opportunity to Self-Determine

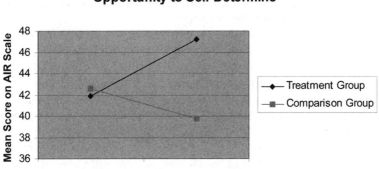

FIG. 11.1. Pre- and posttest self-determination scores for treatment and comparison groups.

structed group and 42.0 for the comparison group. The mean post-instruction score for the instructed group was 47.2, and 39.9 for the comparison group. Again, the difference was significant ($p < .05$).

DISCUSSION

The results support the claim of prescription 3 that teaching problem solving to meet goals that satisfy students' needs and interests increases their prospects for self-determination. This was clearly demonstrated in the study. The instructor provided 31 days of problem-solving instruction to meet personal goals for one group of 36 students but not for a comparable group of 27 students. The instructed group increased self-determination prospects by nearly 10 points, whereas the comparison group did not. In fact, for this group, prospects for self-determination decreased by 4 points. Moreover, data collected on the problem solving of students who received instruction support the claim that instruction was responsible for group differences on self-determination.

Indeed, the procedures that produced these results are similar to those that improved engagement and learning in the previous two chapters: optimized opportunities and adjustments. In those studies, teachers improved the optimality of the learning opportunity through choice, then enhanced students' adjustment capability by teaching a problem-solving strategy. In chapter 9, students chose tasks they wanted to work on, then used a self-regulation card to follow through on those choices while working independently. In chapter 10, students set their own learning goals by solving the discrepancy between what they knew and what they wanted to know. They used a 12-question strategy to regulate their problem solving toward reducing the discrepancy.

In this study, the instructional activities and assignments were optimal in that they were both rewarding and doable from the point of view of the students. Students' adjustments tended to optimize because the teacher helped them use problem-solving strategies to match their needs and interests with their goals, plans, actions, and results. The outcome of these two factors was increased engagement and learning. Student engagement was measured directly by end-of-class reports by students on the frequency of their problem solving throughout the week. The researcher also observed engagement during the classes. For example, after the baseline, she reported these observations of student engagement:

> Students appeared interested in the sessions on famous people. Indicators of interest included lively classroom discussions, attentive posture, smiling and nodding, and expressed eagerness to read class handouts. A few stu-

dents wanted to save the class-read stories and reread them at home.

Certain factors seemed to enhance interest in the lessons. For example, students tended to be more responsive when they could move their chairs to better see and hear each other. Discussion levels also increased with student interest in the celebrity. For example, students who were sports fans participated intensely in the lessons on Michael Jordan and Shaquille O'Neal, and students who were movie fans participated actively in the lesson on Eddie Murphy. Occasionally a student would dislike a celebrity. This happened in the lessons on Oprah Winfrey and Tina Turner. Even here, their dislikes led to enjoyable debates and discussions. . . .

Several teachers also commented on the classes. One teacher stated "most students are rarely taught to think about their interests and goals, and they are *never* taught to make plans. It's a shame because these are things they desperately need to learn." Occasionally students illustrated this limited understanding of the problem solving process. For example, some expressed surprise to discover the struggle that celebrities endured to achieve fame. In one discussion concerning Michael Jordan, a student said, "I would work hard at basketball too if I were making millions of dollars doing it." Others agreed. *But once it was pointed out that Michael Jordan did not start making millions of dollars but had to struggle to reach this point in his life, many students indicated surprise with such comments as "Really?" or "Um, I never thought about it that way."* (DeRobertis, 1997, pp. 91–92, italics added)

After phase 1, the instructor reported on student responses to the challenges of finding goals that matched their needs and interests and then developing plans to meet them. As with the baseline phase, student interest and engagement remained high.

Overall, phase I lessons seemed to help students understand interests, goals, and plans. Each student identified at least one personal goal that matched one of their interests. The word "goal" was defined as "something you want to do or achieve." Long-term goals, particularly career-oriented goals, were frequently selected. The most frequently selected non-career oriented goals were improving their reading and writing and going to college. With practice, students were also able to identify resources to achieve goals. After defining resources as "people or things that can help you," students could elicit many examples of resources to get them what they wanted. (pp. 93–94)

Students had much difficulty developing plans to meet their goals. Often they confused the plan with what would happen if they reached their goal. For example, one student had a goal to be a nurse. When asked to name a plan to meet this goal she said, "I will be working all day in a hospital, taking care of people who are very sick, and getting paid a lot." With practice, students learned to give legitimate plans to meet their goals. Legitimate plans were . . . plans that [were] compatible with one's goals, and . . . possible to achieve. . . .

The majority of the students indicated they liked the workshops. While working on a writing assignment during another class, one student chose to write about the workshops: "She [the researcher] tells the truth about how you can put your life in order. . . . She helps me a lot. She helps me think about what I want to do in life." Similar sentiments were expressed by other students in later phases of the study. (p. 94)

Following phase 2, the instructor noted as well the difficulty students experienced acting on plans, and evaluating and adjusting to results.

During phase II, students identified ways they could adjust their daily schedules to meet their goals. Many students expressed that they should spend less time sleeping late, watching television, and going out with their friends, and more time studying and getting involved in after school activities. These comments also indicated an understanding of the importance of planning to meet their goals.

Students had difficulty carrying out the plans they made in class however. This following-through seemed to be more challenging for them than developing goals and strategies. Students often admitted that they forgot to carry out their plans, or that they were "too tired to do them." Despite these difficulties, the students seemed committed to the goals they chose. When given the choice between continuing with their current goal or setting a different one, they invariably chose to continue with their current goal.

Students also had difficulty evaluating and reacting to their plans and actions. Many students struggled to understand why they forgot, or why they were tired, and how they could prevent this from happening again. Instead they tended to repeat the same plans, by announcing "this time I will remember." Usually students eventually completed the tasks they set out to do. Perhaps they tried another approach that they did not articulate in class, or perhaps the frequent reminder they saw as they monitored their plans on their calendars helped them remember. Either way, most students seemed to enjoy using calendars to plan and monitor their progress. (p. 95)

These observations support student reports on their use of these problem-solving strategies after class. They also support our conclusion that instruction was sufficiently engaging and empowering to produce the effect predicted by self-determined learning theory, that is, maximum gain toward learning to be self-determined. It was engaging in that the opportunities for gain were perceived by the students to be both valuable and doable. Instruction was empowering in that it helped students develop strategies required to adjust effectively to their learning opportunities. Hence, according to self-determined learning theory, the gain toward self-determination must have maximized. But did it?

We attempted to verify this prediction by examining whether the pre- and posttest improvements on self-determination scores were sufficient to conclude that learning had maximized. We did this by comparing the posttest ratings of the groups in this study with the self-determination ratings by successful adults without disabilities. Our reasoning was that if the instructed group ratings maximized, then their ratings would be comparable to those by successful adults. Table 11.5 presents these data, and they support the gain maximization prediction. The first two columns present self-determination posttest scores for the two groups from the present study. The third column presents self-determination scores of community college graduates without disabilities that were reported in chapter 5. The fourth column presents self-determination scores of graduate students in special education. Note that there were marked differences between the noninstructed group of this study and the other groups in the table, but that these differences were all but eliminated for the instructed group. Their scores on capacity and opportunity to self-determine were consistent with the maximization prediction that self-determination prospects would approximate adult ratings. They did. The instructed group's ratings were slightly lower on capacity and slightly higher on opportunity than were the two adult groups' ratings.

Clearly, substantial learning resulted from the 31 days of instruction, as the instructor noted in her report upon completing phase 4.

> Overall, levels of student participation were very high during Phase IV. Students shared personal problems and stories, and showed a greater willingness to discuss and role-play issues about home and school. There was also a continued trend toward greater cooperative learning and class participation
> . . .
>   By Phase IV there was also a noticeable difference in student expressions of self-determination. One of the teachers reported that some of the students have been requesting homework. He added that a few students even re-

TABLE 11.5
Scores on Self-Determination for the Groups of this Study
and Two Adult Groups Without Disabilities

	Present Study of Noninstructed High School Students With Disabilities, $n = 27$	Present Study of Instructed High School Students With Disabilities, $n = 36$	Chapter 5 Study of Community College Graduates Without Disabilities, $n = 117$	Assessments of Graduate Students Without Disabilities, $n = 50$
Prospects for self-determination	80.0	95.0	95.2	95.8
Capacity to self-determine	40.7	47.8	50.0	49.9
Opportunity to self-determine	39.9	47.2	45.2	45.9

minded him to correct the homework and return it to them. He also said that other students requested that he include more reading and acting out plays during class time. The teacher was pleasantly surprised by this and attributed it to their progress in the workshop.

There were other incidents suggesting progress in self-determination. For example, one student was observed asking his gym teacher to help him with his baseball throw. As the gym teacher made suggestions, the student followed through with adjustment movements based on the advice he received. Earlier in the study this same student had stated that one of his goals was to improve in sports.

Another student whose goal was to become an artist shared her art portfolio with the researcher. It included a sketch pad she had won as a prize in a review game. The portfolio and sketch pad were filled with drawings. It was clear she had been practicing her drawing, and making excellent use of her resources. (DeRobertis, 1997, p. 99)

These results are consistent with the instructional prescription derived from self-determined learning theory that claims that when instruction provokes engagement and empowers capable adjustment, learning will maximize. But what do they say about the findings in chapter 4–7 that students with disabilities are less self-determined than are students without disabilities? In our view, the findings suggest that these differences can be eliminated through instruction that optimizes students' opportunities and improves their self-regulated adjustments to those challenges.

Indeed, this is what occurred in the last three chapters. In the description in chapter 9, children between the ages of 5 and 8 years with severe learning and behavior problems learned to improve their adjustments to their own choices as they completed assignments and worked independently. In the description in chapter 12, middle school students with emotional and behavior problems, learning disabilities, and mental retardation learned to choose their learning goals and then to regulate their problem solving to meet them. And in this chapter, high school students with disabilities engaged in similar behavior to learn to self-determine. They learned to identify needs and interests in order to chose goals and then learned to regulate their problem solving to meet those goals.

This suggests a question about how far on the age continuum prescriptions from self-determined learning theory can be extended. Can they be extended to adulthood where the main benefit of self-determination lies — where being self-determined is necessary for success in the free society? If so, can self-determined learning prescriptions lead to improved outcomes for adults with disabilities? The next chapter examines this possibility by showing how a fourth prescription derived from the theory helped adults with disabilities solve the problem of not knowing which jobs they wanted.

REFERENCES

DeRobertis, M. (1997). *The effects of problem-solving instruction on the self-determination of high school students with mild disabilities.* Unpublished doctoral dissertation, Teachers College, Columbia University, New York.

Wolman, J., Campeau, P., Dubois, P., Mithaug, D., & Stolarski, V. (1994). *AIR self-determination scale and user guide.* Palo Alto, CA: American Institute for Research.

12

The Effects of Optimal Opportunities and Adjustments on Job Choices of Adults with Severe Disabilities

James E. Martin
Dennis E. Mithaug
James V. Husch
Eva S. Frazier
Laura H. Marshall

The strong claim for using self-determined learning theory to prescribe instruction for all persons is that it fosters self-determination, which is a basic right in the postmodern world. Supporting this claim is research reported in the preceding chapters showing that students with the capacity to adjust in order to learn also have the capacity to self-determine. It verified the pattern in reverse. Chapters 4–7 showed students with disabilities were at risk for lowered levels of self-determination. Chapter 8 linked the risk to an inadequacy in adjustments to new opportunities, and chapters 9–11 showed that optimizing opportunities and adjustments maximized learning and increased self-determination for those students. Hence we can conclude that learning and self-determination maximize when instruction provokes the optimization of opportunities and adjustments.

In this chapter, we expand the scope of this inquiry to include adults with severe disabilities. We believe this is appropriate, given that the evidence presented so far related to school-aged students and the theory being verified applies to all persons. Hence its prescriptions should apply to adults who are also at risk for learning and self-determination throughout life. Prescription 4 covers this concern by showing how the optimizing conditions affecting the learning and self-determination of school-aged populations can improve vocational prospects for adults with severe disabilities who often fail to adjust to mainstream employment opportunity. It claims that when workers have job options (optimal opportunities) and a means of regulating their adjustments effectively to act on them (optimal adjustments), their prospects for vocational success increase.

Prescription 4: To increase vocational success, give workers a choice of jobs and a means of regulating their behavior to adjust to those choices.

We think this prescription applies equally to adults with severe disabilities, because a supported employment program we developed more than a decade ago revealed the benefits of optimizing opportunities and adjustments for this group of left-out workers. We developed the program because existing supported employment practice ignored consumer choice when placing consumers on jobs. That approach was based on the assumption that people who are eligible for supported employment lack the experience and capacity to make good decisions about the jobs they want and can do (Rusch & Hughes, 1989, 1990; Schaller & Szmanski, 1992; West & Parent, 1992; Windsor, O'Reilly, & Moon, 1993). We challenged that practice, claiming that adults with severe disabilities have the right to choose their own jobs and that the supported employment programs serving them have an obligation to empower that right (Mithaug, 1998).

> To empower means to give authority to make final decisions and to act accordingly. So empowering consumers to succeed means giving them the opportunity to decide what to do on their own.
>   Is this reasonable for persons with severe handicaps? Does it apply to consumers in supported employment? What final decision-making power might this include? Can consumers be trusted to make any of the important decisions affecting their future—what type of work to do, when to work, or even to work or not? (Mithaug, Martin, Husch, Agran, & Rusch, 1988, p. 115)

Then we responded to our own challenge by developing an approach to a supported employment program that trusted consumers to make the important decisions affecting their future (Mithaug et al., 1988).

The unintended consequence of this effort was verification of prescription 4, which maintains that improving choice opportunities and adjustments will increase consumers' on-the-job success. This chapter describes how this happened. It shows how consumer choice and decision-making were included in all phases of the job search and selection process. It also shows how consumer adjustments to those choices led to people making informed decisions about work and jobs they liked, what they wanted to do, and to increased knowledge about the opportunities that were available in their communities.

THE SELF-DIRECTED SUPPORTED EMPLOYMENT PROGRAM

The program that inadvertently verified prescription 4—the Self-Directed Supported Employment Program at the University of Colorado at Colorado Springs—served more than 750 adults with severe disabilities be-

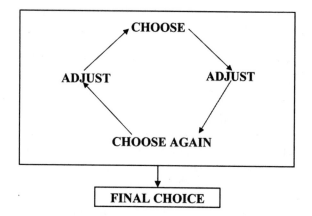

FIG. 12.1.   The choose–adjust–choose again approach to choosing optimally.

tween 1988 to 1999. Included in that group were 234 persons with developmental disabilities, 113 adults with severe learning disabilities, 145 persons with chronic mental illness, 61 persons with traumatic brain injury, 102 adults with physical disabilities, and 96 persons with other disabilities. Of that total, 569 persons completed the choose–adjust process in order to identify their first, second, and third job choices. The procedures and activities of this program and its satellites located throughout the country have been described by Martin and Mithaug (1990), Martin, Mithaug, Agran, and Husch (1990), Martin, Oliphint, and Weisenstein (1994), and Martin, Mithaug, Oliphint, Husch, and Frazier (in press).[1]

A diagram illustrating the optimizing conditions it employed is given in Fig. 12.1, which shows how consumers learned about the jobs they liked, could do, and that matched the jobs available in their communities. It shows choice and adjustment interacting repeatedly to yield optimal choices for community jobs. The process worked in the following way.

Before going to job sites, consumers expressed their preferences for the work conditions, task requirements, and job environments they liked. Then, after experiencing several hours of those circumstances at the job site, they adjusted their preferences by making the same choices again. They repeated this cycle of choosing, experiencing choice, and adjusting to choice until they sampled all available jobs and could make a consistent, rational choice—a choice that was optimal in that it matched their needs, interests, and capabilities with an available job in the community.

---

[1]Funding from the U.S. Department of Education Office of Special Education Program, the National Institute for Disability Rehabilitation Research, the Colorado Division of Vocational Rehabilitation, and the Colorado Division of Developmental Disabilities supported the development of these model programs.

The following examples illustrate how the process worked for two people with severe disabilities. Carl was a 48-year-old man with mental retardation who spent 20 years working in a sheltered workshop where he learned a great deal about social interactions but very little about work tasks. His records indicated that he could read at a second-grade level, walk with a cane, and lift up to 10 pounds. They also indicated he was traumatized when his mother died in a car accident prior to his enrolling in the program.

Carl started our choose–adjust program on March 21 and completed it on July 8. By then, he knew some of the job characteristics that were important to him. He knew he wanted to work with lots of people, in a quiet environment, part-time, and on weekdays only. His first choice matched those conditions, which was to work in a store. His backup choice was a job helping people.

Karen, a 20-year-old woman with Down syndrome and mental retardation, had a similar experience completing the program. The only vocation she experienced was from her high school work-study program in fast foods at a cafeteria site. Karen began the program on August 17 and ended it on December 1. By then she knew that she wanted to work with lots of people, inside with lots of noise, and have easy tasks to do. So her first choice was a job in a retail store, and her second was in food service, which met the requirement of working inside with lots of noise and people.

THE MECHANICS OF CHOOSING AND ADJUSTING

These examples are representative of what happened to 95% of the people who completed the choice–adjust process and found jobs that matched their first or second choices (Martin et al., in press). In this section we describe the procedures that made this possible for adults who many thought were so unemployable they could not choose much less direct the search for their own jobs in supported employment.

The Tools Used

These procedures share one essential feature: They create discrepancy problems consumers must solve each time they make a choice. Discrepancies are created when a preference expressed about working conditions, job tasks, and work sites prior to an experience with those circumstances *is inconsistent with* the preference expressed for those circumstances after the experience. They are resolved when a change in preference leads to a choice that is consistent with on-the-job experience.

The procedures that provoked discrepancies to produce adjusted choice making gave consumers repeated exposure to various working conditions, job tasks, and job environments in the community. They also tracked the before and after experiences with forms consumers used to express what they liked and what they could do in these environments. Mithaug et al. (1988) explained:

> As consumers perform tasks at different assessment sites in the community, they ask themselves two questions: "What do I like," and "What can I do." They answer these questions twice each day. They evaluate their preferences and abilities during job club each morning before leaving for the site. Two hours later, after completing their work, they evaluate again.
>
> Before- and after-site evaluations indicate consistency. As their experience at each site increases, consumers become more reliable in expressing what they like and what they can do. (Mithaug et al., 1988, p. 131)

These self-evaluations defined problems that consumers solved on subsequent visits. After they made a choice, they evaluated whether their experience at a job site was consistent with it and, if not, how they could adjust subsequent choice so that it was. They did this repeatedly until they solved the problem of not knowing what they liked and what they could do. They expressed that understanding with a choice based on what they knew was consistent with their interests and abilities.

Discovering What I Like.   The preference areas covered by these problem-solving episodes were "Work conditions I like," "Tasks I like," and "Jobs I like." Each preference type had an evaluation form consumers used to find out what they liked about various settings. As Mithaug et al. (1988) explained the process:

> *The Work Conditions I Like* [form] . . . allows consumers to indicate preferences for working conditions such as: inside, outside, with people or things, alone or with many, fast or steady, while standing or sitting.
>
> They complete the form by circling their choice "Before Work," and then again "After work." Next, they compare the two by counting the number of choices that were the same (matches). They answer the question "Do I know What Conditions I Like?" by indicating if they were consistent.
>
> In *The Tasks I Like* [form] . . . consumers indicate preferences for tasks at different job sites. The Consumer-Directed SEP has six assessment sites and 12 tasks, two at each site. . . . Consumers complete the forms before and after working the tasks. Then they compare their results, record their matches, and indicate if they know what tasks they like.
>
> *The Jobs I Like* [form] . . . follows the same format, with consumers indicating their preferences before and after working at the six assessment site jobs: laundry, office, outside maintenance, store, factory, and food service.

Consistency of choice is also evident when comparing consumers' selections across the three forms. Preferences for working conditions and tasks should match choices for jobs. For example, consumers who want a laundry job should also like working: alone, inside, with things, at a steady rate, while standing, and using large muscle groups (physical). They should also indicate preferences for working laundry and insert tasks. (Mithaug et al., 1988, pp. 132–133)

The employment staff summarized these before–after evaluations so consumers could track their own progress toward finding out what they like. One of the forms used is in Fig. 12.2. In the bar chart, this consumer likes to work alone, in noisy places, on weekends, and doing easy jobs that require a uniform.

Discovering What I Can Do. The same discrepancy-reduction problems guided consumers to discover their strengths and weaknesses relative to various jobs. Before work they rated themselves on worker behaviors, and after completing their work at each site they gave the same form to their job coach, who rated their behavior and performance. Following this, they compared the ratings with their own to identify discrepancies. They repeated these self-rating and job-coach-rating comparisons until the two matched, as Mithaug et al. (1988) explained.

Self-assessments focus consumer attention on strengths and weaknesses that affect getting and keeping a job. They rate themselves in work, social, and personal areas. Next they compare their evaluations with their trainers' and then revise their self-assessments as needed.

The assessments follow the same format. First, consumers complete their self-assessment in "What I Think." They circle the pictures and phrases that best describe themselves. Next, job coaches assess consumers' strengths and weaknesses on the same form under "What My Job Coach Thinks."

Now consumers can compare their assessments with their trainers'. They record matches between the two evaluations on the "Number of Match?" line. Then they answer the question: Do I Match My Job Coach?

This procedure gives consumers an opportunity to become more accurate and realistic about what they can do. When they see discrepancies between how they evaluate themselves and how their job coaches view them, they may decide to improve themselves in those areas. . . .

The self-evaluation form for *My Work Strengths & Weaknesses* . . . assesses consumer performance in such areas as: attendance, continuous work, safety, responsiveness to feedback, promptness in returning to work, speed, and accuracy.

The form for *My Social Strengths & Weaknesses* . . . assesses behavior in such areas as: initiating contact with others appropriately, behaviors appropriate on the job, asking for help, and following instructions.

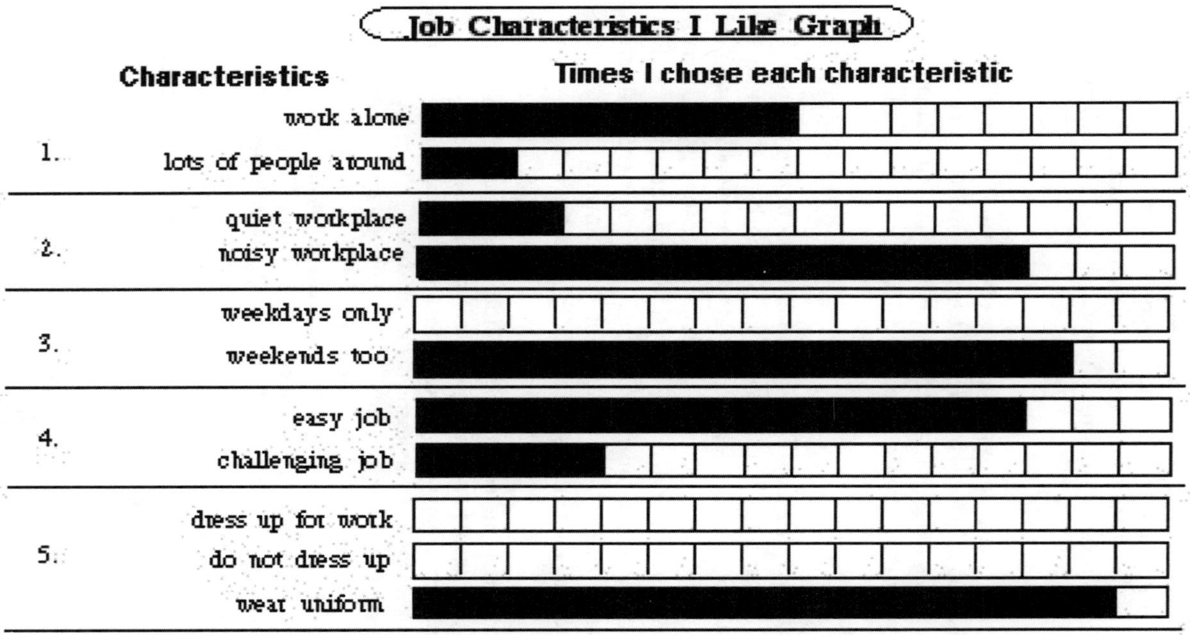

FIG. 12.2. Sample bar chart used by consumers to track learning about what they like. From Marshall, Martin, Maxson, and Jerman (1977), with permission.

194

194

And . . . *My Personal Strengths & Weaknesses* form . . . assesses behavior in such areas as communicating needs, grooming, hygiene, and mealtime behaviors. (Mithaug et al., 1988, pp. 136–137)

Finding Jobs I Like and Can Do.   As consumers learned what they liked and could do, they also learned to evaluate prospective jobs on that basis. They went to job sites knowing what they liked and could do in order to find the job that matched those interests and capabilities. Then they rated the job along those lines, using a form much like the one illustrated in Figs. 12.3 and 12.4. Figure 12.3 presents information in written form and Fig. 12.4 presents information using pictures and words. Both make comparisons between consumer preferences and job characteristics. On the left consumers indicated what they like, in the middle they indicated what the job offers, and on the right they indicated whether the two matched. They evaluated results by noting how many characteristics matched. The job with the most matches was the job that was best for them.

Choosing the Job for Me.   The choice–adjustment process ended when consumers chose the job they wanted. To make this choice, they used a form similar to the one in Fig. 12.5, which was developed for nonreaders. By this time they were ready to make final choices because they were familiar with every job represented on the form. Indeed, they had used the form daily or weekly throughout the choice–adjust process. Hence they knew how to use it to express what they wanted to do, and it made sense for them to have a first, second, and third choice for the job they wanted and could do in the community.

The Time Required

As you can see from this description, the procedures we used in this supported employment approach gave consumers control over their job searches. It gave them the opportunity to learn from experience what they liked, what they could do, and what they wanted from their jobs. It gave them the chance to choose the job they wanted based on that learning through experience. In this regard it accomplished what other supported employment programs had not. It empowered consumers to decide their own futures.

The procedures also followed the advice offered by prescription 4, which claimed that for vocational success, workers need to have job choices and a means of adjusting to them. Our community development program provided consumers with job choices, and our before–after evaluation forms gave them a means of adjusting their preferences and choices to match those options.

JOB CHARACTERISTICS I LIKE WORKSHEET

NAME: _____   JOB SITE: _____   DATE: _____

Directions: WHAT I LIKE column: Circle the job characteristic that you like best in each box.
WHAT IS HERE column: Circle the job characteristic in each box that best describes what is at this job.
MATCHES column: Circle YES if the first two columns are the same.   Circle NO if they are not.

	WHAT I LIKE	WHAT IS HERE	MATCHES
1.	work alone lots of people around	work alone lots of people around	YES NO
2.	quiet workplace noisy workplace	quiet workplace noisy workplace	YES NO
3.	work close to home distance to job doesn't matter	work close to home distance to job doesn't matter	YES NO
4.	weekdays only weekends too	weekdays only weekends too	YES NO
5.	easy job challenging job	easy job challenging job	YES NO

FIG. 12.3.   Written version of Job Characteristics I Like form. From Marshall et al. (1977), with permission.

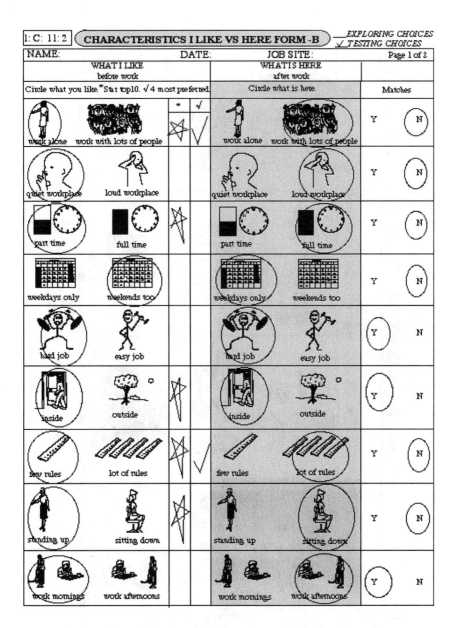

FIG. 12.4. Pictorial version of Job Characteristics I Like form. From Marshall et al. (1977), with permission.

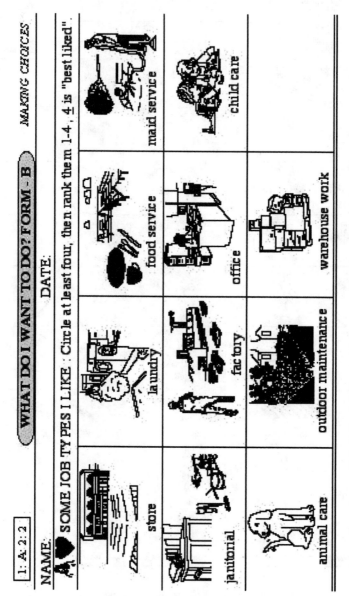

FIG. 12.5. Sample pictorial version of a "What I Want to Do" form.

TABLE 12.1
Breakdown of Hours Spent Finding Optimal Job Placements
for Consumers With Development Disabilities

Type of Service	Placement Activities	Mean Hours per Consumer
Indirect service	Site setup	2.5
	Travel	8.0
	Reports	3.0
	Meetings	2.0
	Referral	1.0
	Consultations	1.5
	Family contacts	1.0
	Subtotal	19.0
Direct service	Initial choices	4.0
	Job shadowing	6.0
	Job internships	24.0
	Subtotal	34.0
All Services	Total	53.0

All of this took time. To give you an idea of what was required, we calculated the average time it took for consumers with developmental disabilities, the group that required the most time to gain enough experience to make rational choices, to make a good choice and find a job (Martin et al., in press). For this group, it took an average of 53 hours distributed over 6 weeks for consumers to make a first, second, and third job choice. The time was distributed between 19 hours of indirect services provided by staff to set up choice-making experiences and 34 hours of consumer experience with different jobs to learn what they wanted and could do. Table 12.1 presents averages per consumer over a 4-year period.

The Jobs Chosen

But the time spent empowering choice was worth it because the result was a very different employment distribution for consumers. In a study that compared placements resulting from our choice-based approach with placements by nonchoice approaches, we found that the choice approach yielded more jobs in clerical and fewer jobs in custodial work (Martin et al., in press). Figure 12.6 presents data comparing jobs secured by consumers from our self-directed supported employment program with jobs found for consumers by supported employment personnel in Illinois and in a national sample. Note that custodial jobs were the least frequently selected occupational category by our consumers (5%) and the most frequently chosen jobs for consumers by supported employment personnel in other samples (23–30%). On the other hand clerical work was the most

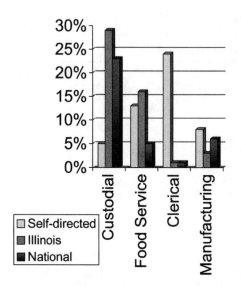

FIG. 12.6. Comparison of different consumer jobs across three supported employment programs.

frequently selected occupation by our sample (24%) but the least frequently selected occupation in the Illinois and national samples (2%). Also, consumers in our program were more likely to secure manufacturing jobs than were consumers in either the Illinois or national samples.

CHOICE AND SUCCESS

But what about the relationship between choice making and success — is there evidence for the claim in prescription 4 that providing choice options and adjustment supports will increase vocational success? We tried to answer this question by comparing the employment outcomes of 569 people who completed the choice–adjust process with the outcomes of 181 consumers who chose not to complete the process. And we found that consumers who completed the choose–adjustment process *before* making a job choice were significantly more likely to be employed than consumers who did not (Martin et al., in press). Table 12.2 presents these data. In this analysis, employment success was defined as having a job and being "closed" by Colorado Rehabilitation Services. As the table shows, consumers who completed the choice–adjust process were 50% more likely to be employed than were the consumers who did not complete the process. We also found that the jobs secured by consumers with development disabilities — the largest group served in the program — matched their first (71%) or second (21%) choice. Only 8% of the that group found jobs that matched their third choice.

TABLE 12.2
Employment Status of Completers and Noncompleters
of Choose–Adjustment–Choose Supported Employment

	Percent of Consumers Still in Program	Percent of Consumers Successfully Employed	Percent of Consumers Unemployed
Completers of choose–adjust–choose again	8	60	32
Noncompleters of choose–adjust–choose again	9	40	51

Note. Chi square, $p < .01$.

It should be noted, however, that optimal matches between interest, ability, and available work were not always possible and successful employment did not always result, as the following examples demonstrate. In the first case, choices and adjustments optimized and Avi succeeded in keeping his job and enjoying its benefits. But in the other two examples, choices and adjustments optimized at first, then deteriorated after that.

When Choice and Adjustments Optimize

Avi was 20 years old when he enrolled in the program. He had a history of mental retardation, could tell time, could read simple work phrases, and knew how to ride the city bus on his own. Avi was shy and easily upset when told to do something that he didn't want to do. His only job experience was provided by his school's transition program where he learned custodial work, which convinced him he didn't want to do that again.

Upon completing the first phase of choose and adjust, Ari completed an internship two days a week at four different sites. He worked at a dog kennel cleaning cages, moving animals, and cleaning floors and decided he didn't like that. He also completed internships at a grocery store, a music store, and a retail department store. After he left the grocery store he commented, "I want to work in a real store—not one that sells food." But after the department-store internship he said he loved working in the toy department. His preferred work characteristics included working part-time, easy work, and working weekdays with lots of people, inside, standing up, and with lots of supervision. His first choice was to work in a toy store.

Two weeks later he accepted a job at a national toy-store chain and began work a week later during the holiday rush. By April of the following year his supervisor reported that she wished all of her employees "worked as hard as Avi. He gets to work on time and does a great job." She also said "his customer relations skills are excellent." When the supported employment program closed in December 1999, Avi was still working happily full-time at the store. The State Office of Rehabilitation

Services closed his case a few months after he started work, and he has continued on his own with no follow-along support since. Occasionally his friends from the supported employment program check on him when they shop there.

When Choices and Adjustment Don't Optimize

Unfortunately, not all job placements end this way, as Cindi and Chris illustrate. For them, initial choices were optimal in that they matched their interests and capabilities. Their initial adjustments were optimal as well in that both of them received good job ratings and were considered successfully employed by Vocational Rehabilitation. However, within months of those initial adjustments, new circumstances developed, they adjusted poorly, and they lost their jobs.

Cindi's Factory Job.   Cindi entered a supported employment program when she was 20 years old. Her records revealed a history of mental retardation, seizures, hydrocephalus, incontinence, and motor coordination dysfunction, and her parents and teachers reported that she was socially immature and a likely victim of abuse in social situations. She graduated from high school with basic academic skills but limited vocational experience. She also needed a job close to home because there was no bus service where she lived. Cindi was eligible for Vocational Rehabilitation support to get a job but not for follow-up support once she was employed.

During four weeks of choose–adjust, Cindi spent 21 hours with supported employment staff and an average of 9.4 hours per week in the community at various job sites. By the end of that period, she discovered that she wanted to work inside, while standing, with other people, during the day, with little supervision, and with few work rules. And after internships in a factory, music store, and hotel, she decided she wanted factory work where she had learned that she could assemble boxes, insert Styrofoam pieces, and operate a machine to bind box stacks and stack bundles. She liked the other jobs too but they were less optimal, given her interests and abilities. At the music store, she liked stocking CDs and videos but had difficulty with other tasks. In fact, she liked that job better than the factory job but did not think she could do the work as well. She tried housekeeping at a hotel and had difficulty with tasks there too. Although she liked her coworkers, she did not like the work. Consequently, she settled on factory work for her first choice and store work for her second. The job developers acted on her first choice by finding an assembler job at a large factory near her home. It was an optimal choice in that it had 100% of the characteristics she wanted.

That phase of the job search and placement was successful in that Cindi took the job and during the first month adjusted optimally. She stayed close to her station and worked continuously. She appeared to be well adjusted. After the first 3 months, her supervisor reported her production had increased, and during the fourth month he made accommodations to her machine duties so she could get her production rate to that of the average worker. This allowed her to maximize her production as well. During the same period Cindi began carpooling with coworkers to get to work. At this point the Department of Vocational Rehabilitation closed her case, defining it a success.

Unfortunately, the closing of Cindi's case also terminated her eligibility for on-the-job support, requiring her family to pay for the follow-along services she needed to adjust to new challenges on the job. They refused to pay, and by the fifth month Cindi's production rate was down from 90% to 72% of the acceptable level. She received repeated warnings to work faster from supervisors but did not improve and was eventually terminated.

Chris's Factory Jobs. Chris was 25 years old when he entered the program from a sheltered workshop where he had worked since high school. His records indicated a history of mental retardation and behavior problems, including rebelliousness and theft. At the workshop he was reported to be impulsive, immature, and socially insensitive. He had a few word recognition skills, could use money to make small purchases, but could not make change or complete two-digit addition or subtraction problems.

Chris received 19.5 hours of direct support from staff and 43.5 hours of job experience (4.5 hours per week for 14 weeks). By the end of that period Chris knew that he wanted to work in a quiet place, with lots of people, weekdays, daytime work only, at a steady (not fast) work rate, and with lots of supervision. With parents and staff, Chris chose factory work as his first choice and store work as his second. A month later, Chris had a job in a computer supply factory working 20 hours a week doing assembly packaging at a starting salary of 75 cents above minimum wage. His social integration rating was the highest possible due to frequent positive interactions with coworkers. Colorado Rehabilitation closed his case as a successful placement.

Chris kept his job for 9 months until he was rotated to the night shift, which contradicted his preference for day work. This caused adjustment difficulties almost immediately, as his production rate decreased and problems with coworkers increased. He was terminated soon after due to low productivity and excessive socializing. A month later he went to work at a large industrial laundry located in a resort hotel where he made 25

cents per hour more and received full benefits. But similar problems occurred again. After a month his supervisor suspended him for swearing,
being violent, and treating coworkers with disrespect. The rehabilitation
office canceled his funding and Chris left the program.

CONCLUSION

The problems experienced by Cindi and Chris are common among people
with limited experience adjusting to challenging circumstances when they
are suddenly on their own. Neither worker had much experience optimizing adjustments to on-the-job challenges, nor was there external support
available to make those adjustments for them. In both cases, they lost their
jobs. Looking back, these results may have been predicted in that Cindi
entered the supported program from high school and Chris entered from
a sheltered workshop where he had worked since high school. Neither
learned to adjust independently before leaving school. In this respect,
their prospects for success were similar to other special education students who leave school without learning the self-regulation behaviors
needed to adjust optimally to adult challenge.

Regrettably, Cindy and Chis were not alone. Even the best effort by our
program to build consumers' adjustment capability yielded a modest 60%
success rate, which by some standards is still significant. Nonetheless, it
left 40% of the people we served unemployed and for what we believe
were preventable reasons. These data are comparable to the 40% of special
education graduates who end up unemployed, too (Fardig, Algozzine,
Schwartz, Hensel, & Westling, 1985; Hasazi, Gordon, & Roe, 1985; Hasazi,
Gordon, Roe, Hull, Finch, & Salembier, 1985; Mithaug & Horiuchi, 1983;
Mithaug, Horiuchi, & Fanning, 1985; Wehman, Kregel, & Seyfarth, 1985).
We believe these poor adjustments are also preventable if students learn
to adjust to their own choices while in school (Mithaug, Martin, & Agran,
1987).

But they don't, and we believe this is due to the reasons suggested by
the prescriptions for instruction introduced in previous chapters. We believe that if teachers systematically helped young people with disabilities
succeed by teaching them to regulate their behaviors in order to adjust optimally to challenge, then students would leave school with a generalized
adaptive capacity to succeed at many, if not most, of the challenges they
will face. This raises the question of what prospective special education
teachers should learn in order to help their students achieve better outcomes. We consider this next.

REFERENCES

Fardig, D. B., Algozzine, R. R., Schwartz, S. E., Hensel, J. W., & Westling, D. L. (1985). Postsecondary vocational adjustment of rural, mildly handicapped students. *Exceptional Children, 52*, 115–121.

Hasazi, S. B., Gordon, L. R., & Roe, C. A. (1985). Factors associated with employment status of handicapped youth exiting high school from 1979–1983. *Exceptional Children, 51*, 455–469.

Hasazi, S. B., Gordon, L. R., Roe, C. A., Hull, M., Finck, K., & Salembier, G. (1985). A statewide follow-up on post high school employment and residential status of students labeled, "mentally retarded." *Education and Training of the Mentally Retarded, 20*, 222–234.

Marshall, L. H., Martin, J. E., Maxson, L., & Jerman, P. (1997). *Choosing employment goals*. Longmont, CO: Sopris West.

Martin, J. E., & Mithaug, D. E. (1990). Consumer-directed placement. In F. R. Rusch (Ed.), *Supported employment: Models, methods, and issues* (pp. 87–110). De Kalb, IL: Sycamore.

Martin, J. E., Mithaug, D. E., Agran, M., & Husch, J. V. (1990). Consumer-centered transition and supported employment. In J. L. Matson (Ed.), *Handbook of behavior modification with the mentally retarded* (2nd ed., pp. 357–389). New York: Plenum Press.

Martin, J. E., Mithaug, D. E., Oliphint, J. H., Husch, J. V., & Frazier, E. S. (in press). *Self-directed supported employment: Infusing self-determination into transition and supported employment practices*. Baltimore, MD: Paul Brookes.

Martin, J. E., Oliphint, J. H., & Weisenstein, G. R. (1994). ChoiceMaker: Transitioning self-determined youth. *Rural Special Education Quarterly, 13*, 16–23.

Mithaug, D. E. (1998). Your right, my obligation? *Journal of the Association for Persons with Severe Handicaps, 23*(1), 41–43.

Mithaug, D. E., & Horiuchi, C. N. (1983). *Colorado statewide followup survey of special educaiton students*. Denver, CO: Colorado Department of Education.

Mithaug, D. E., Horiuchi, C. N., & Fanning, P. N. (1985). A report on the Colorado Statewide Follow-up survey of special education students. *Exceptional Children, 51*, 397–404.

Mithaug, D. E., Martin, J. E., & Agran, M. (1987). Adaptability instruction: The goal of transitional programming. *Exceptional Children, 53*, 500–505.

Mithaug, D. E., Martin, J. E., Husch, J. V., Agran, M., & Rusch, F. R. (1988). *When will persons in supported employment need less support?* Colorado Springs, CO: Ascent.

Rusch, F. R., & Hughes, C. (1989). Overview of supported employment. *Journal of Applied Behavior Analysis, 22*, 351–363.

Rusch, F. R., & Hughes, C. (1990). Historical overview of supported employment. In F. R. Rusch (Ed.), *Supported employment: Models, methods, and issues* (pp. 5–14). De Kalb, IL: Sycamore.

Schaller, J. L., & Szmanski, E. M. (1992). Supported employment, consumer choice, and independence. *Journal of Vocational Rehabilitation, 2*(4), 45–50.

Wehman, P., Kregel, J., & Seyfarth, J. (1985). Employment outlook for young adults with mental retardation. *Rehabilitation Counseling Bulletin*, 90–99.

West, M. D., & Parent, W. S. (1992). Consumer choice and empowerment in supported employment services: Issues and strategies. *Journal of the Association for Persons with Severe Handicaps, 17*, 47–52.

Windsor, J., O'Reilly, B., & Moon, M. S. (1993). Preference: The missing link in the job match process for individuals without functional communication skills. *Journal of Vocational Rehabilitation, 3*, 27–42.

13

The Effects of Choice Opportunities on the Engagement of Prospective Teachers in Student-Determined Learning

Deirdre K. Mithaug
Dennis E. Mithaug

Our discussion of direct instruction in chapter 3 suggested that when students adjust to teacher-delivered cues and consequences they learn because those challenges are optimized for them; hence, the optimality of student adjustments is proportionate to the optimality of teacher deliveries. Under these conditions, teachers' cue-consequence deliveries match student adjustment capabilities to maximize learning as teachers and students adjust together. Teachers learn to deliver cues and consequences effectively and students learn to adjust to them optimally.

This analysis of interplay between teacher and student adjustment during direct instruction explains why it is both effective and limiting. Direct instruction is effective because optimizing learning opportunities for students eliminates the need for them to improve their adjustments in order to learn. However, it is limiting for that reason, too. Direct instruction eliminates the need for students to improve their adjustment capabilities, which inadvertently encourages their dependence on teachers for the optimization of difficult challenges.

The study in chapter 8 revealed this to be a problem by showing that although students in general and special education experienced the same externally improved learning opportunities, the gains they exhibited during those improvements were due to different factors. The gain by students in special education was due exclusively to a change in opportunities, while the gain by students in general education was due as well to their own self-improved adjustments. Clearly, this reveals the limitation of instruction that produces learning through the optimization of opportunities rather than through the expansion of adjustment capability.

The procedures described in the last four chapters addressed this problem by building the adjustment capability of a full range of learners. Chapter 9 showed how young children with severe disabilities could learn to adjust to their own choices while working and learning independently. Chapter 10 showed how secondary-level students with disabilities could learn to adjust to their learning goals. Chapter 11 showed how secondary-level students with disabilities could learn to adjust to their self-determined pursuits. Chapter 12 showed how adults with severe disabilities could learn to adjust their choice of jobs to the working conditions in their communities.

In each of these demonstrations, reluctant learners improved their adjustments and learning because teachers provided them with a strategy for choosing and adjusting repeatedly to improve their choices, actions, and results. This yielded self-determined learning because the learners could control what and how they learned by making choices and then adjusting to them to get what they needed and wanted from new situations. Table 13.1 contrasts this type of instruction with the teacher-directed instruction that characterizes direct instruction.

TABLE 13.1
Teacher Education Prescriptions for
Teacher- and Self-Directed Instruction

Prescription for Teacher-Directed Instruction: To maximize teacher-determined learning, optimize student adjustments to teacher-delivered cues and consequences.

Prescription for Student-Directed Instruction: To maximize self-determined learning, optimize teacher adjustments to student-delivered cues and consequences.

TEACHING TEACHERS TO ADJUST
TO STUDENT-DETERMINED LEARNING

These prescriptions summarize what teachers do when they are effective. Teachers are effective at direct instruction when they *choose* the cues and consequences that students can adjust to, in order to learn. They are effective at student-directed instruction when they optimize *their* adjustments to the cues and consequences that students *choose* in order to learn. The problem, as we see it, is that the preference for direct instruction in teacher training programs for special education tends to eliminate serious consideration of the student-directed alternative. Moreover, lack of experience preparing prospective teachers in this mode of instruction perpetuates student dependency on teachers for learning throughout the school years.

Our solution is a prescription for teacher training that identifies the key procedures prospective teachers must employ to reverse these cycles of learner dependence and replace them with patterns of self-determined learning.

The procedures used in chapters 9–12 identified key factors to be included in this prescription for teacher training—choice opportunities and self-regulation supports. The following prescription includes them in a recommendation for preparing future teachers. It claims that when choices and self-regulatory supports are present and when prospective teachers are required to promote student-determined learning, they learn by adjusting their instructional methods to their students' choices and adjustments.

Prescription 5: To teach student-determined learning, optimize teacher adjustments to students' cues and consequences by providing teachers with (a) instructional choices, (b) strategies to regulate their adjustments to those choices, and (c) strategies their students can use to adjust to their own choice of cues and consequences.

In the study described next, we investigated the effects these conditions had on teacher adjustments. We examined whether choice opportunities, self-regulatory support, and student choice making and adjusting would improve teacher adjustments as claimed by the prescription.

Setting

The study was part of a teacher education program in special education at a university in a Midwestern state. It was conducted during a course on learning strategies taken by prospective special education teachers. The course had a practicum component that required prospective teachers to work with Grades K–4 elementary students at a local school. The participants worked one on one with practicum students in a tutoring space adjacent to the classroom. One group of teachers worked with tutees in a 30-minute morning session, and the other group worked with tutees during a 30-minute afternoon session.

Participants

The participants were 37 undergraduates enrolled in two sections of the practicum course. Group 1 consisted of 15 prospective teachers and Group 2 consisted of 21 prospective teachers. Participants from Group 1 worked with tutees during the morning sessions and participants from Group 2 worked with practicum tutees in the afternoon sessions. Table 13.2 describes the groups. There were more females than males in both

TABLE 13.2
Characteristics of the Two Groups of Undergraduate Practicum Students

	Number of Male Undergraduates	Number of Female Undergraduates	Mean Years as Undergraduate	Mean GPA
Group 1	1	14	4.4	3.4
Group 2	2	19	3.6	3.0

groups, and Group 1 was further along in the undergraduate program and had a slightly higher grade point average (GPA) than Group 2.

Design

The study employed a multiple baseline across groups design. The group comparison contrasted teacher choice and professor choice conditions, and the multiple baseline contrasted the baseline of a no-adjustment contingency with three treatment conditions that employed an adjustment contingency. It permitted an examination of the effects of the student-directed learning that was introduced in the last condition. The reversal of teacher and professor choice sequence for the two groups during Conditions 2 and 3 permitted an examination of possible sequence effects.

Table 13.3 illustrates the design and use of teacher self-regulation cards (Fig. 13.1) to measure teacher adjustments across conditions. During baseline conditions, teachers were free to use the self-regulation card in the absence of directions on teacher or professor choice of goals or on the adjustment contingency. During subsequent conditions, teachers used self-regulation cards during a teacher choice condition with an adjustment

TABLE 13.3
Group Comparison With a Multiple-Baseline Design

	Condition 1	Condition 2	Condition 3	Condition 4
Group 1, $n = 15$	No adjustment contingency Teacher Self-Record Card	Teacher choice and adjustment contingency Teacher Self-Record Card	Professor choice and adjustment contingency Teacher Self-Record Card	Student choice and adjustment contingency Teacher Self-Record Card
Session day:	2–4	5–9	10–14	15–20
Group 2, $n = 21$	No adjustment contingency Teacher Self-Record Card	Professor choice and adjustment contingency Teacher Self-Record Card	Teacher choice and adjustment contingency Teacher Self-Record Card	Student choice and adjustment contingency Teacher Self-Record Card
Session day:	2–6	7–11	12–16	17–20

Teacher-Tutor Self-Regulation Card		
Circle Goals Set	Check Goals Worked	Circle Goals Met
1. Letter/number recognition/identification	1. ____	1. Yes
2. Sight word vocabulary	2. ____	2. Yes
3. Reading comprehension	3. ____	3. Yes
4. Spelling worlds	4. ____	4. Yes
5. Math problems	5. ____	5. Yes
6. Handwriting	6. ____	6. Yes
7. Games, art, puzzles (other fun things)	7. ____	7. Yes
8. Appropriate classroom behavior	8. ____	8. Yes
9. Data collection	9. ____	9. Yes
10. Child Behavior Contract	10. ____	10. Yes
TOTAL SET	TOTAL WORKED	TOTAL MET

FIG. 13.1. Teacher self-regulation card used in Conditions 1–4.

contingency, during a professor choice condition with an adjustment contingency, and during a student choice condition with an adjustment contingency. The adjustment contingency was a point given to participants for the day's tutoring session when their instruction during tutoring matched their choices on the self-regulation card.

Experimental Conditions

The four experimental conditions included a *no adjustment contingency, a teacher choice plus adjustment contingency*, a *professor choice plus adjustment contingency*, and a *student choice plus adjustment contingency*. During the no contingency adjustment condition, participants received points for completing their self-regulation cards correctly. During the other three conditions with adjustment contingencies, participants earned a point for working all goals circled in the "Goals Set" column of their self-regulation card.

During teacher-choice conditions, participants made all of the goal selections on their self-regulation cards. During professor-choice conditions, the professor randomly selected two of the goals for participants to work by circling those selections in the Goals Set column of their self-regulation cards. However, the professor never selected goal 10, the Child Behavior Contract, because that would have required participants to initiate self-determined instruction with their students. Participants were free to choose (circle) any of the other eight goals to work.

During the student choice condition, the professor only circled goal 10 on the self-regulation card, the Child Behavior Contract goal. To complete

Student Tutee Self-Record Card			
Goals to Meet?	# To Do?	# Done?	#To Do = #Done?
1. Science	1. ____	1. ____	1. Yes/No
2. Reading	2. ____	2. ____	2. Yes/No
3. Math	3. ____	3. ____	3. Yes/No
4. Social Studies	4. ____	4. ____	4. Yes/No
5. Geography	5. ____	5. ____	5. Yes/No
			# Yes's

FIG. 13.2.   Sample Child Behavior Contract listed as goal 10 in teacher self-record card and required in Condition 4.

that goal, participants could use the sample contract in Fig. 13.2, or they could construct their own form to manage their tutee's instruction. During this condition, participants were also free to choose the other goals (1–9 in the self-regulation card) to work on during their tutee session.

Teacher Adjustment Indicators

The adjustment indicators were participants' choices, actions, and results during tutoring. We measured them by analyzing teachers' responses to their self-record cards and by examining the self-record cards they constructed to help their students direct their own learning. These data revealed teachers' choices, actions, and results during the four conditions. We evaluated their self-determined instruction by comparing the self-record cards they developed for their tutees with a sample self-record card available in their folders throughout the study.

Choices, Actions, and Results.   Figure 13.1 presents the teacher self-record card used to collect data on teachers' choices, actions, and results. Prospective teachers used it each day to set goals before tutoring (first column), record work on goals after tutoring (second column), and evaluate goals completed after tutoring (third column). Hence, responses in the first column indicated their *choices*. Responses in the second column represented their *actions* on those choices. And responses in the third column represented *results* of those choices and actions—whether goals met equaled goals set.

Participants used a new card each session. Before a session they set goals in the first column of the self-regulation card. After the session they recorded the results of their work in the second and third columns of the card. Next, they totaled the number of goals set, the number worked, and the number of goals met. A "met goal" was a goal that both was circled and worked. Goals that were circled but not worked or worked by not circled did not qualify as met goals. Participants returned their self-record cards to the professor at the end of each tutoring session. They received a point for completing the contract correctly, which was added to their accumulations and used to calculate their grade for the practicum portion of the course.

Optimal Adjustment Measure.   Participant adjustments were the average optimality scores for their choices (goals set), actions (goals worked), and results (goals set that equaled goals worked). Choice and action optimality indicators were based on the expectation that five goal selections and five goals worked per tutoring session was the most a participant could do in the time available. Baseline data on participant work with tutees confirmed this to be the upper limit of what could be accomplished in the time allotted. Optimal goal setting and optimal goals worked were defined as a percent of that upper limit. Therefore, selecting one goal to work or recording one goal worked would yield a 20% optimality score for goals set and goals worked. Selecting two goals to work or recording two goals worked would yield a 40% optimality score for those adjustment indicators, and so on. Results were optimal when goals selected equaled goals worked. They were calculated by dividing the number of matches between goals selected and goals worked by the total number of goals selected. For example, if a participant selected 10 goals to work but only worked 5, the person would have accomplished 50% of what she set out to do. That participant's results optimality score would be 50%. The adjustment optimality measure was the average of these optimality scores for goals set (choices), goals worked (actions), and goals set = goals worked (results).

Student-Determined Instruction.   Following each tutoring session, participants handed in a folder of the materials used during tutoring. The folder included the day's self-regulation card and all instructional materials used. One of those additional materials included a blank Child Behavior Contract that appeared as goal 10 on their self-regulation card. Participants were free to choose that goal and use the contract or to construct one of their own to encourage student learning at any time in the study. All participants received instructions on the purpose and use of the contract prior the study. The contract was similar to the teacher self-regulation card that participants used in the course. The participants could if they chose use a similar form with their tutees.

All the contracts used in tutoring were sorted according to their correspondence with the Child Behavior Contract in Fig. 13.2. The four categories were (a) duplicate contracts, (b) similar contracts, (c) original contracts with student-directed features, and (d) original contracts with no student-directed features. Duplicate contracts were copies of the Child Behavior Contract in Fig. 13.2. Similar contracts were forms with two or more features in common with the forms in Fig. 13.1 or Fig. 13.2. Original student contracts with self-directed features had one or zero features in common with the cards in Figs. 13.1 and 13.2 but included a choice, self-monitoring, self-evaluation, or self-reinforcement feature. Original contracts without student direction had nothing in common with Fig. 13.1 or Fig. 13.2 and did not include student choice, self-monitoring, self-evaluation, or self-reinforcement features.

Reliability

The professor collected agreement data on the number of teacher goals assigned, worked on and completed for 10 out of the 20 days of the study. The average agreement between professor and teacher was 95% across all sessions of the study.

RESULTS

Table 13.4 compares the average adjustment optimality scores for the two groups of participants during each condition. During the baseline condition when there was no reward for work that matched the goals set on the self-regulation card, there were no group differences in adjustment scores. Both groups adjusted similarly, with group 1 averaging 65% and group 2 averaging 64% of the optimal adjustment. When conditions changed to teacher choice plus the adjustment contingency for Group 1 and professor choice with adjustment contingency for Group 2, adjustment optimality scores changed significantly for both groups. Group 1 increased its adjustment optimality to 76%, and group 2 decreased its adjustments to 55% of optimal. These differences were also significant. When conditions reversed for the groups in the subsequent condition, optimality scores reversed as well. The scores for Group 1 decreased significantly to 57% during the professor choice condition, and the scores for Group 2 increased significantly to 62% during teacher choice. Again the differences between groups were significant. Finally, in the last condition when the professor selected student choice, goal 10 in the Child Behavior Contract, adjustment optimality scores increased significantly for both groups, and there were no significant differences between groups. Also, these scores were significantly higher than scores for the two groups during Condition 1 when there was no adjustment contingency.

TABLE 13.4
Mean Adjustment Optimality for Groups 1 and 2 by Condition

	Condition 1	Condition 2	Condition 3	Condition 4
Group 1	No adjustment contingency	Teacher choice and adjustment contingency	Professor choice and adjustment contingency	Student choice and adjustment contingency
	.65	.76*	.57*	.77
	< Condition 2	> Condition 3	< Condition 4	> Condition 1
Group 2	No adjustment contingency	Professor choice and adjustment contingency	Teacher choice and adjustment contingency	Student choice and adjustment contingency
	.64	.55*	.62*	.76
	> Condition 2	< Condition 3	< Condition 4	> Condition 1

Note.   < Score is significantly lower ($p < .03$).
> Score is significantly higher ($p < .03$).
*Group scores are significantly different ($p < .03$).

The three components of the adjustment optimality score — choices, actions, and results — are charted in Figs. 13.3–13.5. Figure 13.3 presents the mean goals set for the two groups across conditions, which were introduced in the staggered multiple-baseline design. For Group 1, goal choices decreased from 3.6 goals per participant in the teacher choice condition to 2.0 goals per participant in the professor choice condition and then returned to 3.8 goals per participant in the student choice condition. And for Group 2, choices decreased from 3.5 during the baseline to 2.0 during the professor choice condition, returned to 2.4 during the teacher choice condition, and then increased to 3.4 during the student choice condition. For both groups, professor choice had a depressing effect on goal choices.

A similar effect was evident in Fig. 13.4 for goals worked during tutoring. The mean number worked by Group 1 participants increased from 2.6 during baseline to 3.2 during teacher choice and then decreased to 2.1 during professor choice before returning to 3.4 during the student choice condition. Group 2 participants also worked fewer goals during the professor choice condition. Here levels decreased from 3.0 during baseline to 2.7 during professor choice and remained at 2.7 during teacher choice before increasing to 3.6 during student choice. Again, the professor choice condition seemed to constrain work on goals.

Figure 13.5 charts the success of participant work, as measured by the match between goals set and goals worked. For Group 1 the mean number of goals met increased from a baseline of 67.7 to 89.6 during the teacher choice where the level maintained during subsequent conditions. For group 2 the mean number of goals met increased from the baseline of 64.9

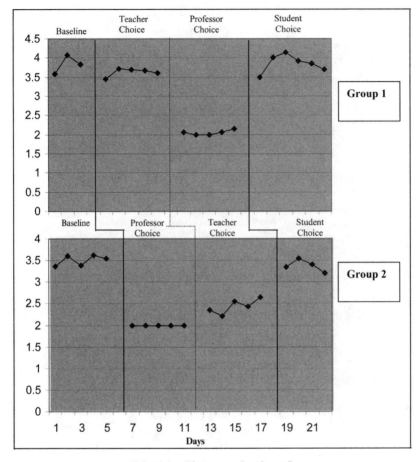

FIG. 13.3.   Choices on "goals set."

to 70.8 during professor choice and increased again to 81.2 during teacher choice and then again to 87.4 during student choice.

These results indicate that the first condition after baseline improved success rates for both groups, with greater increases occurring for Group 1, which experienced the teacher choice condition. Moreover, when conditions changed to professor choice in the third condition for Group 1, levels maintained though the last condition. This did not happen for Group 2, which exhibited a small increase from baseline to the professor choice condition and then a substantial increase during the teacher choice condition, and another significant increase during student choice condition. These data indicate a sequence effect. When teacher choice followed baseline, levels increased and maintained. However, when professor choice followed baseline, levels increase marginally and then improved signifi-

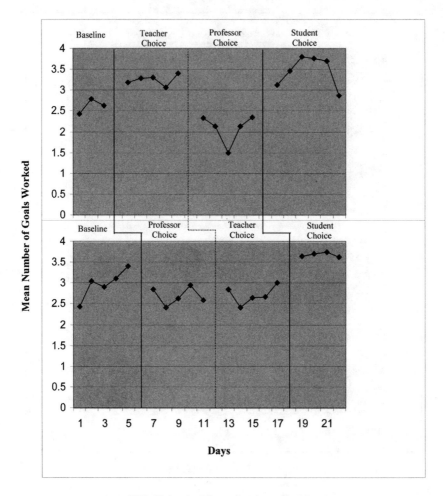

FIG. 13.4.   Action on "goals worked."

cantly during teacher choice and then again during student choice. Again professor choice was less effective than teacher choice in improving teachers' adjustments.

Instructional Contracts Used

The indicator of learning about self-determined instruction was the teachers' use of the self-regulation card with their practicum students. Throughout the study, they were free to choose goal 10 and use the Child Behavior Contract in their folder to introduce self-determined learning to their stu-

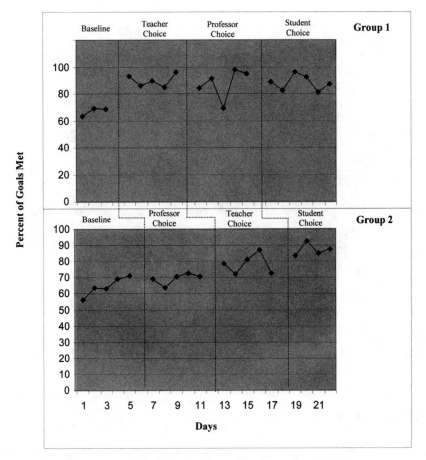

FIG. 13.5.   Results on "goals met."

dents. However, none chose that instructional approach prior to Condition 4, when the professor required it by choosing that goal for them to work. Then they responded by using the Child Behavior Contract in their folders, constructing contracts that were similar to it, or constructing original contracts of their own.

Figure 13.6 presents these results. It shows that most participants used contracts that encouraged self-determined learning. As indicated in the figure, 26 of the 37 participants (70%) engaged in self-determined instruction during that condition. Slightly more than half used their own version of the contract in their folder. The 11 students who used teacher-directed contracts were also split between constructing an original contract (7) and using a contract similar to the one in the folder (4). This evidence plus data on

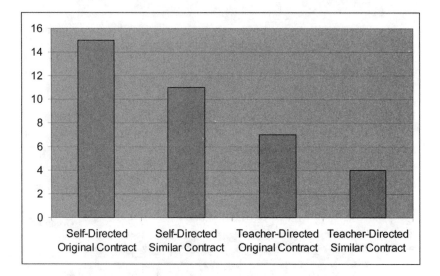

FIG. 13.6.   Number of participants using original and facsimile self- or teacher-directed contracts during the student choice contingency.

participants' optimizing of goal selections, goals worked, and goals met in Figs. 13.3–13.5 and Table 13.3 support the claim that teachers adjusted optimally to student deliveries of cues and consequences in the last condition.

DISCUSSION

The results of this study support the prediction that prospective special education teachers would optimize their adjustments to student-directed learning when (a) they had choices on what to teach, (b) there was an adjustment contingency for acting on those choices, and (c) they were required to promote student-directed learning. When these three conditions were present, the optimality of teacher adjustments was highest. However, when the adjustment contingency was absent during baseline or when professor choice replaced teacher choice, the optimality of their adjustments declined. Finally, when student-determined learning was required and an adjustment contingency was in effect, the adjustment optimality of both groups was highest. This suggests that perhaps the best way to teach teachers to encourage self-determined learning is to give them choices on how to adjust to their students' self-direction and then require that they give their students a self-regulation card to use during their learning. This is what happened in the last condition when they were required to use the Child Behavior Contract with their practicum students. In that condition they were the most adaptive and showed the most learning about student-directed learning. Many of these teachers created original contracts to help their students determine their own learning.

These results are similar to the findings in the chapter 9 that student choice plus an adjustment contingency produces higher adjustment optimality scores for young children with disabilities during independent work than does teacher choice with an adjustment contingency. Apparently, prospective teachers learn to instruct self-determined learners when the same choice-adjustment conditions are in place. By replacing professor with teacher choice during goal selections and by using self-regulation cards with adjustment contingencies to improve their adjustment capabilities, the study showed that teachers would optimize their adjustments to student learning as predicted by prescription 5.

Finally, the comparability of results with those reported in chapters 9–12 suggests that similar conditions provoke all people to direct their own learning: choice opportunities, adjustment capabilities, and adjustment contingencies. When these conditions are present, actors are likely to self-engage and adjust repeatedly to improve their circumstances in order to learn. In contrast, the absence of choice tends to discourage engagement, adjustment, and learning. This was evident in chapter 9 for young children with disabilities and was apparent in this study on prospective teachers. It seems that opportunities are viewed most favorably when actors have options for adjusting to the challenges facing them. Indeed, we have seen this effect in self-determination and in self-determined learning, and now we know why. In both cases, learners engage circumstances that offer choices because those situations offer the best prospects for adjusting in ways that advance their pursuits.

IV

THEORY EVALUATION

14

The Credibility and Worth
of Self-Determined Learning Theory

Dennis E. Mithaug
Deirdre K. Mithaug
Martin Agran
James. E. Martin
Michael L. Wehmeyer

In this chapter we ask whether self-determined learning theory is sufficiently credible and valuable to consider adopting. To find out if the theory is credible, we ask whether its explanation makes sense and is supported by evidence. To find out if the theory is valuable, we ask whether the explanation covers enough of the factors affecting engagement and learning to be worth using. These standards of credibility and value apply to all theories considered for adoption and use (Mithaug, 2000).

To judge the credibility of the self-determined learning theory, we ask whether its explanation provides a coherent, valid, and verified account of the circumstances surrounding engagement and learning. To judge coherence, we determine whether the propositions that comprise the theory hold together logically. To judge validity, we determine whether the theory's concluding proposition follows logically from the premising propositions that explain engagement and learning. And to judge the veracity of the theory, we determine whether results from studies are consistent with its claims.

The value of self-determined learning theory depends on whether it offers a significant, comprehensive, and useful explanation for engagement and learning. To judge the significance of self-determined learning theory, we ask whether it explains the previously discussed factors affecting engagement and learning. To judge its scope, we ask whether the self-determined learning explanation covers a wide range of different situations involving engagement and learning. And to evaluate utility, we ask whether self-determined learning theory offers practical guidance for improving teaching and learning. These six evaluation criteria are both demanding and practical in that they address whether the theory's explanation has sufficient basis in fact and value to be worth adopting. Indeed, they identify the several ways a theory can fail to pass muster (Mithaug, 2000). A theory can prove to be credible, for example, but not valuable, it can prove to be valuable but not credible, or worse yet it can prove to be neither credible nor valuable. Indeed, it is difficult for any theory to be fully credible and valuable. Yet this is what we hope to show for self-determined learning theory.

IS SELF-DETERMINED LEARNING THEORY CREDIBLE?

When we theorized about the problems of student engagement and learning in chapters 1–3, we tried to avoid as many credibility problems as possible by formulating a causal model that could explain factors purported to affect engagement and then by constructing propositions based on those factors to explain learning. Now we examine whether we succeeded in creating a coherent, valid, and verified theory of learning.

Is It Coherent?

In order to answer this question, we must determine whether self-determined learning theory makes sense logically. We can do this by revealing the basis for its claim that optimal opportunities affect learning. Table 14.1 presents the theory again so we can trace the reasons for its claims. An examination of propositions 1–3 reveals that they are connected in a causal chain with the affected variable in one proposition functioning as a causal

TABLE 14.1
Self-Determined Learning Theory

---

1. The closer to optimal the opportunities for experiencing gain (A), the more likely is the regulation of expectations, choices, and actions to produce gain (B).
2. The more often the regulation of expectations, choices, and actions to produce gain (B), the more likely it is that adjustments optimize (C) as expectations, choices, actions, and results become adaptive, rational, efficient, and successful.
3. The closer to optimal the adjustment to an opportunity (C), the more persistent the engagement to produce gain, the greater is the feeling of control over gain production, and the closer to maximum is the learning from that adaptation (D).
4. Therefore, the closer to optimal the opportunities for experiencing gain (A), the more persistent is the engagement, the greater is the sense of control, and the closer to maximum is the learning (D).

---

variable in the subsequent proposition. Let's trace that sequence beginning with the first proposition, which claims that optimal opportunities affect engagement (the regulation of expectations, choices, and actions to produce gain). Proposition 2 continues from there claiming that engagement affects the optimality of adjustment. Proposition 3 ends the sequence by claiming that the optimality of adjustments affects learning. This logic takes the form: A causes B (proposition 1), B causes C (proposition 2), and C causes D (proposition 3). Table 14.1 uses these alpha indicators to trace the sequence and reveal the theory's coherence.

Is It Valid?

Here we want to know whether the conclusion in proposition 4 is implied by the reasons stated in propositions 1–3. Proposition 4 claims that as opportunities optimize, engagement persists, sense of control increases, and learning maximizes. This follows logically from claims in propositions 1–3 because if opportunities affect self-regulation, self-regulation affects the adjustments; and adjustments affect engagement, sense of control, and learning, then opportunities must also affect engagement, sense of control, and learning. Stated in terms of alpha indicators, we have the following

1. If A causes B (proposition 1),
2. B causes C (proposition 2), and
3. C causes D, (proposition 3), then
4. A must cause D (proposition 4).

Another way of assessing a validity claim is to ask if a break in the chain will alter the conclusion. Let's say we discover that A does not cause B, B does not cause C, or C does not cause D; then would the conclusion A causes D be supported? Of course not, the basis for the conclusion is the causal chain indicated in 1–3. Because the conclusion in D depends on the three premising propositions, a false claim among those propositions will render the conclusion false as well. The conclusion depends on the premises in that it follows logically from them; hence, it is a valid conclusion.

This dependence works in reverse as well. Consider, for example, what happens when we test the conclusion in 4 and discover it is not supported. This means that one or more of the premising propositions must be false. A false conclusion in a valid argument means that one or more of the premising claims must be false. In this case, a false conclusion in proposition 4 means there is a false claim among the premising propositions 1–3.

Is It Verified?

We presented studies in chapters 4–13 supporting the veracity of self-determined learning theory. One of these was the deduction from the theory's claim that opportunities and adjustments affect learning. The reasoning from this claim was that if learning is a function of learner opportunities and adjustments, then high-achieving learners should report higher adjustment capacities than low-achieving learners. The studies in chapter 4–7 tested this prediction and found that students in special education reported lower adjustment ratings than did students in general education. Table 14.2 lists these verified claims, which showed that ratings on adjustment capacities for self-determination were consistently higher for students without disabilities than for students with disabilities. Chapter 4 found this in comparisons between students from general and special education. Chapter 5 found it again among community college graduates with and without disabilities. Chapter 6 reported the same result for middle school students with and without disabilities in another country. Then chapter 7 presented evidence indicating that the lower adjustment ratings were associated with disability and not group identity or instructional placement, which suggests that disability affects adjustment and hence learning, to some extent.

These four studies found the association between adjustment and learning that was predicted by proposition 3. But they did not find a consistent association between reported opportunities and achievement differences. This is because students in special education in this country tended to report more favorable opportunities for self-determination than did students in general education. Chapter 8 tested the prediction again by examining the separate effects of opportunities and adjustments on point gains of students in special and general education. It found that as opportunities improved, learning for all students improved regardless of their adjustment capability (proposition 4). The study also found the differential adjustment effects on gain predicted by proposition 3. Students from special education tended to adjust less optimally than did students in general education, which reduced their production gain. Taken together, the results indicated that the optimality of students' opportunities and adjustments explained more variance in gain than did either condition alone. This meant that learning maximization during optimal opportunities could be constrained by students' adjustment capabilities. Consequently, when those adjustments improved, maximization levels increased proportionately.

The chapter 8 study also supported the other propositions of the theory in that the optimal opportunity condition increased students' regulation of exceptions, choices, actions, and results (proposition 1), and this tended to improve adjustments (proposition 2) to maximize gains (proposition 3).

TABLE 14.2

Verified Predictions From Self-Determined Learning Theory Chapter Studies

Chapter 4: Verified predictions

1. Teachers rate self-determination prospects of students in general education higher than they rate self-determination prospects of students in special education.
2. Teachers and students report higher capacities to self-determine for students in general education than for students in special education.
3. Students in general education receive higher self-regulation ratings than do students in special education.
4. Teachers and students report more favorable school opportunities to self-determine for students in special education than for students in general education.
5. Teachers and students report more favorable home opportunities to self-determine for students in general education than for students in special education.

Chapter 5: Verified predictions

6. College students with and without disabilities report similar opportunities to self-determine at school.
7. College students with disabilities report lower capacities to self-determine than do college students without disabilities.
8. College students with disabilities report lower prospects for self-determination than do college students without disabilities.

Chapter 6: Verified predictions

9. In The Gambia, West Africa, middle school students without disabilities report higher prospects for self-determination than do middle school students with disabilities.
10. In The Gambia, West Africa, middle school students without disabilities report higher capacities to self-self-determine than do middle school students with disabilities.
11. In The Gambia, West Africa, middle school students without disabilities report more opportunities to self-determine than do students with disabilities.
12. In The Gambia, West Africa, community elders report higher self-determination levels for students without disabilities than students with disabilities report for themselves.

Chapter 7: Verified predictions

13. Students with different sensory impairments report similar inclusion preferences and group-identity ratings, but they report different levels of self-determination, capacities to self-determine, and self-esteem levels, and they have different achievement levels.
14. Students with sensory impairments report lower self-esteem and capacities to self-determine when they are in special schools than when they are in resource rooms.
15. Students with sensory impairments report lower group identity and higher inclusion preferences when they are in resource rooms than when they are in special schools.
16. There are no correlations between group-identity scores and adjustment or achievement scores for students with sensory impairments, but there are positive correlations between inclusion preferences and self-determination, self-esteem, and achievement.

Chapter 8: Verified predictions

17. Students in general and special education are more productive during optimal choice opportunities than during suboptimal choice opportunities.
18. Students in general education are more productive than are students in special education during both suboptimal choice and optimal choice opportunities.
19. Students in general education adjust more effectively than do students in special education during both suboptimal and optimal choice opportunities.
20. Students in general education regulate their expectations, choices, actions, and results more effectively than do students in special education during both suboptimal and optimal choice opportunities.

This was evident in comparing student gain during the opportunity conditions. It was also evident in comparing gain by students in general education with gain by students in special education. In the first comparison, gain was greater for both groups in optimal opportunity conditions. In the second comparison, gain was higher for the group making optimal adjustments. Hence, students from general education who were better adjusters and produced more gain in both conditions produced the most gain during the optimal opportunity condition. As predicted by the theory, optimal opportunities and optimal adjustments maximized gain.

Taken together, the studies in chapters 4–8 support the prediction that students with different learning and achievement histories will exhibit corresponding differences in their ability to adjust to different opportunity conditions. One set of predicted differences was reflected in student ratings of their capacity to adjust in order to self-determine (chaps. 4–7), and the other was reflected in actual adjustments to different opportunities to learn (chap. 8). Both sets of predictions were supported, which suggests that differences in adjustment capabilities are responsible for differences in learning and achievement.

To verify this claim further, we tested whether interventions to improve students' opportunities and adjustments would increase their engagement and learning, as predicted by the theory. Chapters 9–13 reported these results. Chapter 9 found that improving opportunities through student choice and adjustments through use of a self-regulation card helped young children with severe disabilities optimize their adjustments and maximize their learning, as predicted by the theory. Chapter 10 found that improving opportunities to choose learning goals and improving adjustments to those goals through use of a problem-solving strategy increased learning and sense of control among students with disabilities. Chapter 11 found that increasing opportunities for personal goal setting and teaching problem-solving strategies to meet those self-set goals increased prospects for self-determination among secondary students with disabilities. Chapter 12 found that increasing job choices and providing a means of adjusting to those choices improved employment outcomes of adult workers with severe disabilities. And chapter 13 found that giving prospective special education teachers choices and a means of adjusting to choice when required to teach practicum students to direct their learning improved the prospective teachers' adjustments and learning, as predicted by self-determined learning theory. Table 14.3 summarizes these findings.

This completes our assessment of self-determined learning theory's coherence, validity, and veracity. Our view is that this account shows the theory is coherent in that it has a logically articulated set of propositions explaining the relationship between opportunities, engagement, adjust-

TABLE 14.3
Verified Prescriptions From Self-Determined
Learning Theory Chapter Studies

Chapter 9: Verified prescription
1. To increase the self-engagement of young children with disabilities during independent learning, provide a choice of learning goals and a method of regulating their expectations, choices, actions, and results to meet self-set goals.
Chapter 10: Verified prescription
2. To increase discovery learning, teach students to solve problems of not knowing what they want to know.
Chapter 11: Verified prescription
3. To increase prospects for self-determination of students with disabilities, teach students to regulate their problem solving to meet self-set goals.
Chapter 12: Verified prescription
4. To increase vocational success, give workers a choice of jobs and a means of regulating their behavior to adjust to those choices.
Chapter 13: Verified prescription
5. To teach student-determined learning, optimize teacher adjustments to students' cues and consequences by providing teachers with (a) instructional choices, (b) strategies to regulate their adjustments to those choices, and (c) strategies their practicum students can use to adjust to their own choice of cues and consequences.

ment, and learning. The theory is valid in that its concluding proposition can be logically deduced from the preceding propositions. And the theory has veracity in that studies cited in chapters 1–3 lend support to the factors it covers in those propositions, and the studies that were reported in chapters 4–13 verify the predictions and prescriptions derived from the theory. Based on this, we conclude that the theory is credible enough to consider adopting.

IS SELF-DETERMINED LEARNING THEORY VALUABLE?

Now we must determine whether the theory is valuable enough to adopt too. The criteria for judging a theory's value are significance, scope, and utility (Mithaug, 2000). These three standards offer different but equally important ways of judging whether a theory is worth adopting. The significance standard focuses on how much of the unusual circumstance the theory explains. In our case, theories that account for all factors affecting engagement and learning would be judged to be more significant than theories that do not. The scope standard focuses on how many different situations of the circumstance in question the theory explains. Again, the more different situations of questionable circumstance the theory explains, the more comprehensive it is. Finally, the utility test assesses the benefits of knowing about the theory's explanation for the unusual circumstance. Here, the greater the benefits of having that knowledge, the more useful is the theory. Let's consider each of these value standards in turn.

Is the Theory Significant?

Answering this question is a common way of evaluating the value of a theory. In our case it requires a determination of whether self-determined learning theory accounts for all the factors believed to affect engagement and learning. We think it does. Chapters 1–3 reviewed research on the cognitive, behavioral, and emotional factors believed to affect learning. We identified these variables to be beliefs, challenging circumstances, expectations, choices, actions, results, and experiences.

Figure 14.1 presents the causal model we constructed to show how the seven factors interact to produce new adjustments and learning. Beliefs (factor 1) about circumstances determine whether an event is perceived to be an opportunity or obstacle for gain from the situation (factor 2). This, in turn, affects the probability of engaging the circumstance by adjusting expectations for producing a gain from the circumstance (factor 3), regulating choices about how best to produce that gain (factor 4), and taking actions to produce the expected gain (factor 5). The gain produced by these changes (factor 6) yields an experience (factor 7) that affects subsequent beliefs about the circumstance and its promise for future gain (factors 1 and 2).

As indicated by the model, any change in one of these factors can affect the others to alter prospects for engagement, adjustment, and learning. A change in beliefs can affect engagement by interpreting a circumstance as being valuable and manageable enough for engagement or too worthless or impossible to engage. A change in circumstance also can confirm or refute a belief about whether the situation is doable and valuable enough to engage successfully. And a change in expectations, choices, or actions can alter the situation sufficiently to make the circumstance consistent (or inconsistent) with beliefs and expectations for gain. This can alter experiences of control over the circumstance, which in turn can influence subsequent beliefs about engaging in it to benefit.

Self-determined learning theory translates this causal reasoning into the following explanation. A learner's experience (7) and belief (1) about a problem circumstance (2) interact to produce an *opportunity optimality effect* on engagement. Consequently, as that optimality increases, engagement is more likely. If there is engagement in the circumstance then it can yield new expectations for gain (3), new choices to produce that gain (4), actions based on those choices (5), and results that may or may not match what is expected (6). The result is an *adjustment optimality* that produces

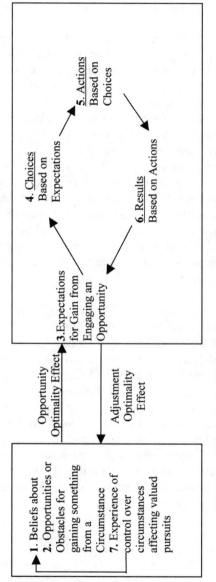

FIG. 14.1.   Effects of beliefs about circumstances, self-regulation, and experiences of control on the optimality of opportunities and the optimality of adjustments during engagement and learning.

1. Beliefs about
2. Opportunities or Obstacles for gaining something from a Circumstance
7. Experience of control over circumstances affecting valued pursuits

Opportunity Optimality Effect

Adjustment Optimality Effect

3.Expectations for Gain from Engaging an Opportunity

4. Choices Based on Expectations

5. Actions Based on Choices

6. Results Based on Actions

new experiences and perhaps new beliefs about the circumstance. The theory predicts that as the optimality of opportunities and adjustments improve, engagement persists, feelings of control increase, and learning maximizes.

We believe this explanation is significant in that it covers many of the same factors affecting learning that cognitive and behavioral theories cover. Our argument is that because it includes more of the key variables of those theories, it is more significant. Covering more key variables allows the theory to explain more of the variance in learning. Figure 14.2 summarizes this argument, showing for example how the key variables of both cognitive and behavior theories are covered by the opportunity and adjustment optimality factors of self-determined learning theory. The experiential, cognitive, and learning circumstances central to theories of optimal experience, cognitive learning, and programmed instruction theory, for example, are covered by the optimal opportunity factor of self-determined learning theory. And the expectation, choice, action, and results variables that are central to expectation theory, rational choice theory, and behavior theory are covered by the optimal adjustment factor of self-determined learning theory. In the following sections we argue that this coverage increases the significance of self-determined learning theory.

Theories That Cover Factors 1, 2, and 7.   We begin by considering theories based on factors located on the left side of Fig. 14.2. As indicated in the diagram, those theories include Csikszentmihalyi's (1990) optimal experience theory, which employs factor 7, Brunner's (1967) theory of cognitive adjustment that employs factor 1, and Gagne's (1985) theory of programmed instruction that uses factor 2. First consider the Csikszentmihalyi (1990) theory of optimal experience, which explains why some types of engagement and learning tend to persist. He claims that when people engage in a challenging circumstance, the experience of control that comes from being able to deal with a challenge successfully maintains engagement and learning. Csikszentmihalyi claims that this experience of control is due to the match between self-set goals and the skills required in meeting them.

> The optimal state of inner experience is one in which there is order in consciousness. This happens when psychic energy — or attention — is invested in *realistic goals, and when skills match the opportunities for action.* The pursuit of a goal brings order in awareness because a person must concentrate attention on the task at hand and momentarily forget everything else. These periods of struggling to overcome challenges are what people find to be the most enjoyable times of their lives. . . . A person who has achieved control over psychic energy and has invested it in consciously chosen goals cannot help but grow into a more complex being. By stretching skills, by reaching toward

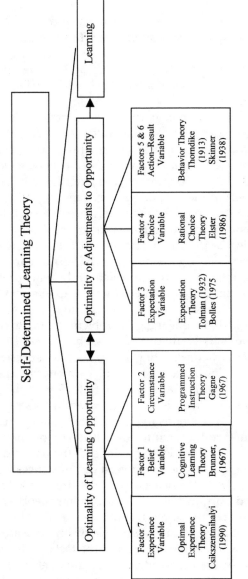

FIG. 14.2. Learning variables and theories covered by the opportunity and adjustment factors of self-determined learning theory.

higher challenges, such a person becomes an increasingly extraordinary individual. (Csikszentmihalyi, 1990, p. 6, italics added)

Self-determined learning theory covers similar ground in Fig. 14.1. Using this reasoning, an experience of adjustment (factor 7) affects beliefs about subsequent challenge (factors 1 and 2), which affect engagement to improve the situation. Hence, when these adjustments optimize, the resulting experiences create cycles of adjustment and learning that Csikszentmihalyi called "flow."

Bruner's (1967) theory of cognitive development is also based on key factors affecting engagement and learning. According to his account, learning is a function of the learner's attempt to construct beliefs about circumstances that match experience with those events: factors 7 and 1 in Fig. 14.1. Bruner claimed that learners use language, imagery, and action to construct models of their world (circumstances), and that when these models contradict each other or the experience of a circumstance, actors engage in problem solving to eliminate the contradiction. The result is a new representation of the circumstance, which is what is learned.

We made a parallel argument for learning in chapter 3 when we showed that discrepancies between beliefs and events provoke problem solving to resolve discrepancies. Recall what happened to John Dewey's traveler who came to a fork in the road and did not know which way to go. He was provoked into engaging in problem solving to find the correct path. Using Bruner's theory to explain what happened, Dewey's traveler solved the problem by constructing a new internal representation for the correct path to his destination. Figure 14.1 covers this causal sequence with the arrow connecting the experience factor 7 with the belief factor 1. When experiences are inconsistent with beliefs, actors regulate their expectations, choices, and actions to produce information that resolves the inconsistency. This would seem to cover Bruner's prediction that cognitive inconsistencies provoke learning. Indeed, the only reason actors adjust is to resolve inconsistencies between circumstances and an existing adjustment (which includes beliefs about the situation). The assumption of self-determined learning theory is that all adjustments are a function of matches between circumstances and expectations based on beliefs (knowledge) about those events. Therefore, when there are discrepancies between beliefs about circumstances and the facts of the case—between expectations and experiences—adjustments are likely to be provoked to resolve them. This assumption is suggested by Bruner's theory, too.

The last factor on the left side of Fig. 14.1—factor 2, the environmental circumstance—also affects learning. This factor reflects what happens when change in a situation renders it more or less valuable or manageable for an actor to engage in, in order to gain. Theories of programmed instruction are based on this factor and its effect on learning. The premise of these theories is that some arrangements of the learning circumstance lead to more learning than do others, the most effective being the graduated easy-to-difficult sequence (which makes learning more manageable for the learner). Gagne's (1985) theory of instruction provides prescriptions for instruction based on this task sequencing principle, showing that when learners progress through carefully sequenced learning challenges they end up mastering the content without noticing the difficulties of the challenge. Self-determined learning theory makes a similar prediction that learner engagement will persist and learning will maximize when challenge circumstances (of learning) place minimal adjustment demands on learners. In Chapter 2 we predicted a similar effect for direct instruction, which provides optimal matches between instructional cues and student responses so students learn with minimum change in their adjustment capability. This is what happens when challenges are carefully sequenced *for* learners, the hallmark of programmed instruction.

This completes the first half of our assessment of self-determined learning theory's significance. The argument we are making is that the theory is significant because it covers more of the key factors central to learning. The theory's optimality of opportunity prediction covers the experience variable in Csikszentmihalyi's theory (1990), the belief variable in Bruner's theory (1967), and the circumstance variable postulated in Gagne's theory (1985). Our claim is that because self-determined learning theory covers all three factors through this optimality of opportunity effect on engagement (proposition 1), it can explain more of the variance in engagement and learning than can theories postulating fewer variables.

Theories That Cover Factors 3–6. The same argument applies to factors 3–6 in Figs. 14.1 and 14.2. Again, several theories of learning cover one or more adjustment variables, but none covers all of them in a single, coherent account. This is apparent in the theories of Tolman (1932) and Bolles (1975) that postulate that expectations (factor 3) are influenced by cognitive factors, in rational choice theory that claims choice (factor 4) is influenced by rationality, and in behavior theory that claims responses and results (factors 5 and 6) are influenced by reinforcement contingencies. Each of these accounts covers some but not all the factors responsible for the change in adjustments necessary for learning. The following review describes these limitations, beginning with theories about expectations.

Tolman (1932) was the first theorist to employ a cognitive factor in learning theory. He argued that there was a goal-directed influence on behavior caused by this intervening variable. Bolles (1975) empirically tested for the cognition effect by hypothesizing two types of cognition, the S–S* cognition formed by associations between neutral and reinforcing stimuli, and the R–S* cognition formed by associations between responses and reinforcing stimuli. He found that when learners respond to new circumstances they develop S–S* and R–S* cognitions that affect their expectations for gain from different choices and actions.

Figure 14.1 shows how these cognitions affect engagement through the optimality of opportunity effect. When S–S* cognitions are formed from associations between neutral and reinforcing stimulus events and when R–S* cognitions are formed from associations between responses and reinforcing stimulus events, learners believe they know what events produce gain (S–S* cognition) or what actions produce it (S–R* association) in those stimulus situations. Hence they believe they know enough about the situation to produce gain from it should they act. This, according to self-determined learning theory, produces an opportunity optimality effect. As actors learn more about the factors affecting the gain they want from a situation, they are likely to act on that knowledge to produce the result they want. The optimality effect is a change in their expectations for gain from the situation, factor 3 in Fig. 14.1.

Of course, expecting gain based on beliefs about what causes what in a given situation does not always suggest how to produce it. Sometimes we face several ways of acting and struggle with deciding which one to pursue. This presents yet another variable to consider in explaining the variations in adjustment that affect learning. Rational choice theory offers one of the most robust accounts of how choices are made to produce optimal adjustments. It claims that people adjust optimally to conditions of choice when they engage in rational decision making to find the best way to reach their goals. Elster (1986) described this theory as follows.

> The theory of rational choice is, before it is anything else, a normative theory. It tells us what we ought to do in order to achieve our aims as well as possible. It does not tell us what our aims ought to be. . . . Unlike moral theory, rational-choice theory offers conditional imperatives, pertaining to means rather than to ends. . . .
>
> In order to know what to do, we first have to know what to believe with respect to the relevant factual matters. Hence the theory of rational choice must be supplemented by a theory of rational belief [about what causes what]. Again, this is a normative theory before it is anything else. While the rationality of an action is ensured by its standing in the right kind of relation to the goals and beliefs of the agent, the rationality of beliefs depends on their having the right kind of relation to the evidence available to him. . . .
>
> Once we have constructed a normative theory of rational choice, we may go on to employ it for explanatory purposes. We may ask, that is, whether a given action was performed because it was rational. To show that it was, it is not sufficient to show that the action was rational, since people are sometimes led by accident or coincidence to do what is in fact best for them. We must show, in addition, that the action arose in the proper way, through a

proper kind of connection to desires, beliefs and evidence. (Elster, 1986, pp. 1–2)

Rational choice theory predicts that actors who know the costs and gains of their options select the one that produces the greatest net gain. Becker (1986) based this theory on Bentham's pleasure–pain principle. "Jeremy Bentham was explicit about his belief that the pleasure–pain calculus is applicable to all human behavior: 'Nature has placed mankind under the governance of two sovereign masters, pain and pleasure. It is for them alone to point out what we ought to do, as well as to determine what we shall do ... they govern us in all we do, in all we say, in all we think' " (Becker, 1986, p. 113). According to Becker, the rational calculus of economic theory explains all human behavior involving choice.

> Indeed, I have come to the position that the economic approach [rational choice theory] is a comprehensive one that is applicable to all human behavior, be it behavior involving money prices or imputed shadow prices, repeated or frequent decisions, large or minor decisions, emotional or mechanical ends, rich or poor persons, men or women, adults or children, brilliant or stupid persons, patients or therapists, businessmen or politicians, teachers or students. (Becker, 1986, p. 112)

This frequently used predictor of human behavior is covered by proposition 2 of self-determined learning theory, which connects the optimality of a challenging situation with persistent engagement. It claims that when situations are favorable and actors persist in engaging them, expectations become adaptable, choices become rational, actions become efficient, and results become successful. This means that when other adjustment factors are optimal, choice tends to be rational in that it yields the best path to a desired end. In chapter 3 we showed how use of this rational choice calculus in various decision-making strategies was claimed to solve a full range of adjustments problems. The assumption supporting these strategies is that calculating costs and gains of various action alternatives more often than not identifies the best route to the optimal adjustment.

Still, this is another single-factor explanation and hence does not fully explain variations in adjustment that affect learning. It does not explain, for example, how actors discover which of their choices work and which of them do not. On this score, behavior theory is perhaps more helpful in that it links more adjustment factors together in an account that explains how choices are learned. According to this theory, choices are learned when they are connected with a stimulus situation and a consequence for responding to it. Thorndike (1913) presented the first of these stimulus–response–consequence explanations in his Law of Effect. He claimed that learning occurred when a stimulus-response association produced a satisfying state but not when it produced an unsatisfying state, as Hill (1985) explained:

> His primary law of learning, however, was the *law of effect*. This stated that the stamping in of stimulus–response connections depended not simply on the fact that the stimulus and response occurred together but on the effects that followed the response. If a stimulus was followed by a response and then by a satisfier, the stimulus–response connection was strengthened. If, however, a stimulus was followed by a response and then by an annoyer, the stimulus–response connection was weakened. Thus satisfying and annoying effects of responses determined whether the stimulus–response connections would be stamped in or stamped out. (Hill, 1985, p. 45)

Skinner's (1938) theory covered similar ground, claiming that two causal relationships accounted for instrumental or operant learning. One was between discriminative stimuli and responses, and the other was between responses and reinforcing stimuli. He claimed that when a response followed a stimulus and when a reinforcing stimulus followed that response, a three-term contingency was formed and learning occurred.

> *The Behavior of Organisms* is often placed, quite erroneously, in the S–R tradition. The book remains committed to the program stated in my 1931 paper in which the stimulus occupied no special place among the independent variables. The simplest contingency involves at least three terms—stimulus, response, and reinforcer—at least one other variable (the deprivation associated with the reinforcer) is implied. This is very much more than input and output, and when all relevant variables are thus taken into account, there is no need to appeal to an inner apparatus, whether mental, physiological, or conceptual. The contingencies are quite enough to account for attending, remembering, learning, forgetting, generalizing, abstracting, and many other so-called cognitive processes. In the same way histories of satiation and deprivation take the place of internalized drives, schedules of reinforcement account for sustained probabilities of responding otherwise attributed to dispositions or traits, and so on. (Skinner, 1938, p. xii)

You can see the three-term contingency functioning in Fig. 14.1 if you interpret factors 2–4 to be stimulus cues, factor 5 to be responses, and factor 6 to be consequences. Focusing on these factors alone yields the behavioral explanation for learning. When a reinforcing event (result factor 6) is contingent on a response (action factor 5) that is contingent on a cue (factors 2–4), learning is likely. Of course, this conflating of the factors in the figure to conform to Skinner's three-term contingency contradicts our argument for significance, that considering all the factors in Fig. 14.1 explains more variation in learning than considering a few of these factors in isolation.

This concludes the significance argument for self-determined learning theory. The diagram in Fig. 14.2 summarizes the central claim that adjustment and learning are not due to one or two factors functioning independently, but rather are due to all seven interacting to alter the relationship between new circumstances and the learner. Moreover, when these seven factors function together, they produce two main effects — an optimal opportunity effect and an adjustment optimality effect. According to the significance argument, these net optimality effects explain more variation in learning than can be explained by any of the seven factors functioning alone or in alliance with one or two other factors.

Is the Theory Comprehensive?

To evaluate this theory's scope we want to know how many different situations of engagement and learning it can explain. We want to know, for example, if the theory can explain the engagement and learning of young and mature learners, and whether it can explain learning in different situations. On both tests, self-determined learning theory appears to be comprehensive. The theory's prediction–verification studies in chapters 4–8 included a wide range of age groups, and its prescription-verification studies in chapters 9–11 covered learning in elementary and secondary classrooms, in community job sites, and in higher education.

Beyond these demonstrations of scope, there is the more difficult question of whether the theory covers transfers of learning across situations. This is perhaps the most difficult test of a learning theory because circumstances vary so dramatically across situations that predicting whether learning will transfer for a given learner in a given situation is difficult. Indeed, this test limits the scope of most learning theories. But it does not limit the scope of self-determined learning theory because this explanation is based on the adjustment model of learning that explains how a *difference* or *discrepancy* between expectations and new circumstances provokes problem solving to produce adjustments that eliminate those differences. The behavioral theory explanation, in contrast, is based on *similarities* across situations. Hence, the more similar a previous situation is to the present situation, the more likely it is that there will be learning transfer from the previous situation to the present one.

The account offered by self-determined learning theory is markedly different. According to this explanation, all learning transfers involve some type of adjustment to new situations and all adjustments require self-regulated problem solving to find out what effect a *difference* between a previous and a present circumstance will have on current pursuits. Hence, self-regulated problem solving to meet the goal of these pursuits determines the learning that will transfer at the same time it determines the adjustment that will match the new situation. The resulting adjustment may be a change in beliefs about what causes the situation, a change in expectations for the gain possible, an adjustment in choices about how to produce gain, or a change in responding to produce gain. And what remains from the past adjustment is the learning that transferred. This is what the learner discovered worked in past and present situations. What did not work, the learner altered or eliminated in the new adjustment. Therefore, all new situations are occasions for learning transfer. All learning transfer requires a discovery of what works and what does not through *self-regulated problem solving to meet goals in those situations*. So it matters not that situations are slightly different, somewhat different, or completely different from previous situations. It only matters that the actor determines what works and what does not by figuring out what to change from past adjustments that will improve present adjustments.

According to this view, learning transfer is part of the process of adjusting to change and hence is also a function of problem solving to meet goals in new situations. People who are effective at solving the adjustment problem are also effective at transferring their learning to new situations. Conversely, people who are poor adjusters are also ineffective at learning transfers for the same reasons. They do not know how to regulate their problem solving to meet goals in new situations. Of course, if they were to develop this regulatory capability, then their adjustments would improve and along with that their learning transfers would improve. This was demonstrated in the study in chapter 9. When young children with disabilities learned to use a self-regulation card to regulate their adjustments and learning in another setting, the demonstrated learning transferred to that setting. They generalized their self-regulated problem-solving skills as they worked and learned independently in the different setting.

This is our assessment of the scope of self-determined learning theory. We believe the theory is comprehensive because it can explain learning in any situation. It can explain learning in classrooms where formal instruction is offered and in daily activities where people adjust and learn as they strive to get from one place to another or from one goal pursuit to another. The theory explains learning that applies to new circumstances because the adjustment process requires problem solving to figure out what present-state experiences, beliefs, expectations, choices, and actions will work in new situations. And that process of problem solving to meet goals determines what is kept, revised, or discarded to adapt successfully to the new situation. The residual is what is transferred. This is how learners sculpt their adaptations to fit new circumstances at the same time as they figure out how to benefit from what they learned from previous situations. It is also how they use previous adjustments to improve their prospects for future ones. This, in summary, is the reach of self-determined learning theory. It is the basis for our claim that the theory is comprehensive.

Is the Theory Useful?

The last evaluation of a theory's worth is its utility. It determines whether a theory offers a useful explanation for the phenomenon in question, which is why disengagement impedes learning. The answer provided by self-determined learning theory is that the optimality of opportunities and adjustments affect engagement and learning. The closer to optimal the opportunity, the more likely the engagement. And the more persistent the engagement, the more likely it is that adjustments will optimize and learning will maximize. This explains why engagement is central to learning. It produces the adjustments in expectations, choices, actions, and results that are necessary for learning. This information is useful in solving the problem of disengagement or ineffective adjustment because both yield minimal learning.

The theory suggests solutions to these problems, too. To solve the disengagement problem, teachers must make learning opportunities valuable and doable for learners. And to solve the ineffective engagement problem, they must provide learners with a means of regulating their adjustments effectively in new situations. Table 14.4 summarizes these prescriptions for teaching and learning. The first column of the table lists the key variables of the theory. The second column lists the instructional variables used to test predictions and prescriptions for engagement and learning. The third column lists the engagement effects of choice opportunities, which are expectation setting (goal setting), choice making, action taking, and circumstance changing. It also lists the effects of self-regulation interventions, which are new patterns of expecting, choosing, responding, and

TABLE 14.4
Relationship Between Theory, Instruction, Engagement, and Learning

Theory Variables	Instructional Variables	Engagement Effects	Learning Outcomes
Opportunity optimality Doable Valuable	Choice Opportunities	Expectation setting Choice making Action taking Circumstance changing	Change in Experience Beliefs Circumstances
Adjustment optimality Expectations Choices Actions Result	Self-regulation strategy Expectation-results contingency	Patterns of expecting, choosing, responding, and gaining	Change in Expectations Choices Responses Results

gaining (toward goals). The fourth column identifies learning outcomes predicted from these adjustments to new circumstances. They include changes in experiences, beliefs, and circumstances (variables 7, 1, and 2 in Fig. 14.1), and changes in expectations, choices, responses, and results (variables 3–6 in Fig. 14.1).

Chapters 9–13 revealed the utility of these prescriptions for engagement and learning. Chapter 9 showed that when a choice opportunity, self-regulation strategy, and result-expectation contingency were combined, adjustments and learning of young children with severe learning disabilities improved, as predicted by the theory. Chapter 10 study produced similar results by combining choice opportunity and a problem-solving strategy to help middle school students with disabilities learn what they wanted to know. The study in chapter 11 combined goal choices with problem-solving strategies to help high school students with disabilities become more self-determined. Chapter 12 used a similar approach to help adults with severe disabilities optimize their choice of community jobs. And chapter 13 used this prescription to help prospective special education teachers learn to teach practicum students to direct their learning. These studies demonstrated the utility of combining choice opportunities, self-regulation strategies, and expectation-results contingencies to increase engagement and learning.

Finally, the theory is useful because it explains the suspected connection between in-school learning and after-school self-determination. It shows that the variables affecting the former also affect the latter. Chapters 4–7 demonstrated the usefulness of this account by showing that students in special education report lower capacities to self-determine than do student in general education, and chapter 8 related these differences to the optimal opportunity–adjustment variables of self-determined learning theory. The useful implication here is that the factors affecting engagement, adjustment, and learning also affect prospects for self-determination. Apparently, how teachers teach affects whether students engage self-determined pursuits after school. When teachers give students frequent opportunities to decide how to adjust in order to meet their own challenges at school, and when they teach students to use self-regulation strategies to guide adjustments to those challenges, students learn to improve their prospects for self-determination when they are on their own.

In summary, we believe that using this theory to prescribe instruction will make a significant difference in the lives of every student. If teachers teach students to learn from the challenges they set rather than from the challenges teachers set, a different learning environment and achievement ethic will unfold. At first, students will work just enough to meet one or two of their expectations. But after succeeding at that, they will try to exceed their goals a small amount, by setting expectations just a little higher.

Then after that success, they will be off in a race with themselves that provokes more persistent engagement, more continuous adjustment, and greater learning than their parents or teachers would have imagined possible. This can happen for all learners, regardless of their talent, ability, or disability. And it will happen if teachers teach students self-regulated problem solving to meet self-set goals, an approach to instruction that is no more expensive or difficult than teacher-directed instruction but that is much more powerful over the long term. Students who learn to regulate their own problem solving to get what they need or want in school become lifelong learners, which, in turn, allows them to control their self-determined pursuits long after they leave school. Understanding this relationship between self-determined learning and self-determination offers, in our view, a powerful reason for adjusting all instruction along the lines suggested by self-determined learning theory.

IS THE THEORY CREDIBLE AND VALUABLE ENOUGH TO ADOPT?

We conclude by asking whether you think self-determined theory is credible and valuable enough to adopt. Recall that we began the book asking why students who are frequently disengaged in school also underachieve. Then we answered by constructing a theory of learning to explain the relationship between opportunity, engagement, and learning. According to this account, students disengage from new challenges when they view their opportunities to learn to be irrelevant to their pursuits or too difficult to manage. Based on this we revealed two undesirable consequences of disengagement. One was that without engagement there would be no adjustment to challenge and hence no learning from it. The second was that without engagement there would be neither the learning of new adjustments nor the building of regulatory capacity to produce those adjustments.

We discussed both difficulties by explaining that when teachers attempt to engage reluctant learners, they tend to focus on the first consequence rather than the second. As a result, when they strive to make learning circumstances more valuable and doable, they encourage students to engage and adjust based on their existing regulatory capabilities. This has the unintended consequence of making their engagement and learning short-lived, depending as they do on optimal opportunities for adjusting and gaining from new situations.

The theory we developed to explain these problems and their solutions yokes opportunities to learn with learner adjustments to deal with them. It predicts that when these conditions interact in positive cycles they produce persistent engagement, feelings of control, and the maximization of learning. But when they interact in negative cycles, they lead to disengagement, feelings of helplessness, and the minimization of learning. The propositions of the theory trace the development of these cycles, from the effect of opportunities on engagement in proposition 1, the effect of engagement on self-regulatory behavior in proposition 2, and to the development of new adjustments and effects engagement, control, and learning in propositions 3. The conclusion of the theory is consistent with what teachers know about learners and learning: that the more optimal the learning opportunity, the more likely the engagement, control, and learning. However, what teachers may not know, which is now evident from the first three propositions of the theory, is that optimal opportunities have the greatest effect on learning when engagement involves self-regulatory behavior that produces optimal adjustments. Then learning maximization approximates the learning potential of learners.

Our evaluation of self-determined learning theory's credibility showed that it offers a coherent, valid, and verified account of engagement, adjustment, and learning. Our evaluation of the theory's value showed that its explanation is significant, comprehensive, and useful. Now you can decide for yourself whether our assessments are sufficient to render a plus rating on your believability scale and a plus rating on your value scale. If they do and if you decide to adopt the theory for your own use, then you may also want to adjust other beliefs you hold about learning.

On this final point, we leave you with a quote from Winston Churchill, who said, "Personally, I am always ready to learn, although I do not always like being taught." Self-determined learning theory explains Churchill's readiness to learn as being a consequence of perceiving challenges as valuable and manageability enough to engage. It explains his "always" being ready to learn as being a function of his effectiveness in regulating his expectations based on his beliefs about the challenging circumstance, his choices based on his expectations, and his actions based on his choices. Because when Churchill produced results that were consistent with his expectations or that indicated progress in that direction, he engaged in repeated cycles of adjustment that yielded successively higher and more complex levels of learning and accomplishment. Understanding this is possible with self-determined learning theory, which reveals what is common to all learners who self-determine what and how they will learn. It explains why Churchill was always ready to learn but not always ready to be taught.

REFERENCES

Becker, G. (1986). The economic approach to human behavior. In J. Elster (Ed.), *Rational choice* (pp. 108–122). Washington Square, NY: New York University Press.
Bolles, R. C. (1975). *Learning theory*. New York: Holt, Rinehart and Winston.

Bruner, J. S. (1967). On cognitive growth. In J. S. Bruner, R. R. Olver, & P. M. Greenfield (Eds.), *Studies in cognitive growth: A collaboration at the center for cognitive studies*, pp. 1–29. New York: John Wiley & Sons.

Csikszentmihalyi, M. (1990). *Flow: The psychology of optimal experience.* New York: Harper & Row.

Elster, J. (Ed.). (1986). *Rational choice.* New York: New York University Press.

Gagne, R. M. (1985). *The conditions of learning and the theory of instruction.* New York: Holt, Rinehart and Winston.

Hill, W. F. (1985). *Learning: A survey of psychological interpretations.* New York: Harper & Row.

Mithaug, D. E. (2000). *Learning to theorize: A four-step strategy.* Thousand Oaks, CA: Sage.

Skinner, B. F. (1938). *The behavior of organisms: An experimental analysis.* New York: Appleton-Century-Crofts.

Thorndike, E. L. (1913). *The psychology of learning.* New York: Teachers College.

Tolman, E. C. (1932). *Purposive behavior in animals and men.* New York: Appleton-Century-Crofts.

Author Index

A

Achenbach, T., 45, *52*
Acosta, N. K., 48, *52*
Adelman, H. S., 48, *52, 55, 57*
Affleck, J. Q., 77, *87*
Agran, M., 11, *16, 17*, 46, *52, 56*, 77, *87*, 161, 165, 168, 169, *170, 171*, 189, 190, 192, 193, 195, 204, *205*
Albarez, V., 48, *52*
Algozzine, R. R., 204, *205*
Anastopoulos, A. D., 28, *36*
Anderson, J., 28, *34*
Andrews, D., 50, *56*
Andron, L., 48, *57*
Aponik, D. A., 28, *33*
Arlin, M., 43, *52*
Arnold, J. H., 28, *33*, 78, *87*

B

Bailer, I., 23, *33, 34*
Baird, J. R., 49, *52*
Bandura, A., 8, *16*, 23, *33*, 41, *52*
Barbaranelli, C., 41, *52*
Baron, J., 48, *53*
Bash, M., 46, *53*

Battle, J., 110, *120*
Becker, G., 237, *244*
Belmont, J. M., 45, *53*
Bendell, D., 23, *33*
Beyth-Marom, R., 48, *53, 54*
Bickel, D. D., 7, *16*
Bickel, W. E., 7, *16*
Biemiller, A., 30, *33*
Blanchard, C., 46, *52*, 165, 168, *170*
Boersma, F. J., 23, *34*
Bolles, R. C., 233, 235, *244*
Bolstad, O. D., 28, *33*
Bonner, S., 3, 4, *18*, 29, *36*, 49, *57*
Borkowski, J. G., 49, *53, 56*
Bos, C. S., 49, *53*
Bourbeau, P., 50, *56*
Brim, G., 51–52, *53*
Bron, S. P., 41, *55*
Brown, A., 11, *17*
Brown, A. L., 28, *33*, 49, *53, 56*
Brown, F., 11, *16*
Brown, R. V., 48, *53*
Bruner, J. S., 232, 233, 234, *245*
Bryan, T., 23, *35*
Budoff, M., 45, *53*
Bumgardner, M., 42, *56*, 143, *157*
Burgio, L. D., 45, 46, 50, *53, 57*
Butkowski, I. S., 23, *33*

Subject Index

A

Adaptation, 14

Adjustment, *see also specific topics*
  to circumstances, 29–30, 33
  definition and measures of, 144–147
  effects on achievement and self-determination, 74–76, 85–86, 119–120
  learning through, 33

Adjustment effects, 19, 20, 233

Adjustment optimality, 151, 152, 155, 156, 230–232
  defined, 128
  measures of, 146, 212

Age effects on self-determination (ratings), 101, 102

AIR Self-Determination Scale, 63–67, 108–110

AIR self-determination study, 63, 66
  results, 67–74

Attribution theory, 32

B

Behavioral opportunity interventions, 41

Behavioral problems, students with, 28

Beliefs

Beliefs
  about circumstances, 19–24
  about opportunities, 19, 20
  knowing what to believe, 21

Bentham, Jeremy, 237

Blindness and visual impairment (BVD), *see* Sensory impairment

C

Capacity interventions, 39, 44–45
  that optimize choices, 46–48
  that optimize expectations, 45–46
  that optimize results, 49–51

Causal attribution, 8

Child Behavior Contract, 211–213, 216–218

Choice making, rational, 236–237
  measures of, 146

Choice opportunities and adjustments, prescriptions for improving, 142–143, 150–156

Choice opportunity, 42–43

Choice optimality, *see* Optimal choice

Choose-adjust-choose again approach, 190

Churchill, Winston, 244

Classroom structures, 7–8

Cognitive approaches that optimize opportunities, 40